'This engaging, excellent and insightful book is a great read. It is thought-provoking, heart-warming and potentially life-changing. Highly recommended – read it and share it.'

Rev'd Canon J.John

'Dan's book demonstrates that the future will belong to the peacemakers – the true heroes among us.'

Bear Grylls, adventurer

'This is one of the most inspiring books I have read for many years. I hope you will travel with Dan Morrice on his phenomenal journey. You will meet the Chilean miners who were freed from imprisonment seven-hundred metres underground to become role models of unity in a bickering world. You will meet Syrian refugees who were "released from a prison of tribalism and fear to become voices of love and service to other refugees, regardless of their race of religion." You will also meet peacemakers in Bethlehem "setting people free from a conflict that has existed for millennia, giving a new generation the chance to overcome fear with love."'

Baroness Caroline Cox

'As someone who has known and worked with Dan over the last few years, I've had the privilege of sharing in little parts of this adventure. The power of this book is that it's written by an ordinary guy who took a leap of faith and found himself in extraordinary places meeting extraordinary people. It is an inspiring and uplifting book for our time, by someone who lives out the call to be a peacemaker on a day-to-day level here in Bristol.'

Dan Green, Founder & Director of Bridges for Communities

'This book is a game-changer; its power lies in the fact that it's forged from true stories of real-life heroes on the coalface – people Dan has journeyed with in the corners of the globe. The ideas that flow from these pages are not plucked from the air, they flow from the witness of lives well lived – people who have overcome seemingly insurmountable obstacles and who are transforming the world around them with faith, hope and love. Be warned, these are powerful stories from radical people: they will challenge you, inspire you and invite you to join them in a brave new world.'

Simon Guillebaud, Founder of GLO Burundi
and author of *Choose Life*

'Dan is no ordinary geography teacher. He is more like Indiana Jones. Overflowing with an adventurous spirit and inquisitive mind, he hunts not for buried artefacts but for buried stories. And in these pages, you meet the real people behind the news headlines. Dan weaves their stories together, giving us all an opportunity to reflect upon our own lives, and asks how we can be peacemakers in the world today. Best of all, his international escapades are not the end of the story. The lessons learned from the mines of Chile and the deserts of the Middle East are shaping his own story in his home city of Bristol. Whether you have a faith or no faith, this book is powerful challenge to follow in the way of Jesus.'

Andy Frost, author of *Long Story Short*

'Dan's book is truly inspirational. His journey and insights into the lives, cultures and hearts of people from different countries and continents across the world are an encouraging and awesome read. Miracles are happening all around us.'

Pat Lam, Director of Rugby at Bristol Bears

FINDING THE PEACEMAKERS

FINDING THE PEACEMAKERS

A Journey of Faith from the Mines of Chile
to the Deserts of the Middle East

DAN MORRICE

HODDER

'Blessed are the peacemakers,
for they will be called children of God.'

Matthew 5:9

CONTENTS

PROLOGUE

MYSTERIES IN THE WILDERNESS

AS THE SUN rose over the mountains of Jordan, the vast sands of Egypt appeared in the west. I paused for a moment on the shores of the Red Sea and waved goodbye to civilisation. As the dark ridges of Israel's Negev Desert stretched into the horizon, I prepared to enter a landscape that looked like Mars.

Days of being cooked by an inescapable sun were just beginning, and they would continue for weeks, interspersed by lying awake in the freezing hours of the night. Wild dogs and wolves waited for me further north and not a drop of water could be tasted for miles.

Staring out into the unknown on that first day, I was gripped by fear.

Though I didn't know it at the time, in the desert trials that lay ahead I would encounter an unparalleled beauty, not in the tapestry of stars that lit up the night sky, but in the hearts of strangers who saved me in my hour of need.

I found the peacemakers.

There are unsung heroes from every tribe and tongue who, right now, are carving out a brave future in the apex of the Middle East, a future many have never considered, at least not those in power. That is why this is not a book about politics; it's a book about people.

How did I end up on this bizarre quest? I'm not a paratrooper, or a secret agent, or an investigative journalist. I'm just a humble geography teacher with a few questions that the headlines weren't answering, and my search for truth got a little out of hand.

My desert survival skills leave a lot to be desired and I have no connection to the Middle East. I'm more at home wandering the lush green hills of England and then heading to the pub. But the Negev didn't seem to have any lush green hills. Or pubs.

I was out of my depth from the moment I set off.

Only one thing drove me on.

Curiosity.

I was retracing the footsteps of a child, a refugee in Africa, who had walked those desert paths many years previously on his way home to an obscure village in the region of Galilee, hundreds of miles to the north. That child would grow up to change the world more than anyone else in human history. For someone of such influence, his early years were unimaginably vulnerable.

How did he make it through the desert?

How would I make it?

This journey was the final part of a bigger investigation that had started three years earlier and had taken me around the world, from disaster zones to war zones. I found an unbreakable peace in the most surprising of people, from Chilean miners to Syrian refugees to former English football hooligans. Beneath the headlines of cohesive fear, I discovered stories of subversive grace. Stories that are rarely heard. Until now.

In a world increasingly indoctrinated by bad news, it can be easy to wonder whether anything good is happening ... with anyone ... anywhere. Perhaps the good news has been hidden from us because it's only bad news that sells. Apparently.

But this is a book about good news, and it appears you're reading it. Touché.

The people I have met are as varied as the cultures they come from, but the golden thread running through every interview is the life and teaching of that refugee child, who became a rabbi, who became a revolutionary. Ye'shua was his name, common at the time. In English it is translated as 'Joshua', or in the Greek form it is 'Jesus'.

I was brought up to hold a healthy suspicion of people who talk about Jesus, for the religious baggage that accompanies them is something we could really do without. But what if we could take off the grubby lenses of European history, with all its greed and violence, and journey back to the man behind the movement, before his story was hijacked by religious armies and corrupt governments?

When people say to me, 'But religion has caused so many problems,' I don't have a comeback. To be honest, I agree. I've just had the privilege of meeting people in this generation who are the opposite, people who have recaptured his original vision, those whose faith has given them an appetite for peace rather than conflict.

Perhaps the West can learn from the East in this phenomenon.

EAST MEETS WEST

For Jesus' followers in the Middle East, the events of this generation have offered them a stark choice – give up your faith or die fighting. Yet I've also met those who have chosen a third way, which is neither to back down nor to fight back. Rather than hating their supposed enemies, they bless them, and their mercy is having a transformative effect.

Amid bitter conflict, they walk the bravest path of all: the way of the peacemakers.

Their movement is still ablaze today, right across the world, smouldering below the surface of society. Despite the fears of those in authority, this spiritual uprising is no enemy of the state, for their war is not against military forces or tribal leaders. Their battle is with the source of evil itself, in every human heart, even their own.

They are not peace*keepers*, but peace*makers*. They don't negotiate political stalemates; they love their enemies – which is a bit different. They are quietly courageous, eternally content to spend themselves serving the last, the least and the lost in the poorest corners of the land, their humble lives shining ever brighter in the fading shadows.

And there are millions of them.

Now, a new generation in the West is starting to learn from its Middle Eastern brothers and sisters. People are finding their faith while serving their communities, in pubs and clubs reconciling former rivals, and in refugee camps being a friend to millions of lost and lonely souls who are far from home.

These are the people who line the pages of this book, prophets in a tide of negative press, servants in a society of self-promotion, miracle-workers in a material world and peacemakers in a culture of polarised politics.

This is the hour, I believe, for these stories to be heard. I share the journey, not as an expert or an academic, but simply as a witness.

I'm honest about my own faith along the way, imperfect though it is, and I don't have all the answers; if anything, I have more questions. All I offer are stories from people I've laughed and wept with on this road through uncharted territory, beacons of hope in this generation. They have changed me, and whatever your faith or perspective on life, I hope they change you too.

Some people's names and identities have been disguised for their safety; other people were happy for me to record or film their interviews. You can access them for free at www.lukex.org.

My first glimpse into this remarkable world came not so much *in* a desert, but *under* a desert.

Part One

IN THE BELLY OF THE EARTH

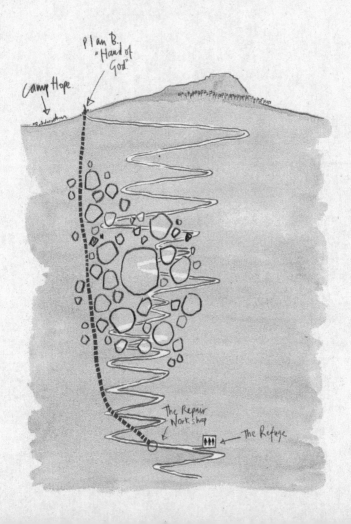

Part One

IN THE BELLY OF
THE EARTH

1.

SOUND OF THE UNDERGROUND

LONDONERS ARE A funny bunch. Every day up to five million of them cram into metal cages and huddle under the armpits of complete strangers. The hum of collective existence saturates the air, as a thousand tribes and a thousand tongues weave to and fro, like giant ants, racing to fulfil their daily tasks in the underground labyrinth of trains and tunnels.

There is a paradox in the diversity, for everyone is following the same stories from their newspapers and screens, feeling the same emotions as they travel together on their unspoken journeys. People download the day's events, desensitised to the sagas that rattle our generation, occasionally pausing over a rare story of triumph: a refugee rescued from the ocean, a moment of ceasefire in an endless war, Olympic Gold for a rags-to-riches athlete.

Reports of good news are few and far between, but once in a while something shifts in the culture of the underground; a story catches everyone off guard, and millions share the same shock reaction with simultaneous delight.

I was travelling from Bristol to London to meet a team of fellow geography teachers from across the country, having been granted a rare break from the classroom. After swapping stories about our latest field trips and sharing the same nerdish excitement about a colour-coded map, we would spend the day making wildly ambitious plans over luke-warm coffee and preparing to breathe new life into our lessons.

I'm a geographer by nature, as well as by trade. I'm no sociological expert, just an ordinary guy with too much curiosity for my own good. I've known the buzzing intensity of Middle Eastern cities and the beckoning silence of Patagonian mountains. Yet there's something about the ordered chaos in the London Underground that always fascinates me – the brisk wind signalling an approaching train, the Cockney voice casually telling me to 'Mind the gap,' and an ocean of people sipping their caffeinated fix of choice, rubbing the sleep from their eyes.

This day was different. There was a tangible lightness in the air, as if the impending burdens of the week had been momentarily lifted and carriages of overworked people were collectively celebrating some unspoken victory.

The headlines were dominated by a sixty-nine-day saga that had just come to fruition, and the morning papers were unpacking the mystery in all its detail – thirty-three Chilean miners, once given up for dead, now stepping into the light, every one of them a marvel of human survival.

As a billion stars in the desert sky faded into the dawn, the miners savoured the warm touch of the morning sun on their faces, sunglasses veiling their squinting eyes, tears cutting through dirty cheeks. Some knelt and prayed, others embraced their wives, kissing them again and again, while drilling teams high-fived the President, and the melody of the elated masses echoed out across the Atacama.

It was impossible not to be moved. Perhaps the story represented a subconscious metaphor of the daily commute for millions of Londoners as they looked forward to the moment when they'd stream up the escalators at the end of the day, leaving their underground world behind them.

Maybe it was just a moment of collective relief after sixty-nine days of tense waiting.

Or was it merely a rare treat in the hustle and bustle of the daily grind; a pure, untarnished, happy ending to a story that had had all the initial hallmarks of tragedy?

Two months earlier, journalists had dined out on the bitter truth with morbid curiosity – thirty-three men buried alive under a mountain of rock, with only three days' emergency rations, no clean water, no ventilation, no electricity, no medicine and probably no light.

The largest segment in the collapse was a 770,000-tonne slab that geologists referred to as the 'megablock'. It was so vast, writers had to make gargantuan comparisons to help people grapple with it. The most common was 'two Empire State Buildings'; another made it '150 *Titanics*'.[1]

I measured it in elephants.

When the mountain imploded, this skyscraper-sized megablock dropped through the heart of the mine, choking every pathway, sealing every ventilation shaft and triggering rockfalls in every direction, crushing diggers like matchboxes. Above ground, dust and rocks spewed from the mouth of the mine for hours, 'like a volcano', in the words of a miner preparing for the next shift.

The chances that anyone would survive 200,000 rock elephants plummeting through their workplace seemed painfully implausible. Even if one or two miners were desperately clinging to life, there was no way they'd be able to hang in there for more than a few days.

Or was there?

Only one way to find out.

SHOT IN THE DARK

Chile's elite rescue team, GOPE, disappeared into the disaster zone, along with one miner's father. Hours later, after narrowly escaping a further collapse, they emerged with a depressing conclusion: there was no way through.

The rescuers prepared for battle.

Never surrender.

Plan B was to drill them out, but to find a drill powerful enough to reach them and yet gentle enough to avoid causing a further collapse was a near-impossible task. The mine lay like an underground house of cards: one wrong move . . .

Nobody had ever performed a rescue at that depth before; it would take weeks, not days.

To add insult to injury, drills deviate by as much as five degrees in this kind of operation, so by the time they got to the bottom of the mine, even the slightest slant would become a massive misdirection. They barely knew which way to aim in the first place, for maps of the San José mine were woefully inaccurate.

The designated safe place in the event of an emergency was a tiny room called the Refuge near the base of the mine, about two thousand feet below the surface. If there were any survivors, that's where they'd be.

Hopefully.

An underground vacuum left by the collapse meant that drilling vertically was even more dangerous, so the solution was to start to the side of the mine and drill at an angle, hoping the natural deviation in the drill's path would curl it in the direction of the Refuge. Or where they thought the Refuge might be.

It was like trying to score a goal with a bend-it-like-Beckham free kick.

From outside the stadium.

Blindfolded.

'It could end up anywhere,' said Eduardo Hurtado, the leader of one of the engineering teams, tasked with finding them. As Hurtado stepped up to the platform and the drill rumbled into action, he invited his band of brothers to pray, for he knew their rescue attempt was a shot in the dark.

'Let's all put our trust in the skinny guy,' he told them, referring to the skinny guy on the cross. They held hands for a minute, heads bowed, an elite team of engineers humbled by the task in front of them, desperate for some divine inspiration.[2]

The first attempt curled the wrong way.

That cost them three days.

They started again.

If there was the slightest chance that there were beating hearts down there, the engineers would keep fighting, whatever the cost. It became the biggest, most expensive and most widely viewed mine rescue in history.

The irony was that for the first few days, the thirty-three miners, the prize for which everyone fought, knew nothing of the rescue above them. Some doubted a rescue would even be attempted. Yet as the gnawing vibration of tungsten-carbide teeth chewed through the mountain above them, they heard the unmistakable message of hope: 'We haven't given up on you yet.'

How sweet the sound.

How cruel the aftershock.

What must they have felt as they heard the drill missing its target and winding back up?

The rumble of redemption turning back into the sound of silence.

The thought that you might be left to die at the bottom of a mine is bad enough, but how do you cope with the knowledge that people have attempted to rescue you and failed?

News of the first fruitless results seeped into the media with predictable melancholy. After a few days without contact, the drillers kept going optimistically. After a week, they kept going faithfully. After two weeks without a sound, nobody knew why they were still trying. All they had to show for their efforts were a catalogue of dead ends and a string of broken drill bits.

Against all rational judgement, something beckoned them on.

After seventeen days without so much as a whisper of life, Hurtado's drill deviated the wrong way, hundreds of metres down. It was a fatal setback. Or so they thought.

Swinging in at an unexpected angle, the drill chomped through a final few metres of rock, punctured an air pocket and stopped. The engineers heard a sound that sent shivers up the backs of their necks.

There was banging on the end of the drill.

Someone was down there.

Alive.

Slowly and tentatively, they pulled the drill back up to discover a dirty, crumpled note clinging to the end, bearing news that few dared to dream.

'We are all well, the thirty-three.'

The sheer rawness of human emotion was captured by the cameras in a moment of unhinged euphoria. Grown men dropped to the sand weeping with joy, drilling crews embraced each other like brothers returning from battle, technicians raced down the hill to the waiting families who were camped out in the desert, and the shock of beautiful news rippled out to the watching world. Against all the odds, the lost had been found.

'It was like looking for a needle in a haystack, seven hundred metres underground,' one of them later told me.

For the thirty-three, this was the watershed moment on a tumultuous journey. Even after that moment of blind success, their ordeal wasn't over; it would still take many weeks to widen that initial borehole until it was big enough to get them out. All that time they waited on tenterhooks, desperately praying that a further collapse wouldn't sabotage their rescue, as the mountain growled around them and fresh rockfalls made their hearts sink.

But this is a story that refused to end in disaster.

Sixty-nine days after they had entered the mine, the sight of thirty-three husbands and fathers emerging from a bottomless pit into the arms of their families stopped the world in its tracks.

Even the anaesthetised environment of the London Underground was moved. For a moment, the city forgot its troubles, the personal woes of a million commuters faded from memory and every heart rejoiced with the families of the miners.

Broadsheets and tabloids evoked almost spiritual language to explain the serendipity of the rescue, the front page of *The Times* projecting the words, 'The Miracle of San José', and the *Mirror* calling it 'Salvation'.

Like millions of others across the world, I watched and wondered. How did they do it?

CALL ME WHEN YOU LAND

With classic journalistic predictability, a few papers started to mine some gloomy conclusions from within the seams of joy. Would the men be deeply traumatised for years afterwards? What would happen to the owners of the mine, whose negligence had triggered the collapse? How would the miners cope with the sudden stardom?

But there was something about this occasion that couldn't be tarnished, an unexpectedly triumphant ending and, ultimately, that can never be taken away.

Years later, when I mention the Chilean miners, people remember the rescue as if it were last week; the story can flood back in an instant. In fact, when twelve boys and their football coach were stranded in a Thai cave, people joked that we should send in the Chilean miners. One of the miners even sent them a video message, promising, 'We will be praying for each one of you and your families.'[3] It was a similarly gruelling rescue in which one of the elite rescue divers lost his life, a modern hero if ever there was one.[4] Yet despite the odds stacked against them, every one of those Thai boys emerged into the light of day, a flashback to the Chilean miners, a valiant rescue which seems to linger in the spirit of our nation, and countless others.

But for me, there were too many unanswered questions regarding that Chilean mine.

How did every one of them cheat death in the initial collapse?

Where did they find light . . . and water . . . and oxygen?

What would have happened if the drill hadn't swung off course, all by itself, two thousand feet down, to hit the corridor outside the Refuge?

How did the miners keep the peace when they could so easily have turned on one another (especially after some of them had raided the emergency rations on day one)?

Was this really a miracle? What about disasters where people aren't so lucky?

I devoured *Deep Down Dark* by Héctor Tobar, the account commissioned by the miners in the aftermath of the rescue, and I carefully dissected every interview. I studied every news story and considered every analysis. There were countless articles, scores of motivational talks by the miners, even a Hollywood film.

The more I read, the more it seemed there was a deeper level in this story.

Hungry to uncover the full picture, I decided to write to one of them. A year later, I received a message from José Henríquez, the one they had nicknamed 'the pastor', for his ability to impart an unwavering sense of peace in the miners throughout their epic battle.

His email was refreshingly candid.

'Brother Dan,' he wrote, 'here is my cell phone number . . . Call me when you land.'

Just like that, it was happening.

I booked my flights, picked up a book on beginner's Spanish and soon learned that I was still as useless at languages as I had been at school. I called Ross, an English teacher in Madrid, and asked him to join me as a translator. He quickly agreed, partly as an old friend doing me a favour and partly because I described the trip as a wine tour of South America, stopping briefly en route to meet some miners, for which he may need to do a bit of interpreting.

Our mutual friend Louise, a physics teacher from Northern Ireland, was recruited using the same persuasive 'wine tour' line and we reasoned that if she could teach her students about sound and light, she'd be more than qualified to capture the story on film. She adopted the role of camerawoman, sound technician and film producer, and the team was complete.

Setting off from Bristol in the school holidays with moth-eaten rucksacks and a pile of books, we looked more like a trio of middle-aged friends on a belated gap year than a team of investigative journalists, but we had one phone number and that was our key. Tenacious curiosity can get you a long way. We were about to discover just how deep the rabbit hole went.

2.

SURVIVAL

SHORTLY AFTER TOUCHING down in the capital Santiago, we were wandering the wet streets of Talca, a small town nestled in Chile's lake district, searching for a hostel that could shelter three scruffy Brits and a tonne of kit.

After battling a storm that had swept in from the Pacific, my camera stuffed under a waterproof jacket, and with white-knuckled hands clutching a crinkled map of the town, we checked into a small hostel with a smiling hostess, and Ross called José to set up our first interview.

Early the following morning, with jet lag still wearing off, we heard a thud on the door and José ambled in, grinning from ear to ear and greeting the hostel staff like they were family.

Perhaps they were.

We soon felt part of the family too. He was unusually tall for a miner, with broad shoulders and an unshakable grin. When he laughed, the room laughed with him. When he cried, we all sat motionless, paralysed by his broken voice. He wasn't overly dramatic, just happy to be vulnerable before us, speaking honestly about the roller coaster of emotions that they'd experienced underground. He shared the struggle of near starvation and then tapped his stomach with a cheeky grin and said, 'I've had a few steaks since then.'

On the morning of the collapse, José had been asked to help fix a faulty wheel by one of the engineers as a one-off favour.

'I was in a different part of the mine from normal,' he said. 'My usual work area was completely crushed.'

Lucky escape.

As cracks started to form in the rocks around them, José finished his work and went to get a cup of water in the Refuge. 'It was less contaminated than the rest of the mine,' he explained. As I started to build a mental picture of this little room of sanctity, he gave me a reality check.

'It wasn't a very good place for humans to be in . . . the temperature never went below 38°C (100°F). It was so hot, you had to take off your overalls and just sit in your underwear.'

There aren't many offices in the UK where you have to sit in your underwear just to survive.

The Refuge was only designated the 'safe place' because it was the most structurally sound part of the mine. But the conditions inside weren't exactly comfortable.

At the apex of the collapse, when the skyscraper-sized rock sheared off from the mine and bulldozed through their underground world, it sent a shock wave down every tunnel, sweeping the miners clean off their feet. One of the youngest was picked up and thrown against the wall of the mine, knocking out his front teeth, like a boxer in a street fight. Another described the blast as if they were 'inside a cardboard box that someone had decided to shake'.[1]

With the explosion still ringing in their ears, half of the miners fled upwards to escape, but when they hit the impenetrable wall of rock they hurried back to the Refuge, dodging slabs of stone that were falling from the roof of the corridors. One of them remembers feeling as if 'the mountain was about to eat us'.[2]

At the base of the mine, the men were gripped by a sudden pressure shift, which squeezed their chests like an invisible python and rendered one of them temporarily deaf. Another said it felt like his head 'were a balloon being inflated'.[3]

In the aftermath of the shock wave, as men crawled into the Refuge from the farthest corners of the mine, bleeding and broken, they were consumed with one thought.

How many had survived?

'Because of the dust we couldn't see each other; we could just see the teeth and eyes,' José said, pointing at his teeth, to help me with my rusty Spanish.

I tried to imagine how I would feel, trapped in a small room of petrified miners, the sound of explosions in the rocks above, sweat pouring down my body in 38°C heat, choked with dust, seeing nothing but the faint glow of eyes and teeth, wet with blood, staring back at me. If ever there were a horror movie set in a sauna, this would be it.

'Most were very traumatised,' José said. 'There were different personalities, different ages and levels of experience. Some had never worked in a mine before.'

That's a tough first day.

José had been working in mines for more than thirty years, and he became a great source of strength to the younger men who hadn't yet been hardened by the road of suffering that comes with the mining life. He was old enough to be a grandfather to some of them.

'I've been intoxicated by fumes, I've endured rockfalls, I've experienced rocks exploding, I've been in mudslides . . . these kinds of experiences help you to get used to accidents.'

The constant awareness of his fragility had taught him to depend on prayer to survive.

'Every day, when I go to work, I pray.'

José's unshakable peace in the aftermath of the collapse made him stand out instantly.

'I took on the positive role because we were okay, we were alive.'

Later in my journey, I met other miners who credited José for holding them together.

'The pastor that we had inside blessed us every day,' said Carlos Barrios, a strong, sporty miner in his late twenties. 'He helped us a lot.'

From the very start, José saw the whole ordeal as a test, which God, in his mercy, would lead them through.

'In those moments, faith is activated. For me, this was just another test of my faith.'

José never doubted they'd be rescued, even after weeks of starvation. When other men were starting to write goodbye letters, he calmly reminded them of the facts that could fuel their faith, like the sheer improbability of their survival in the first place.

'When we all gathered in the Refuge, we realised that nobody had died, and this was a very good thing,' he said, with signature understatement.

Miners had died in San José before; others had narrowly escaped. Exactly one month earlier, miner Gino Cortés had been caught by a slab of rock that dropped out of the ceiling and severed his left leg clean off, like a guillotine. He was carried out in two pieces, thanking God that he still had his right leg. And his life.[4] Soon afterwards, miner Alex Vega narrowly escaped after inhaling toxic gases. Now Alex was one of the thirty-three at the bottom of the mine, wondering why he had gone back to work so soon.

As José pointed out, if falling slabs, poisonous gases and exploding rocks had taken out miners when the mountain *wasn't* collapsing, how on earth did they manage to escape death when it *was* – when rocks the size of skyscrapers were descending on them?

When the mountain gave way, every one of them just happened to be in a place that narrowly avoided being crushed.

One of the most unusual accounts came from two miners who'd been driving down one of the long tunnels to the Refuge in a truck, when a flash of white fluttered past the windscreen. A butterfly had flickered by and, for a few seconds, it grabbed the men's attention.

Butterflies don't live underground, certainly not at this depth. How could this be? A trick of the imagination, perhaps? The reflection of the headlights on a seam of minerals? As they continued down the underground road to the Refuge – the driver processing the strange sight and his colleague questioning his imagination – they wondered how they were going to share the event with their fellow miners. In a workplace like this, you can't claim to have enjoyed watching a pretty butterfly and not expect to get some backchat.

But as they assembled in the wake of the collapse, a soul-searching realisation dawned upon them. Because they had paused to watch whatever it was fly past the windscreen, they fortuitously missed the rockfalls that tumbled across the road all around them. If they hadn't stopped for a few seconds, they might never have lived to share the story of this butterfly effect.

THE POWER OF HUMILITY

The initial relief of survival turned to a cocktail of emotions. Some accepted the gravity of the situation and took refuge, waiting to be rescued. Others made desperate attempts to escape through precarious ventilation shafts that all led to the same dead end – a wall of rock, 550 feet tall. José summarised their effort in those first fragile days.

'We did everything we could to get out of that place, every possible human effort.'

As the dust settled, they could read the truth on each other's faces – they were utterly dependent on help from above.

But for José, help from above didn't just mean the engineering teams.

'There was no telephone to the surface,' he said, holding his right fist to his cheek. 'Only the telephone to God.'

He pointed to the ceiling and chuckled to himself. We soon learned that this was no joke – over the next few weeks, their 'prayer phone' became remarkably clear.

One of the miners, Mario, who called himself 'Braveheart', took up the role of motivational leader after the collapse. The miners needed to keep their spirits up, and he knew how to rally the troops. In a moment of despair, he cried out, 'We need to pray,' and looked to José.

'Lead us in prayer, José.'

Perhaps it was José's age and experience, the quiet strength of his faith or the peaceful temperament he maintained throughout the collapse, for when he was called out as the spiritual leader, everyone agreed.

He knew there were men of many faith expressions down there, so he told them he was going to keep it simple. He prayed only to Jesus, for every denomination agrees that Jesus is central, and he invited them to kneel in the dust and be honest before God.

When you're that far down, you might as well be on your knees.

It was not a moment of panic, but a posture of meekness.

There was no complaining about their situation or pointing the finger at heaven. Later in our journey, Carlos Barrios confessed, 'All of us knew that that mine wasn't very stable. There had been deaths, but all the same we worked.'

Despite the risks, it paid well, and for the rewards that lay beneath, they had all taken the gamble. José shared with us the prayer he had offered with the thirty-three on that first day.

'Lord, we are not the best of men, but have mercy on us.'

From the moment he uttered those words, something shifted in the culture of the underground.

'We started praying with humility.'

As he shared with us the details of that first desperate cry for help, he leaned back in his chair and smiled as he recalled one of his favourite verses from Scripture: 'God opposes the proud, but gives grace to the humble.'[5]

He would know. Despite the absurdity of their situation, they would receive a mountain of grace in their dark night of the soul.

FLICKERS OF LIFE

There were many reasons why people on the surface doubted the miners would survive. Even if they had all managed to dodge the collapse, their fate would still be sealed. In José's words, 'We were buried alive in a giant grave.'

Without food, they wouldn't last more than three weeks.

Without water, they wouldn't last three days.

Without oxygen, they wouldn't make it past three minutes.

But the thirty-three soon discovered that, against the odds, they had all three.

'We thought that we were going to die without oxygen because there was no circulation of air,' he told us.

They all knew a way to find out. Someone pulled out a lighter. It's not the safest way to test for oxygen. There have been accounts in other mines of trapped pockets of gas catching a flame and torching the miners in seconds, but if they could die from lack of oxygen anyway, it was worth the risk.

'The flame flickered one way and the other, so we realised that there must be air circulating,' he said. 'We had something in our favour.'

It wouldn't be the last time one of them held up a flickering flame to test the wind.

As the designated safe place, the Refuge was where the mining company stored fresh water, emergency rations and medical equipment, but it came as a grave disappointment when they discovered that the San José refuge wasn't exactly well stocked. They had ten bottles of water and three days' emergency rations, consisting mainly of tuna, cookies and milk, one-third of which was already rancid.

On the plus side, there were 240 spoons.

A couple of weeks later, José described their daily ration as 'a teaspoon of tuna per man'.

At least they each had seven spoons with which to eat it.

The mockery of abundant cutlery wasn't the only thing to rattle them in the hunger games that followed. When the mine collapsed, a few of the miners reached the Refuge first, broke into the emergency rations and scoffed a load of cookies before the others arrived. As the days turned into weeks, this proved to be a particularly sore point.

In terms of water, the irony was that, like men lost at sea, there was plenty of water around, just none they could drink. One of them found two industrial tanks further up the mine, filled with water that had sat stagnant for weeks. As they peered over the edge, their head torches picked up an orangey film of industrial chemicals glinting back at them. No rational man would drink such poison, but as the hot and thirsty days continued, desperate times called for desperate measures. If they would die of thirst anyway, they might as well die fighting.

José wasn't concerned. They chose a tank, and he led them in prayer.

'We went to the water tanks and prayed that God would bless the water, that he would make it clean.'

He held up his glass of tap water as he spoke, just to be crystal clear.

'Later on, when they studied the chemical content of both water tanks, the first tank, the one we asked to be blessed, was completely clean, but the second tank was contaminated.'

He paused for a second and raised his eyebrows as if to say, 'Fancy that.'

The clean water sustained them for weeks. When they eventually made contact with the world above, doctors sent them down bottled water and told them not to touch the industrial tanks, for that polluted water could kill them. Apparently.

Another miner later told us that, ironically, it was the bottled water that made them sick. Perhaps they forgot to pray for it.

THE WINDS OF CHANGE

Of all the unusual accounts to emerge from the San José mine, for me there is one that eclipses them all. After interviewing José in Chile's southern lake district, we travelled a thousand kilometres north to the mining town of Copiapó, in the dusty hills of the Atacama.

We met Omar on the outskirts of the town, and he walked us out to his favourite park to see the desert ridges stretching into the horizon. He was friendly and relaxed, sporting a striped polo shirt and the same Oakley sunglasses he had worn when he stepped out of the mine into the light of day. He chatted away to Ross as we walked through Copiapó's suburbs, where many of the miners still lived. As we reached the park, he paused and smiled fondly at the sight of it, his thin white hair rustling a little in the wind.

Like José, Omar was one of the older miners of the thirty-three, and he was quick to thank God that he'd survived all his years in the industry. He wasn't especially religious. 'I believe in Jesus,' he said, but confessed to finding big religious gatherings a little overwhelming.

'I can pray anywhere – my house, my patio, my car . . . Sometimes I leave Copiapó and go to the tranquillity of the countryside.'

It was in one of these tranquil moments, in the very park where we were standing, that Omar had had what he thought would be his last moments with those he loved.

'I'd met at this park here with all my family, even my grandchildren; a granddaughter had just been born. I thought that day had been given to say goodbye; that gave me some peace.'

In the long and torturous days buried in the earth, that family reunion became a bittersweet memory. He was grateful for the precious goodbye moment but haunted by the implication of it.

As time went on, conditions in the mine deteriorated into what José had described as 'not fit for humans'. The air was thick with sweat, the walls crawled with mould and the floor became a quagmire of mud and rubble. Permanent heat and relentless humidity provide a hotbed for fungi which the miners saw flourishing in every crevice and coating the ceiling of the Refuge. Shiny hairs rained down, glinting in the torchlight as the miners breathed in a cocktail of pathogens, night after night, week after week.

As starvation set in, sheer exhaustion sent the men into a zombie-like state, reluctant to move yet unable to sleep. As the toxic filaments took root in the miners' skin, several of them developed red circular rashes filled with pus. For Omar, this was the least of his worries. His struggle to breathe was what really put the fear in him.

'I was feeling really sick, from lack of oxygen.'

Even the slight circulation of hot air had ground to a halt, and his lungs felt as if they were being squeezed by a vice.

'A strong pain had started in my chest, and I couldn't breathe.'

A burning sensation travelled down his arm and his friends desperately searched the Refuge for oxygen tanks and medical supplies. The findings were predictably useless. The men simply gathered around and watched Omar fading away, quietly praying for a miracle none of them expected.

'I felt at that moment that my time had come to leave this life . . . I surrendered myself to the will of God.'

His thoughts drifted back to that day in the park, the last moment he'd been given with his family. But as his imagination rested on that tender memory, he had a flash of conviction.

'I thought, "God isn't going to let me remain in this mine." It wasn't my moment to die; it was my moment to fight.'

His epiphany turned to fervent prayer, and he cried out, not to be taken quietly but to be healed miraculously.

'I prayed with such strength and such faith.'

As he choked out this raspy prayer, an uncharacteristically cold breeze swept up through the mine, rushing over the miners and easing his breathing.

'At that moment, a breeze swept up, and I even began to feel cold.'

It was so peculiar, Omar thought he might be imagining it. I wondered if his body was going into shock, but it turns out he wasn't the only one who noticed the sudden change.

'I was going to mention it to one of my colleagues, but before I asked him, he said, "It's really cold, and there's a lot of wind coming in."'

It lasted long enough to restore Omar's breathing, and as he started to recover, they realised that the breeze could only mean one thing. Their fiery furnace was completely sealed off from the outside world, so for a cold breeze to be penetrating the dark underworld, there had to be contact from the surface.

'We thought that somewhere there would be the drill, so we started to look for it. We used a lighter to see where the breeze came from.'

Unlike the gentle wisp of warm air they had discovered on the first day, this was a strong and steady wind, abnormally cold and powerful enough to bend the flame in one direction.

They tracked it upwind, using the angle of the flame to lead the way.

Bizarrely, it took them not upwards, but downwards, into the narrow corridors at the base of the mine. The Refuge itself was close to the deepest point, so how a breeze could be coming from underneath them was a mystery. No drill could enter from the earth below.

They pressed on.

As they hit a dead end, the breeze evaporated into thin air, just as suddenly as it had come, although by this point Omar's breathing was considerably better.

'The incredible thing was that the air came from the bottom of the mine where there is nothing,' he told us with a slight shrug of his shoulders. 'It's like looking in the bottom of a bottle, where there is no exit.'

The breeze returned for a couple of hours the next day, as if to finish the job and bring Omar to full recovery.

To this day, the origin, healing power and perfect timing of that cool breeze remains a mystery.

3.

BROTHERHOOD

WHEN A TEAM of medics is rushed in to perform a life-saving operation, everyone brings their specialism to the table. There are doctors and nurses, anaesthetists and surgeons, all experts in their field, and only as a united team can they perform wonders. So it was with the San José operation. Their tools may have been the biggest in the world, but they were still a surgical team of sorts and everybody had their role. As the weeks wore on, and signs of life refused to emerge, one group of professionals stepped up to prepare for a new challenge.

Psychologists.

On the slim chance that any of the thirty-three were found alive, there was a growing fear that they might not be the same men who had kissed their wives and children goodbye on a quiet morning in early August.

What if the rescue teams discovered not men, but monsters?

What if one of the miners was dying, while the others were dying of hunger?

While the human body is not equipped to deal with countless days of relentless heat and constant darkness, the mind is perhaps even more fragile. For men imprisoned in the deep, insanity could settle in long before starvation. When thirty-three alpha males are entombed in an eternal night and left to fight for the last scraps of food, the story that unfolds might not be one their families would want to hear. Comparable survival stories have ended with blood on the walls. In the early days after the collapse, the miners even joked about cannibalism. To survive in the gritty mining world, men develop a dark sense of humour, but for the families on the surface, this was no joke.

When the euphoric news broke on day seventeen, and that famous note brought the world to a standstill – 'We are all well, the thirty-three' – for me, the greatest miracle was not that all thirty-three were alive, but that they were 'all well'.

As a phone wire was dangled down an endless labyrinth of pipelines and the Minister of Mines, Laurence Golborne, broke the silence with Luis Urzúa, leader of the thirty-three, doctors and psychologists flocked around the phone to assess the mental state of the miners. They had prepared the families for insanity, but what they heard left them in quiet wonder. A calm, collected and well-organised brotherhood had united in the worst of circumstances and collectively championed faith, hope and love, right up to the point of near-death.

The men were no longer just survivors, but role models to a bickering world.

They were peacemakers.

Psychologists were baffled. The men's medical records revealed a whole host of physical and mental conditions, from diabetes to epilepsy, from depression to bipolar disorder. Yet, despite having survived for weeks in a hellish pit with a bucket-load of cutlery and next to no food, they were inexplicably sane.

It wasn't that they'd somehow become immune to suffering, for the physical pain and mental anguish had been agonisingly real, yet they'd triumphed over adversity as one unit. The 'survival of the fittest' mentality was put to death, and they had pioneered a way of cooperation that inspired the nation. If these men could build a peaceful community in an underground furnace, is anything impossible on the surface?

Like millions of people across the world, I was forced to learn the art of being isolated for weeks on end during the Covid-19 pandemic. It's one thing being in lockdown at home with your family, but it's quite another being involuntarily quarantined in a toxic dungeon for sixty-nine days with your work colleagues and next to no food. I'll never complain about a long wait for a takeaway again. I wonder if the miners ever considered, at that point of crisis, how much their brotherly love would be able to teach the generations to come.

How did they do it?

José shared the key to their unity. In their daily prayers, the men would confess their sins and ask God for forgiveness, not just for past regrets, but also for moments of fracture in the mine.

'I would call them back to one another, make them shake hands, give one another a hug and request to be forgiven,' he told us. 'Praying reconciled them with one another.'

There was plenty of material for heated arguments and fists were raised on more than one occasion, but when skirmishes flared up, other miners jumped in and conflicts were quickly resolved before bitterness had a chance to set in.

Although some men had raided the emergency rations on the first day, this 'hangry' score was settled with tearful confessions and heartfelt forgiveness. There was no place for revenge in their community. Daily rations were then meticulously divided into thirty-three cups so that the three days' rations could be eked out in tiny, thimble-sized portions for days to come. Some of the older miners even planned to share their half-a-cookie-every-two-days with the younger miners.

One of the thirty-three, Carlos Mamani, felt especially vulnerable in the depths of the mine. Not only was the disaster his first day at work, but he was also the only miner who wasn't Chilean, having crossed the border from Bolivia. Mamani's mother had died when he was four, and he had been raised by his siblings, especially his oldest sister, in a remote mountainous corner of the Andes. Now, years later, in the belly of the earth, he found strength in a band of brothers.

'You are as Chilean as the rest of us,' said Mario, 'a friend and brother of us all.'

As the words left his mouth, those friends and brothers broke out in spontaneous applause, and in the half-light of a flickering bulb, faint white tracks could be seen as tears carved their way through dirty cheeks.[1]

As the days wore on, breakthroughs like this continued, as every potential avenue for disharmony was sealed and friendships were forged across all divides. It wasn't that maintaining peace was easy. There were differences of opinion on every matter, from leadership to spirituality, in daily tasks and practical solutions, but unity is not the same as uniformity. Despite their differences, the men forged a community that flourished.

Perhaps that's the heart of a true peacemaker. It's not just about learning to agree; it's about learning to love beyond the disagreement.

Ironically, in their quest for brotherhood, their greatest blessing nearly became their greatest curse. When contact with the outside world brought relief and elation after seventeen days of silence, a narrow tube was installed through the borehole to bring food, water and newspapers to their barren prison. The miners affectionately named this tube 'The Dove'. It would still take another fifty-two days to drill another hole wide enough to get them out, and as news of their stardom filtered down through The Dove in daily deliveries, a new challenge arose. Tabloid journalists were digging for potential conflicts, hungry to sell stories of betrayal and conspiracy, while ludicrous deals were offered to different men for book contracts and film rights.

As Omar explained, in the days before contact was made, 'Real human beings flourished. We were more concerned about the man by our side than ourselves. We gave thanks to God twice a day . . . but in the middle of it, there is the capacity in man to forget.'

Adversity brought out the best in them, but fame and fortune threatened to derail everything they had fought for. The testimony of Abraham Lincoln rang true at that moment: 'Most people can bear adversity; but if you wish to know what a man really is, give him power. This is the supreme test.'[2]

Despite the temptations above and the disagreements below, tussles for leadership were quenched, faults were forgiven, and the men prepared a peaceful solution to the flurry of media speculation.

They recruited a legal attorney to create a written contract so that they could share the profits of their account equally, and they made a pact not to expose details of each other's personal lives. They could each share their own story, as many of them later did in books and interviews and speaking tours, but they were not allowed to tell each other's. Names would be withheld from any written or spoken accounts, and privacy would be respected.

The miners I met were intensely loyal to the pact and kept this practice in our interviews. They took no payment from me and gave no details of other miners. The authorised account was written by Héctor Tobar, and the profits were split equally.[3]

As the man the other miners looked to as their pastor, it would have been easy for José to take some credit for all this camaraderie, especially as he was often the one who led the prayers, counselled the broken-hearted and brought peace to fractured friendships. But José insisted that neither he nor any man should be credited. They all played their part but, in his opinion, the ultimate praise belonged not with men at all.

'The hero of this story is Jesus Christ,' he told us, fighting back the tears. 'We are not the heroes; he is the hero, and he deserves the glory . . . He is a God of love, a God of mercy.'

It wasn't just in the mine where the spirit of brotherhood was forged. As the men knelt shoulder to shoulder in the dirt, fervent prayers were being offered thousands of feet above them, by their wives and children, brothers and sisters, mothers and fathers, holding their ground against the morbid predictions in a makeshift settlement known as Camp Hope.

CAMP HOPE

The ramshackle city of shipping containers and canvas that sprouted up around the mine became a place of sanctuary for government officials, world-class engineers and Chilean mine experts.

They were propped up physically and emotionally by the army of families who cooked for the masses through the early morning fog that rolled in from the Pacific and stoked the fires late into the evening as the heat of the day gave way to the eerie cold of the desert night.

Marta Contreras oversaw Social Services for the Atacama Region during the sixty-nine-day saga of San José, and her life revolved around Camp Hope as she waited and wept with the families of the thirty-three. We caught up with her in the government headquarters in Copiapó, the desert town nearest to the mine. With jet-black hair and a dark-pink jacket, she had an air of distinguished professionalism, yet her tone was affirming and gracious, and we were treated like friends.

As Marta peppered Ross with questions about our journey, Louise set up the camera to film the interview, and I wheeled a black swivel chair into the corner, ducking under shelves of ring-binders and print cartridges. We must have seemed like the clumsiest film crew in history, but Marta was patient and unhurried, honoured to share something of the inspiration she had drawn from Camp Hope.

'People were living together in an exceptional way.'

She was quick to downplay her role in the rescue and credited everyone else, especially the miners' families.

'One thing that caught my attention a lot was the way the families never lost faith, even when on the technical side we thought that they were dead, because the collapse may have killed them. Never did they say, "My husband or my brother is dead." Their faith was unconditional.'

That faith was rewarded when they discovered that their loved ones had spent those torturous days underground, not descending into insanity, but praying for *them*, the families above them.

José told us that, in their daily prayers, 'We said, "Look after our families and look after the young that are down here . . . have mercy on us and our families and our children."'

This spirit of humility and faith was transmitted to the surface in the notes they sent, as Marta explained, 'We would get letters coming up the tube from the miners underground . . . with wonderful words like, "Wait for us with faith; we will meet again."'

One of the thirty-three became a father while the miners were underground. They had settled on a name already, but when his baby girl was born, her mother called from the telephone that now ran from the surface, and they decided to rename their new daughter after the spirit that kept her parents going in their agonising wait.

'Hope.'

As Marta explained, this hope was more than wishful thinking or avoidance of the facts.

'We knew that anything could happen during the rescue; another collapse could occur . . . but even so, we never lost hope.'

Camp Hope became a place of steely resolve, a spiritual rebellion against the challenges before them.

'There were a lot of people praying and seeking God, in congregations, in churches, in prayer chains, all asking for these men.'

It seems faith and hope are active, not passive, and so too were the families. There were no ritualistic routines but a deep and united cry for mercy. With flags fluttering by day and candles flickering by night, the families stood together across denominational divides – Catholics and Protestants seeking not just God's ear, but also his very presence.

'The families were always searching for the presence of God . . . It was all directed by something supernatural.'

Women would wander up onto the hillside late in the evening, wrapped in blankets, and stretch out their hands over the mine, praying into the night for their husbands and brothers, like biblical prophets crying out in the wilderness. Far below them engineers worked around the clock, constantly surprised by the providence in operation, as drills deviated fortuitously towards their targets and setbacks were overcome without explanation.

Marta echoed José's conviction about the power of humility.

'Whatever may happen to us in life, if we pray in faith, with our whole heart, if we cry out in humility, then God hears us, and he will do the impossible.'

When the rescue capsule, the Phoenix II, finally fished the thirty-three from the depths, Marta was standing with the families by the thick concrete platform of the drilling rig as they prepared to see their beloved stepping onto the lunar surface of the desert.

'When I saw Luis Urzúa, who was the last one to come out . . . I was with his wife, waiting for him. I said, "Thank you Lord," and my tears started to fall.'

Her eyes watered as she recalled the moment the last man stepped onto the surface of the desert. 'At that moment, I thought, "It's like when man first walked on the moon . . . a small step for man, but a giant leap for humanity."'

POST-TRAUMATIC SIMPLICITY

We stumbled out of the government offices into the daylight of the central plaza, where a network of tents played host to an artisan market, with fresh coffee and green maté to tempt passers-by with alluring scents. One of the youngest miners, Alex Vega, still lived in Copiapó, and we arranged to catch up with him right there in the town square.

Alex comes from a mining family, and his father and brother were part of the first rescue team that dived into the mountain in the wake of the collapse.

He was noticeably younger than José and Omar, with a mop of coal-black hair, five-o'clock shadow, and smile lines that appeared out of nowhere when he grinned. Like Marta, Alex was open and trusting with us, pausing for Ross to interpret so Louise and I could assemble his story in snippets, as if we were digging up pieces of treasure.

'Every time you go into the mine, you pray to God because nobody knows if you're going to leave. Like the fishermen, they always go to sea, but they don't always know if they're going to come back.'

I sensed the fishing comparison was for our benefit, as he sought to help us grasp the uncertainty of life in the mining world. He talked us through his emotions when the mine gave way.

'I felt anxious and uncertain, for we didn't know what was going to happen to us. We tried to get out ourselves, but it wasn't possible; it had fallen down on many levels . . . it was very distressing.'

Like the other miners, Alex followed José's lead and bared his heart in prayer.

'Day after day, we would come together in prayer with our other colleagues . . . We were always believing in God.'

This was no blind faith, for they all knew a successful rescue was a long shot.

'It was like looking for a needle in a haystack . . . a room so small, four metres by four metres, one drill going seven hundred metres; it's practically impossible.'

Like the other miners we'd chatted with, there was a gentle authenticity to Alex. The 'five years on' reports that I'd read in the news had delivered some grim findings. Miners were apparently gripped by depression and post-traumatic stress, dependent on drugs and wrestling with violent flashbacks. But chatting with Alex that afternoon, it appeared the morbid reports I'd read in Britain weren't doing the miners justice.

Alex was open about the ordeal: he struggled to sleep at times, he had some bad memories for sure, and it wasn't easy to find work.

'I still have difficulty sleeping at night . . . the collapse was very traumatic.'

But while he was honest about the struggles, he wasn't a man trapped in his past or unable to find hope. He was also happy to laugh, to pray, to bare his heart as if speaking to old friends.

'Everything about the rescue was a success,' he said with quiet wonder.

He was a man living with a condition we dubbed 'post-traumatic simplicity'.

PTSD is better known as post-traumatic stress disorder, a medical condition facing countless soldiers and refugees who have left a war zone behind them. But Alex showed us something that many of the miners experienced: a fresh perspective on life after the collapse. They cherished their families, they thanked God for every day of their life, and they marvelled at the sheer beauty of the mountains.

'It was simply a miracle that we were able to see sunlight again and our families,' he told us.

While many journalists were itching for news of a scandal, the miners gave them something different – a spirit of humble gratitude, rarely seen in the media today.

Before they left the mine, they had T-shirts sent down to them with 'Thank you Lord' written on the front, so the world could see the real message they wanted to send out from San José. On the back was a line from Psalm 95: 'In his hand are the depths of the earth, and the mountain peaks belong to him.'[4]

Stepping out onto the surface of the desert, their first taste of freedom for sixty-nine days, many of the miners dropped to their knees, in the same way they had dropped to their knees on the day of the collapse. But this was not a cry for mercy; it was an act of worship, a prayer of 'Thank you' from deep within. Their families knelt with them, holding their beloved in their arms, sharing their holy moment.

It would be easy to think that this divine positivity was simply a reaction to the moment, but five years on, Omar was still as grateful as ever, and he reminded himself daily of what the ordeal had given him. 'I have my faith in God and my beautiful family, my son, my grand-children, my brother and more children since the accident.'

Carlos Barrios, now married to Marta, shared the same perspective when we met him at a friend's house in Copiapó,

'All this has pros and cons. If I hadn't gone through this, I wouldn't have my daughter or Marta, my wife; they are very special to me . . . it has given me some amazing things.'

Contrary to the doom and gloom I'd read before I left, the miners I met were men of peace, unhindered by the trappings of modern life, enjoying the simple things that mattered, like the sight of loved ones that they might never have seen again.

As our interview with Alex drew to an end, he grinned and said, 'God can move mountains.' Then, letting out an innocent chuckle, he added, 'And he did.'

4.

THE PROPHETS

ONE QUESTION REMAINED for me: why did the government undertake this rescue in the first place? It's easy to celebrate the success, now that thirty-three men are above ground, but on the day of the collapse most people thought there would be zero survivors. The San José mine was not one of the government's own; it was a privately owned industry. While Chile was still recovering from the effects of the 2010 earthquake, the last thing a sane government would do would be to turn the spotlight of world media on another disaster zone and go full throttle in an impossible task to redeem what were likely to be thirty-three dead bodies.

When reports of the collapse came back to the capital, the advisors to President Sebastián Piñera told him, 'This is not your battle. They won't have survived. Don't get involved.'

For some reason, he point-blank ignored their advice and ordered the government to take full control of the operation immediately. He instructed Minister of Mines, Laurence Golborne, to hold nothing back in the search and quickly appointed experienced driller André Sougeret to head the operation. (Sougeret later confessed that he didn't even know why he was called into the Presidential Palace. He was whipped in, still clutching a helmet under his arm, and bundled into the President's plane to be briefed en route to the mine.)

Why did Piñera throw everything at this rescue, in the face of all advice to the contrary?

We managed to track down the Presidential Chaplain Rev. Alf Cooper, who invited us to meet him in the capital, Santiago.

Alf is an unlikely character to be a chaplain to the President of Chile. For starters, he's British, not Chilean, and he speaks with a strong Queen's English accent that some people think is the norm in Britain (until they visit). When we met him, we discovered he had the same affirming warmth and infectious grin that we'd found with José and he was delighted that we'd been able to meet some of the miners.

We later discovered that, unusually for a chaplain, he grew up as a staunch atheist and had taken great pleasure in mocking Christians in his university years. But after a mysterious encounter in Portugal, he began to rethink everything. He would never have predicted that, years later, he would be leading a prayer meeting in La Moneda, Chile's Presidential Palace.

As we crammed into his little office between mountains of paperwork and a forest of old coffee cups, he filled us in on the rescue from the government's perspective.

'I was on my day off when I got a phone call saying, "The President would like you to organise a prayer meeting tomorrow."'

Prayer is not an unusual activity for a chaplain, but to witness the government throwing itself on the mercy of God, Alf was caught off guard.

'I sensed there was something very unusual about what was going on. I had never seen a President call for a whole nation to pray.'

When Alf caught up with the miners, months later, he realised the timing of that moment.

'That night on 5 August, at the bottom of the mine, they prayed, one, that God would get them out of that impossible situation, and two, that the President himself would become involved.'

The miners knew the eye-watering magnitude of the drilling operation that would be required to reach them, and they knew the mining company had neither the money nor the resources to make it happen. Only a massive worldwide operation could drum up the expertise and equipment needed for such a rescue, and that could only come from the top. As the thirty-three men knelt in the dirt and asked God to move the heart of the President, Piñera ordered a prayer meeting and commissioned the largest mine rescue in history.

Alf had already conducted a thirty-minute interview with Piñera when he left the office, and he gave us a copy of it to see it for ourselves. It proved to be a valuable resource in understanding the mind of the President.

As he sat down with Alf in the Presidential Palace, Piñera explained that he had a 'deep conviction' that they must search for the miners, regardless of the odds against them. When the drilling team asked how long for, Piñera replied, 'Until you find them.'

There was no cut-off day in this operation.

The collapse had come at an already stressful time for Piñera, for his father-in-law was on the brink of death in the Presidential Palace. Late one night, unable to sleep, Piñera went in to speak to him and he asked about the miners. Piñera didn't want to upset him, but he had to be honest.

'There's no news.'

They'd been searching for more than two weeks by this point.

His father-in-law was unwavering.

'Keep going.'

After a strange prophetic revelation, which none of us fully understood, his father-in-law was convinced that they were alive, and he told Piñera to go up to the mine.

When Piñera told his wife about this midnight conversation the following morning, she said, 'Go today; this means something.'

With the last words of his beloved father-in-law ringing in his ears and the conviction of his wife sending him on his way, he touched down in the desert and marched up to the mine, seventeen days after the collapse, just in time to be handed that famous crumpled note saying, 'We are all well, the thirty-three.'

The timing was exquisite.

As Alf shared the story, I wrestled with the implications of it. Was this a divine connection or merely a coincidence? The fact that the miners and the President were praying simultaneously isn't unlikely. People of all faiths and none often turn to prayer in desperate moments. But as our journey continued, we discovered that Piñera's father-in-law wasn't the only one who had a revelation that the thirty-three were alive.

Long before the President became involved, José had been prepared for this disaster before he entered the mine. Months before the collapse, José's grandmother had dropped round to visit with a haunting message.

'José will enter a dark place, and it will be difficult for him to leave.'

A bit weird.

As José is one of the oldest miners in San José, I couldn't help but wonder how old his grandmother must be. My calculations put her somewhere near ninety.

Perhaps a woman of prayer knows after ninety years on her knees how to discern the voice of God from her own thoughts, but it was hardly an encouraging message.

José's family were understandably confused and troubled by this 'message', but in the days after the collapse, surrounded by despair and standing on the brink of death, José remembered it. If God had prepared him to enter the mine, then God would prepare him to exit the mine, that was his conviction. What else keeps a sane man chirpy, for sixty-nine days entombed in the earth?

While José was spurring on the miners with faith and hope, on the surface the prophecies continued to roll in.

'When I was down in the mine, God was doing great things in Talca,' José told us, referring to his home town. 'A lady came from Mendoza, Argentina, to my mother's home to bring her a message.'

This mysterious lady had been quietly praying in her home town when she had received a clear prophetic message: 'Go to Talca, in Chile, and find his mother and tell her: I will take my son out of the mine and he will testify about me to the nations.'

Now it was getting ridiculous. This wasn't just a promise of an against-all-odds rescue. It was a proclamation that José would share his story with 'the nations'. If I had been in José's family, I might have thought this was a bit far-fetched. They decided to pray and fast, asking God what it meant.

They didn't wait long.

BREAKFAST IN THE WHITE HOUSE

For me, coming from a culture where prayer is often seen as a private affair, it's unusual to hear accounts of such communal dialogue with the Divine. The prayers offered by an army of Chileans during those sixty-nine days in the desert were not formal routines, but bold and courageous cries in ordinary language, from people baring their hearts before God. It wasn't a monologue of grumbling so much as a practice of listening, and they fully expected God to answer.

When José prayed with us at the end of our interview, he spoke like he knew God, not in dead religion but in a living relationship. He prayed like he was talking to a friend, and who parrots formulas at their friends? When I meet a mate for coffee, I do some speaking and some listening; there's no mystery to conversation. That's how the miners prayed.

José explained what it was like, tuning into the divine voice from the depths of the earth.

'Someone had a dream that showed them exactly where the drill was going to come through, in the precise location . . . there were many things like this.'

It would have been easy to write off these 'dreams and visions' as starvation-induced hallucinations rather than reliable predictions. But, surprisingly, they came to pass precisely as the miners saw them.

Carlos Mamani, the miner from Bolivia, had a dream in which he was lifted to the surface in a giant metal bucket, 'like a man riding an elevator . . . to sunshine and safety'.[1]

He dismissed it at the time, for they were expecting a rescue to involve ropes and ladders, like a cave rescue. But a few weeks later, when the purpose-built Phoenix II capsule came down to get them, a metal elevator turned out to be a rather accurate description.

The thing that fascinated me most was the prophetic lady from Argentina. To travel to a distant town, knock on the door of José's family home and tell them that, despite the predictions, he was going to be safely rescued and would then travel the world, sharing God's message with people of every nation . . . that kind of encouragement is either very insightful or very insensitive. Aside from the sheer improbability of his survival, José is not the sort who would want to travel the world anyway. He had never liked being the centre of attention, and he had no desire to get on a plane. But shortly after the thirty-three were rescued, when news of his role as 'pastor' came to light, José received an invitation from President Obama.

'I didn't want it, because I'm afraid of flying,' he said, raising his eyebrows and chuckling to himself. 'So how was I going to go?'

We laughed too, pointing out that a man who'd remained fearless for months underground was anxious about flying business class to The White House.

He grinned and nodded. We weren't the first ones to see the irony. Piñera's chaplain, Rev. Alf, told José that it's not every day you get flown in as a guest speaker to The White House, so he should probably dig deep and find some courage.

José was invited to address the annual presidential prayer breakfast and share his story.

If I were an ordinary Chilean, invited to address the US government (granted both are equally unlikely), I would probably harness the opportunity to voice my opinion on various foreign policies. But José wasn't interested in playing political games. He simply told his story, informed the cabinet that it's prayer that moves mountains, not government policies, and encouraged everyone to humble themselves and put their trust in Jesus.

It was the same message he'd shared with his fellow miners in the belly of the earth, the same message he'd brought to the rural towns and villages in Chile's south for years. As far as José was concerned, everyone is equally valuable in God's eyes, peasant or president (which was just as well for the three shabby teachers in front of him).

Rev. Alf took José to Washington and then to Ireland and then to London. As the invitations continued to flow in, it wasn't long before he was speaking at gatherings all over the world, just as a mysterious lady from Argentina had promised.

ECHOES IN THE ATACAMA

Before we left the Atacama, Omar took us up to Camp Hope in person to show us around the site of the rescue.

When people describe a place as 'spiritual' or profess to some sort of divine encounter, I'm always a little apprehensive. I'm a social scientist at heart and I don't fully trust something that I can't map, quantify or measure. But the miners had taught me to open my eyes to a world beyond my own cultural perspective, and for a moment I sensed something special about this place. Marta had testified to a tangible peace around Camp Hope, with the constant music of prayer filling the night sky and the tenacious faith of the families saturating the atmosphere.

'The joy that I felt was the greatest I have felt in my life,' she told us.

For someone from a secular society, it would be easy to assume that the religious testimonies people shared were the result of their cultural conditioning, the spiritual lens through which they saw the events of San José. But what I discovered in Chile was the opposite. Most of the miners wouldn't have described themselves as men of deep faith before the collapse.

Of course, desperate times bring out drastic measures, but the standard response to life's trials is often fight or flight, not faith.

Then there's the blame game. Why not lament the terrible health and safety record of the mine, or ask why God would allow this accident in the first place? These are all understandable responses. I thought the same myself, but while some tried to force their cynicism on the praying families of Camp Hope, the families were more interested in encountering God than accusing him. One British reporter interrupted Rev. Alf Cooper during an interview at the mine to ask, 'But wasn't the God who pulled them out, as you are saying, also the God who put them in?'

I couldn't help but think it was a fair question.

Alf calmly pointed out what every Chilean already knew. The 'accident' of San José was no freak disaster or divine sleight of hand. The company running the mine was well aware of the dangers – the miners had warned them and the blueprints told them it was time to close, long before the disaster. But they ignored the warnings and willingly sent the men day after day into a deathtrap. The miners knew they were taking a risk. As far as they were concerned, it was the greed of humanity that got them into this mess, but the mercy of God got them out.

Alf explained their perspective to the reporter: 'When selfishness and greed put working conditions in such a way that there are "accidents" like this, there are human victims . . . even under those circumstances . . . God hears prayer.'

Of course, I might have expected Alf to have a faith perspective as a chaplain, but the government ministers overseeing the rescue weren't especially religious people, which is why Alf was so surprised when the President called the cabinet to a prayer meeting.

The engineers were not necessarily men of faith either and, apart from Eduardo Hurtado's team who prayed to 'the skinny guy', most engineers never mentioned religion; they were just ordinary men doing their job. But when the drill swung off course of its own accord and hit the perfect spot on day seventeen, even the hardest hearts couldn't help but wonder. We later discovered this was the exact spot where one of the miners had 'seen' it burst through in a dream a few days before.

The strange providence continued, right up until the final moment. On the last day of drilling, metres before the end, there was a loud pop and the drill stopped dead, blocking the hole they had been working on for weeks. It was like watching a marathon runner collapse at 26.1 miles, with the finish line in sight. For a second, the hearts of the engineers melted. All was lost. But with no explanation, the drill simply started up again and finished the job. To this day, nobody knows how it fixed itself.

As this final drill wound back up, the mountain started to crack and groan beneath them. I wondered whether the rush of air from the surface and the consequent pressure release exacerbated the instability. Whatever the cause, when a rockfall crushed an area where one of the miners had previously gone to pray, they began to panic and called up to the surface, 'Get us out, now.'

André Sougeret, the engineer who coordinated the team, had planned to steel-line the rescue chute, but now this was a luxury they couldn't afford. An unlined chute was more dangerous, for the capsule could get stuck, the walls could crack, and rockfalls could descend without warning. But with time running out, it was a risk they had to take.

As the Phoenix II capsule descended into the mine, screeching and scraping the rock as it went, one man, Manuel González, went with it, to test it out.

The guinea pig.

They needed to prepare for any complications on the way up, and González was tasked with going down to brief the miners for the rescue journey.

That's a brave job.

The first few ascents went well, but as the capsule descended for Omar, they hit a problem. A falling rock smashed the camera on top of the capsule on its way down, killing the visuals. A desperate attempt ensued to get it back, but the line was cut by another rockfall. The mountain was imploding, even as the miners were being hoisted through it.

Omar prized open the now dented door of the capsule with a crowbar and entered what must have felt like a moving deathtrap. The shaft to the surface was more than twice the height of the Eiffel Tower. A free fall would take twelve seconds from the top. Something for Omar to think about on the journey up.

While the rescue team tentatively pulled Omar up without any visuals from the capsule, the media put the supposed 'live cam' on a loop with some footage from earlier in the rescue. Little did we know how close they came to disaster in the final minutes.[2]

Like every other fortuitous moment in their sixty-nine-day ordeal, the miners dodged a bullet.

The rescue team was undoubtedly the best in the world, and nobody could doubt their efforts, yet the name they gave to the drill that finally brought them out of the depths was not 'The Glory of Man' but 'The Hand of God'.

Manos de Dios.

For some, 'The Hand of God' will be remembered, not as an act of controversy in a football match between England and Argentina, but as an act of mercy at a copper mine in Chile.

THE THIRTY-FOURTH MINER

As we wandered up from Camp Hope and into the entrance to the mine, Omar shared with us the name they used to refer to Jesus in that deep underworld.

'Miner number thirty-four.'

He spoke with the peaceful conviction of a man whose very existence was the product of something mysterious.

'He was always with us.'

As we wandered through the dusty paths of Camp Hope, I was surprised to sense something of what they spoke about. There was a paradoxical peace in that lifeless landscape that had to be experienced to be believed. It was a profound moment for me personally. I had built my faith on study, not emotion, but, standing there at a small site in the vast expanse of the Atacama, I pondered the events that had echoed through this desert.

How did the water tank laced with chemicals somehow become clean?

How did an uncharacteristically cold breeze sweep up from the fiery depths of the mine to suck Omar back from the brink of death, seconds after he started praying? Where did it come from? Why that moment? How was it so refreshingly cold?

Omar believed that this rescue, indeed the survival of all thirty-three, carried a message the world needed to hear.

'In those days, when we were inside the mine, people above were talking to each other. When they found us, people who'd never met hugged one another, shook hands and cried. This doesn't happen very easily, so I believe God was sending a strong message to the world, to say, "I am here. You have gone far from me, but look at what is happening."'

As we wandered back towards Omar's truck, I reflected on the dialogue of prayer surrounding the rescue, from the words of José's grandmother to the President's father-in-law to the prophetess from Mendoza who told José's family that he would soon be travelling the world, even while he was still buried in the depths of the earth.

Marta reminded us that when God caught the attention of the prophet Moses in the wilderness thousands of years ago, he spoke to him 'as one speaks to a friend'.[3]

I wonder if the same is true today.

Perhaps the desert is simply the place where people finally stop talking and start listening.

I'm no Moses – far from it; I was just a geography teacher, out in the wild, a long way from home. But Camp Hope became the tipping point that awakened my curiosity for other ordinary places where strange and wonderful things have happened, where the raw beauty of unexplained providence seems to soak the earth like the morning dew.

I rejoiced in the miracles I encountered in the Atacama, but there were still some lingering questions that haunted me as I boarded the long flight home.

What about those people who don't get their miracle?

What about the prayers that don't seem to be answered?

Is there a divine presence in those moments?

A few months after thirty-three men were liberated from their underground prison, another disaster rippled out across the deserts of North Africa, flooding into the Middle East.

Finding people in a collapsed mine is one thing, but what happens when a whole region collapses? It's one thing to be a peacemaker in a disaster zone, but what does it look like to be a peacemaker in a war zone?

I decided to find out.

Part Two

MARTYRS

5.

SECRET BELIEVERS

A FEW WEEKS after the Chilean miners were rescued from their battle with the earth, another conflict grabbed the world's attention, on an altogether different scale.

Tunisian street vendor Mohammed Bouazizi set himself on fire in protest after being arrested for selling vegetables without a permit. His death sparked a wave of protests against Tunisia's authoritarian regime, and within a month the entire country united to overthrow the President and pave the way for a fairer, more democratic future. It was dubbed the 'Revolution of Dignity', or the 'Jasmine Revolution'.

Of course, no political movement is perfect – lives were lost and there is still work to be done – but credit where it is due: the civil war was averted, a new era of freedom and democracy began, and friendships were forged across multiple religious and political boundaries. In fact, the Tunisian National Dialogue Quartet was later awarded the Nobel Peace Prize for establishing 'an alternative, peaceful political process at a time when the country was on the brink of civil war'.[1]

As the movement rippled out across North Africa and the Middle East, it felt as if a whole region could transition into a brave and equitable new era.

But it wasn't long before the 'Arab Spring' started to sound like a bit of an over-promise. For many, it felt more like an eternal winter. Not every dictator was prepared to go as quietly as Ben Ali in Tunisia, and some resorted to insidious methods to punish rebels. When leaders across the international community waded in to 'help', it started to get even messier.

When the world unites against a common enemy, it's only a matter of time before they are conquered, but when various countries back alternative sides, for different ideological and political reasons, the conflict can go on forever. For the average person in Libya or Yemen, life didn't get magically better in the Arab Spring; it got worse.

In Syria, western countries temporarily backed Kurdish forces, which was like a red rag to Turkey, while a group of Middle Eastern donors supported a set of rival rebel groups. Russia and Iran threw their weight behind the government of Assad, whom all the rebels were fighting, and there is no shortage of evidence of nasty tactics on several fronts.

Then there was IS.

Amid the utter breakdown of law and order, one well-funded, well-armed death squad got out of hand. Despite styling itself as an 'Islamic State', field interviews by Oxford University research fellow Lydia Wilson found many young fighters recruited into ISIS were, 'woefully ignorant of Islam',[2] yet, undeterred by their ignorance and motivated by financial rewards, they quickly established an implausibly extreme manifesto and set about killing anyone who didn't bow to it. Kurdish communities, Shia Muslims, Arab Christians and Yazidi minorities were particularly decimated, but pretty much any sane person was a target, and it wasn't long before the world came about as close as we've ever come to a globally agreed 'common enemy'.

Notwithstanding the different motives, almost everybody united against ISIS. The fight was ultimately successful, albeit with untold casualties, and with the understanding that it will never entirely disappear.

Complacency doesn't help anybody.

Even with the diminished power of IS, similar groups are rising in its wake, minority groups are still just as vulnerable and the battle between the Syrian rebels and the government of Assad is still unresolved. Besides the hundreds of thousands who died, more than half the country's inhabitants are displaced, and 5.3 million refugees have fled to surrounding nations.[3]

As the glory of the Chilean mine rescue faded from the news, reports from the Arab Spring suggested that this story wasn't destined to have such a happy ending. It's one thing to stay positive when the whole world seems united in your rescue, but how do you maintain hope when the world is at war in your back yard?

Millions have gone into hiding, others have taken up arms and many pinned their hopes on secret trails and smugglers' paths as they escaped through rugged mountains and stormy seas.

Like most people in Britain, I've read the newspapers, I've seen the pictures, I've felt the overwhelming sense of paralysing hopelessness. Most of us have certain scenes indelibly stamped in our minds – Aleppo's streets piled high with rubble, lines of refugees waiting in camps, small boats packed full of frightened people adrift on the Mediterranean.

As with the Chilean miners, I wasn't content with stories in print; I wanted to meet the people behind the pictures, to hear the accounts first hand. Has anyone found hope in their darkness? It seemed almost cruel to think such a thing, but what if the mainstream media was so inundated with news of war that stories of peace were struggling to get through?

What about those who claimed to be followers of Jesus? For the Chilean miners, their faith was certainly tested by their circumstances, but at least the government was on side. In Chile, as in Britain, there is freedom of religion, but in many parts of the world, to openly celebrate Christmas is a life-or-death decision. The growing persecution of Christians across the globe has long been hidden in the media, but now it seems it's getting harder to avoid. Last year, 260 million Christians experienced 'high levels' of persecution, and eight Christians are killed for their faith *every day*.[4]

In light of the faith crisis in the Middle East, the European Centre for Law and Justice issued a statement asking the UN Human Rights Council to recognise the atrocities committed by ISIS against Christians and other religious and ethnic minorities as 'genocide', partly to garner extra support under international law, but mostly because that is what it is.[5]

A report commissioned by the UK Health Secretary and led by the Bishop of Truro concluded that Christians are by far the most persecuted group globally.[6] The *Spectator* called it, 'The unreported catastrophe of our time',[7] and Former Chief Rabbi, Jonathan Sacks, told the House of Lords that the persecution of Christians across the world is a 'crime against humanity', before adding, 'I'm appalled at the lack of protest it has evoked.'[8]

For years the global persecution of Christians was disguised by the mistaken idea that Christianity is a western thing, and the West has a long history of being the oppressor, not the victim. But this warped political correctness and post-colonial guilt have masked the fact that the early Jesus movement was an eastern revolution of peace and love, long before it was a western engine of law and order. Now, with the flow of refugees into Europe, evidence is surfacing of faith communities who can teach this generation what it *really* looks like to be a follower of Jesus.

Contrary to the deceptive brushstrokes of Italian artists or the perfect smiles of Hollywood actors, Jesus was Middle Eastern, the early church was Middle Eastern and the justice and equality we strive for in the West we learned predominantly from followers of Jesus in the Middle East.[9]

Perhaps it's time to do so again.

LOST

I met Zain in a coffee shop in the heart of a bustling city in southern Europe. People from countless nations swarmed the streets, and the warm air echoed with the nasal buzz of a thousand motorbikes weaving through the traffic like motorised bees.

I leaned forward onto a small round table, clutching a tiny espresso mug, as Dan, our translator, fed back Zain's story in bite-sized pieces. Flecks of grey were woven through Zain's dark hair, which was swept back like an Italian waiter's, and his expressions were animated as he spoke. With piercing eyes and silver-lined stubble, he seemed to convey the passion of youth and the wisdom of an elder at the same time. His English was reasonable, but I prefer people to share their story in their original language. That way, the words come unfiltered, from the heart. At least, that's how it felt with Zain.

'I was studying hospitality in Aleppo, and I started to get to know Christian men and women.'

This isn't unusual; there have been Christian communities in Syria since the time of Jesus, who, technically speaking, was himself born in Syria.[10]

'They started to tell me that faith and religion are not about what's on the outside, the way you pray or what you wear; it's about the inside, your intention and your heart.'

Perhaps that's true for every faith. Zain decided to visit a church in Aleppo to ask them some questions, but when he arrived, they asked him to leave.

'I asked a friend, "Why did they do that?" and he said, "Well, they've had guys who just come to look at the women, or maybe the priest is scared of the secret police." When people like me come to the church, it creates problems in society.'

The Christians in Syria are in a precarious position; when someone of another religion is seen visiting, it can arouse a lot of suspicions. But the more the Christians tried to avoid Zain, the more it fuelled his curiosity.

'I could see that the Christians around me had peace; they were not proud, they were not hypocritical or exaggerated. If they said they loved someone, they did love them.'

Zain's investigations were cut short when he had to leave Syria. His family had joined in peaceful protests, calling for greater freedom for ethnic minorities, and the government didn't respond favourably. Sadly, this was many years before the Arab Spring, an early warning sign that many in the international community seem to have missed.

Zain's family fled to the distant hills of Iraqi Kurdistan to make a fresh start. In this new land, he rekindled his soul-searching and got to know some believers from a minority ethnic group of Christians.

'While I was in Kurdistan, I worked with a lot of different people . . . we used to talk about faith, and one of them invited me to a small city, which is a Christian area.'

Zain was hoping he'd finally be able to see what they believed, but when he arrived, the door was slammed shut. Again.

'When we got to the meeting somebody asked to check my ID, and when they saw my name, they said, "You can't come in."'

So close, yet so far.

'This frustrated me. I felt more motivated to find out what was hidden from me, more determined to find out about Jesus.'

The Christians he met in Iraq seemed to have a serenity he didn't understand, for the religious environment he'd been raised in was more about fear than peace.

'My picture of God was as an old man sitting on a chair . . . holding his rod, that when you did something wrong, he would punish you.'

He stood slightly from his chair, mimicking the swiping hand with the giant rod.

'I thought, "Why am I alive if I'm just destined to go to hell?"'

Curiosity got the better of Dan, our translator, and he asked, a little concerned, 'Why did you think that?'

Zain shrugged his shoulders. 'Because that is the message I received from the scholars. There is a Kurdish scholar, who is very high up . . . I watched him on TV talking about who will go to heaven, and he said in this current generation, the number of people is less than those you can count on your fingers.'

He held out his hand as he spoke, silently counting on his fingers.

'This Mufti then asked, "Will I be one of them?" and he was told, "No."'

Zain still remembers the haunting realisation of those words.

'If this leader is not going to enter paradise, I have no chance.'

It's not just in Islamic subcultures that people can be racked with anxiety. I've met people from every religious background – Jews, Christians, even atheists – who are driven by fear, if not the fear of letting God down, then the fear of letting someone else down, even themselves. But the Christians whom Zain had met in Iraq seemed to be free of all that.

He could never find out why.

Instead, the fear of punishment and the inability to escape it drove him into a state of hopeless rebellion.

'I decided, "If I'm going to hell anyway, it doesn't matter if I continue to do bad things."'

He didn't offer specifics; he didn't really need to.

'Anything bad you can think of, I've done it, whether that's with alcohol or relationships, or anything else, that's where I was.'

He was looking for a way to summarise the day he gave up hope.

'I felt like a lost person.'

He eventually met Layla and fell in love, and they were soon married and starting a family in Iraq. He found a well-paid job and built secure connections all over the Middle East. To the casual observer, it seemed like he had made it, but all the external indicators of happiness disguised a deep sense of hopelessness.

Then death showed up on his doorstep.

'ISIS started taking control of the area. They were less than an hour away from where we lived.'

Zain's diverse group of friends and open-minded discussions would not sit well with ISIS. When Zain and Layla discovered they had friends and family who'd already been killed, they realised they had no choice. Once again, they were forced to flee.

'We decided it was time to move and get to Europe.'

Easier said than done.

TO THE HILLS

Zain and Layla lived in the foothills of Iraqi Kurdistan, with Iran to the east and Syria to the west. To get to the Mediterranean would involve crossing most of Iraq and all of Syria. Not likely. He and four other families banded together and made a decision.

'We fled to Turkey through the mountains.'

It was the least dangerous option. In theory.

'It was very cold; there was snow up to a metre high.'

His eyes widened as the trauma lay fresh in his mind.

'It was so dangerous, there were smugglers, drugs, weapons; it felt like even the animals were waiting for us to die, so they could come and eat our bodies.'

To protect themselves from what lurked in the shadows, they had taken a calculated risk.

'We went with some smugglers, we paid them an amount in Iraq, and they took us up into the mountains.'

At least they were with people who knew the way, even if it involved some shady characters.'

'We were on the way, and the smuggler demanded another payment, but we didn't have enough money.'

This couldn't end well.

'The smuggler left us there in the mountains.'

They were lucky to be alive, but now they were really lost.

'We didn't know where to go, whether to try to go back to Iraq or whether to go on to Turkey, but we couldn't see the way. Everything was just covered in snow.'

They took a guess and set out for what they thought was the way to Turkey.

They didn't get very far.

'We were picked up by the Turkish army . . . taken to a detention centre and locked in a sports hall with a basketball court. To our surprise, when we entered, there were about fifteen hundred people.'

This basketball court in this military compound in the mountains became the setting of an international game, but not the sport for which it was intended. Nobody was shooting hoops.

The long-standing conflict between Kurdish independence fighters and the Turkish government had continued to escalate in the Arab Spring, even though they were fighting a common enemy. As victory over ISIS drew closer, old battle lines were redrawn and, from Turkey's point of view, having a few thousand refugees from Kurdistan in custody was a useful bargaining tool. Zain's family became pawns in a political chess match, which is how they were treated – not refugees with rights, but bargaining chips of little human value.

There were two toilets between fifteen hundred.

'They used to give us old bread and a sort of soup. It took four hours to wait for the toilet, so we just took it in turns to stand in the queue, because if I didn't need to go, then one of my family would need to.'

The sleeping arrangements weren't much better.

'They gave us two blankets for our family of five – one to put underneath and one to put on top . . . you were lucky if you could get any sleep because of all the noise and the babies crying.'

For some it was worse than others.

'They were dangerous times; there was a lady who gave birth in that camp, and there was an old lady who died on the way.'

Everyone was desperate to leave, even if it meant going back to Iraq.

'Every three days, they would come and read out a list of names of people who could be released, and we would all go and listen to see if it was our turn.'

Those who didn't hear their name were in for a double disappointment.

'While that was happening, other people were stealing your blankets.'

He looked for a way to sum it up.

'It was tough.'

Then his daughter got sick.

'My eight-year-old daughter got very sick during that time and had a temperature of 40°C (104°F), but the person who was responsible for health was the same person who was cleaning the place . . . at night he would give the same medicine, with the same spoon, to all the kids.'

It was more of a disease-spreading operation than a treatment plan.

'I told the man that the "medicine" was making people worse, but he told me, "That's not my problem. If you don't want it, don't take it." So I refused to give it to my daughter.'

The family sleeping next to Zain had been watching his daughter fading away over several days. When they overheard his debate with the fake doctor and their refusal to take the dodgy medicine, they decided to help.

'The family next to us were Kurds from Iran . . . they had recently become Christians, and they asked if they could pray for my daughter who was sick.'

In many situations, people fleeing from Iran and others coming from Iraq might have been old enemies, but not in this case.

'The Iranian lady placed her hands on my daughter's head and prayed for her.'

Zain and Layla watched and listened intently.

'Within an hour, the fever had gone and she was completely well.'

In their darkest trial, Zain and Layla stumbled across something wholly different from the despair around them. They found the peacemakers.

I have spoken to several medics since I first heard that story, and I phoned Zain and Layla in the months that followed to double-check the details. There are many theories; some say it was a coincidence, or a placebo, perhaps. Others call it what it is: an answer to prayer, a miracle. Whatever your opinion, Zain and Layla were convinced that something extraordinary was going on, something that couldn't be ignored. Whatever motivated that Iranian couple to pray for their daughter, it wasn't fear, but love.

And therein lies a world of difference.

6.

THE SEARCH

THE LOVE THAT the Iranian family showed to Zain and Layla was not a soppy or sentimental love, but a love that offers to pray for someone from a different nation and a different religion, which, in the Middle East, is no small risk.

'After my daughter was healed, this family started telling me, "We're Christians. We were Muslims in Iran, but we believed in Christ and then our lives were in danger, so we fled to Turkey."'

Zain was fascinated, but for Layla, their story felt strangely familiar.

'From the age of fourteen, my wife had been having dreams where she would see this person, a figure, and it always happened during the festivals, like Eid. In this recurring dream, the person would say to her, "My daughter, your place is not here."'

At the time, Layla didn't understand the dreams, and when she asked her mum about them, she was none the wiser. All these years later, when they took to the hills, these strange dreams became a distant comfort. She never expected to have to flee her country, but now she wondered whether she had been prepared for this day all along. In the unlikeliest of places, as the Iranian family shared their story of becoming followers of Jesus, Layla started to join the dots.

She wanted to know more about this elusive figure in her dreams, but none of them knew how much time they had, so the Iranian family gave Layla a rather dangerous gift.

'They gave us a copy of the New Testament on an audio MP3 player for my wife to listen to.'

Zain had been taught in the past to avoid the Bible because of the belief that it had been 'corrupted', Apparently.

'At school we were taught that the original version has been corrupted . . . this idea is spread throughout the Arab world and especially in Syria.'

As a consequence, most people in the Arab world have never read the Bible, but Zain had friends in Syria and Iraq who knew the corruption rumour was a myth, especially after the discovery of the Dead Sea Scrolls.

'"It is not corrupted," they told me.'

In fact, the Qur'an actually advises Muslims to consult those who read the 'earlier books' – both the Torah and the Gospels[1] – so, in theory, reading the New Testament should have been encouraged, but getting hold of a Bible in Arabic was easier said than done.

Now, all these years later, he and Layla finally had a chance to read it, or listen to it, in their mother tongue. A military detention centre is not an ideal place to be seen discussing religious texts, but on audio it was a little easier to disguise. Both families began opening up to one another, but as their friendship began to deepen, they were off, just as suddenly as they had met.

'We became friends, but then we had to leave.'

After twenty-seven days of hopeless waiting, they managed to get a bribe to one of the guards and seized a rare moment for escape. The journey to Istanbul was not without danger, but compared to the weeks they'd spent in the camp, any risk felt worth taking.

'We made it to Istanbul. It was tough; the mafia was running the smuggling business.'

They weren't there for long.

'We took a boat, like you see on TV, and got lost on the Mediterranean.'

For Zain, those memories were not as traumatic as I thought they might be.

'We were actually rescued by one of the EU boats.'

As they made their first small steps onto the sand of a new continent, Zain was in for a surprise.

'When we arrived, we were received by organisations and volunteers from churches who smiled, gave us their time, gave us blankets . . . these were people who didn't know us, didn't know our story. They knew that we were Arab Muslims, but they received us with love.'

As European coastguards pulled them off the water, he stood in awe as volunteers gathered round and threw blankets around his family. There were men and women, young and old, united in a common task – rescuing families like Zain's for no other reason than that they were fellow human beings.

He started to rethink everything.

Many in Iraq are taught that Iranians are the bad guys, but the Iranian family in the camp had been there for his family in their darkest hour. And as for Europeans, despite the centuries of conflict, the people he met were nothing but kind to Zain and his family.

It wasn't that it was plain sailing from that moment on – for the first two weeks they were literally living on the streets. But little by little, as EU systems and an army of volunteers kicked in, he began a new journey, to finish his soul-searching and to find out about the faith he'd stumbled across in the mountains of Turkey.

To his initial frustration, people in Europe seemed very awkward when he asked them about religion; it was sensitive and personal and very politically incorrect. The refugee camps had a strict culture of banning religious discussions, and most people he met were too unsure or too afraid to answer his questions.

He kept digging.

Many churches across southern Europe opened their doors as distribution centres for clothes and food and to offer help with asylum applications. There were numerous centres in cities all over the Mediterranean, but most people were so busy taking care of practical needs, they didn't stop to talk about their faith. Zain wandered between shelters looking for someone who could tell him about Jesus.

One guy asked him what he needed, and he replied, 'Nothing. I have food and shelter; I just want to know about Jesus.'

The man was shocked. Zain was the first person to ask that.

They found someone willing to talk – a former refugee who was working in a distribution centre, and this new friend sat down with Zain to explain Jesus' story.

After all those years, he finally heard about the figure at the heart of the Christian faith, one who, like Zain, had seen his world torn apart by conflict and prejudice and hatred. Zain's new friend explained that Jesus' solution to the battle around him was to absorb the consequences of evil on his own shoulders rather than let humanity destroy itself. He explained how, on a cruel Friday morning, on a cross outside another Middle Eastern city, Jesus carried the burden of human selfishness all the way to the grave. And left it there.

Zain was speechless. The idea that God would take a bullet for his own people was news to him. As he shared this story with Layla, his wife, they made a radical move. Leaving their past behind them, they decided to put their faith in this compassionate Saviour. Perhaps this was the elusive figure Layla had seen in her dream, and he was certainly the one to whom the Iranian family had prayed before their daughter was healed. As they listened to their audio Bible, they discovered that Jesus had been a Syrian refugee himself. He knew the world Zain and Layla came from, and he knew the path they had walked.

They soon decided this news was too good to keep to themselves; they wanted to share their story and live the sort of life that Jesus had lived, demonstrating love to every people group, including their own. When they finally got their papers to leave the camps behind and settle into a comfortable life in Germany, they made a surprising move – they turned it down.

To this day, they work full-time helping other refugees in centres around the Mediterranean, in the same way their Iranian friends helped them: providing for people's practical needs, fighting for their freedom and sharing the news that God is not waiting to punish people, but to love them.

THE HAPPIEST PLACE ON EARTH

Zain and Layla weren't the only people I met who'd taken the unusual step of turning down a comfortable life and going the other way. On a separate trip, I met another couple who had voluntarily returned to a war zone. It became one of my litmus tests to find people whose faith was the real deal, for not everyone who claims to be a Christian knows what that means. For some, it's just a label they're born with; for leaders in the West it can be a political tool to win votes; and for refugees, it can be a ticket to safety.

When ISIS let out a war cry to 'kill the Christians', refugee agencies stepped up support for Middle Eastern Christians, along with other minority religions like Yazidis, as they were singled out by extremists as critical targets.

But as news of this genocide filtered through refugee communities, lots of people started claiming to be a 'persecuted Christian', in the hope that it would bump them to the top of the list. I can't blame people for trying. When you're desperate to get your family to safety, who wouldn't say whatever was necessary to save their loved ones?

But how can anyone 'prove' their faith?

For me, one of the signs that someone has really become a follower of Jesus is when they turn down their resettlement place and return to the danger zone to share their faith in Jesus, at every risk to themselves. That's real commitment.

One of those was Reza. I caught up with him in an undecorated tea house in a side street of a Mediterranean town, and he greeted me like an honoured guest. His eyes seemed to hold the entire fractured history of his nation, yet his beaming face was brimming with hope. He was running a refugee centre in a busy European city and spoke more languages than anyone I have met, which is always embarrassing for a Brit who speaks . . . one. I introduced myself as a friend of a friend of a friend, and he graciously reassured me that any friend of a friend of a friend is a friend of his.

'The war came to my country, and one night I lost everything. I had a good job, I had a good life, and I lost it all in one night.'

For many years, Reza had been supporting refugees in Syria who had fled from other nations. When the roles switched, and he became one of the ones on the receiving-end, it came as a cruel shock when he was left in a makeshift camp, forgotten by the outside world.

At first, naturally, he was grateful to be rescued, to have made it out alive, to be free. But stuck in the camp, as the weeks turned to months, the initial delight turned into a growing despair.

He was anything but free.

'I'd prefer to die in Syria than be here in this situation,' he told his fellow refugees.

A group of volunteers from a local church visited the camp. Reza was surprised by how willing they were to help, so he asked one of them, Salah, what motivated him.

'I am your neighbour; I came because I care about you,' Salah replied.

Reza laughed. 'I'm surrounded by neighbours, and nobody cares here.'

Salah gave him a bit more detail. 'I'm a believer in Jesus Christ.'

Reza was having none of it. 'No, my friend, there is no God in this world. If there is, we shouldn't be here.'

Salah didn't want to get into a religious argument, so he simply encouraged Reza to pray and let it go. But Reza was adamant that prayer didn't work – he'd done that as a child, and it had made no difference.

'I found myself calling the wrong number,' he said with a sarcastic chuckle, holding his fist to his cheek.

Despite his conservative religious upbringing, Reza doubted that God even existed, but Salah had got him wondering. How could a rational, intelligent human be so sure about Jesus?

It was strictly forbidden to talk about religion in the camps, and Salah didn't want to cause any trouble, so Reza asked if he could speak with him outside the camp. He negotiated a short break with the authorities and met Salah in a nearby forest, out of earshot, to ask him some questions.

'We were in the forest. Nobody knew, not the government, not the soldiers . . .'

It sounded like a Middle Eastern version of Robin Hood.

Salah didn't want to get into the complexities of religion and politics; he simply encouraged Reza to pray to Jesus, whom he described as 'the way and the truth and the life'.[2]

Reza was curious. Maybe prayer was worth a second shot.

'My first prayer in Jesus' name was, "Use me as your worker."'

Out of the blue, Reza got a phone call from the biggest relief organisation in the country who called him in for an interview. He had given his CV to the UNHCR but had never heard anything, yet weeks later, as he prayed that tentative prayer, a partner organisation stumbled across his application and called him.

He went in for an interview, they snapped him up, and he was soon back in the refugee camp serving his own, the people he knew and loved.

Reza worked harder than anyone in that camp for he understood the despairing mindset of a refugee, and he wanted everyone to experience the new lease of life that he had been given. Contrary to some of the political propaganda in the West, most refugees entering Europe are not helpless victims waiting on handouts, but men and women with skills and talents, longing for the dignity of work and the opportunity to contribute to their new communities. When Reza was given that chance, he ran with it, doing everything in his power to help other refugees get the same break.

As he excelled in this work, he continued to quietly explore his faith. When he got hold of a Bible and stumbled across the story of Joseph (as in Joseph and the technicoloured dreamcoat), he instantly found a connection.

'I saw how Joseph was in prison, but God was using him in prison . . . I was a community leader in the camp, and I started to see myself in the story.'

When the paperwork came through for his permanent residence in a European country, it seemed he'd lucked in.

Finland.

For a number of years, Finland has been designated the happiest country in the world.[3]

Which makes it all the more surprising that Reza turned it down. The Finnish ambassador gave him a second chance.

'Go and take a breath and relax, and come back to us in ten days,' he told Reza.

Nobody turns down the Scandinavian countries, apparently.

'After ten days I went back and said, "No, I want to stay here."'

He turned down the happiest country in the world, to work with possibly the unhappiest people in the world – not grudgingly, but willingly. Joyfully. He didn't want to tap out and live a life of quiet comfort when others still needed help.

Reza's work has now expanded into a whole spectrum of different programmes, from language classes to legal advice to sports coaching – anything that can give people hope.

'We have two football teams, we do sports ministries . . . Tomorrow is International Women's Day, so we have activities just for women . . . Other times we make a trip to the sea . . . We don't want to be in front of these people or behind them, but beside them.'

When the relief organisation that Reza was working for moved on, it was so impressed with him that it decided to leave all its resources in his hands to carry on the work long term. It was an unexpected blessing and an unprecedented opportunity.

'We are so grateful to God for using us in this way, for giving us this opportunity.'

Reza now runs one of the most effective refugee programmes in the region, and is happy in the knowledge that another refugee has been gifted with that coveted place in Finland.

One of his co-workers in the centre was Zara, a beautiful Syrian lady, who had the same passion and kindness that lived in Reza. As their friendship deepened, Reza decided to be honest about his future. In the excitement and success of his relief work in Europe, he'd felt a gentle nudge in his spirit towards a different calling.

To go home.

'My vision changed. Before, I was looking for a better life; now, I want to go back to my country to share the word of God.'

He was no longer simply turning down a comfortable life of steamy saunas in Finland; he was planning on going back to Syria. He shared this nervously with Zara, expecting her to say, 'OK, bye,' but it materialised that she'd already sensed God speaking to her about the very same thing.

They are now married, a family team, working every hour they can to love and empower refugees in the camps and squats of Europe, while preparing to go back to the apex of the conflict itself. They've made three reconnaissance trips to camps in Syria already.

It's not an easy life, nor is it a safe one, but for Reza and Zara, it's the happiest place on earth.

7.

SCARS

AS I CONTINUED to interview new believers from different parts of the Middle East, I discovered a recurring theme. When they spoke about encountering Jesus, they weren't talking about a change in their religion, but a transformation in the way they viewed faith itself. They no longer focused on what rules to keep or which tribe to identify with. Their desire was for a relationship with the God who welcomed every people group.

I have interviewed believers from Muslim, Christian, Jewish and atheist cultures and, despite their religious differences, they all spoke about their experience of Jesus as something entirely new. Of course, you might think the Christians would know something about Jesus already.

Not necessarily.

Some of them seemed to know less than their Muslim neighbours. In Islam, Jesus is revered as one of the greatest prophets, but in some Christian cultures it seems he is little more than a glorified mascot, bolted on to a religion that people are fighting for, without really knowing why they are fighting.

My final interview was with a man who learned this the hard way.

And I do mean the hard way.

When I first met Karim, he flung wide his arms and embraced Dan, my translator and me, as if we were returning prodigals. We soon discovered that he was like this with everyone. It was as if the joy inside him simply could not be contained within his body and it burst out of him with slaps on the back and spontaneous laughter, like a football manager celebrating with his team after a resounding victory.

He was well built and full of energy and you could be forgiven for thinking he was twenty years younger than he really was, were it not for the thin wisps of white hair and the fact that when he grinned, his eyes squinted and smile lines rippled across his face.

Given this unquenchable joy, it came as something of a shock when I discovered that his story was more traumatic than, well, anything I've ever heard. When I felt the physical scars on his body, his innocent smile became something of a paradox.

'When I was thirteen years old, something happened to me,' he said, as we sat down around a small, square table in the corner of a busy meeting room.

Karim was born a Syrian Christian.

Or so he thought.

I'm not sure Jesus ever thought that anyone could be 'born' a Christian – quite the opposite.[1] But Karim didn't really know what a Christian was; he just loosely identified with the religion of his family and, despite knowing almost nothing about it, he was ready to fight for the crew.

'I was sitting with some of the guys in my community, and we were talking. Somebody insulted my faith, and I insulted his faith. We started fighting.'

It sounded like a story that could end badly.

'This person picked up a can of petrol from by the fire and threw it on me.'

That was worse than I thought it would be.

He was lucky to survive, but was not without injury.

'I had third-degree burns . . . For some time, I was not able to see.'

I felt sick.

'My father paid all the money he could to bring me back to normal.'

After many days in hospital, unable to move, Karim started to make a few tentative improvements.

'The doctors started giving me injections, and I began to get better

. . . After three months, I was able to see the difference between day and night.'

It was a long time before he was able to regain some semblance of a normal life.

'For about eighteen months, I was just in bed . . . After a year and a half, I began to walk again.'

When the time finally came for him to leave the hospital, he had no desire to face the world he came from.

'I refused to go to school. I didn't even want to talk Arabic.'

The scars on the outside may have appeared to have healed, but the wounds on the inside were as raw as ever.

Throughout all this trauma, he had one saving grace.

'God had given me a gift as a musician; from the age of eight, I could play the notes of anything on the electric guitar. It was just a natural gift that I could play by ear.'

Music became his lifeline, his escape route. He left his family home on the banks of the Euphrates and moved to Aleppo to pursue a new career.

'I became a professional musician and brought in a lot of money.'

It was a relief to hear some good news, and I wondered if this would be where his story hinged.

'Now I look back on that time and see it as another period of darkness.'

After everything he'd been through, I couldn't help but wonder what could be so bad about being a professional musician. He'd left the trauma behind him, he had crowds of people hanging on his every note and he was being paid to do what he loved.

But Karim didn't see it that way.

'I was just a young man, sixteen or seventeen years old, bringing in a lot of money, and I didn't know how to handle it. It was just all about me and my reputation.'

Not all his family and friends were supportive of his new-found success, either.

'My father rejected the idea of me becoming a musician because he was an officer in the army.' Apparently, music wasn't the prestigious career his father had wanted for him.

After his parents died, he had a heated argument with one of his siblings and made a knee-jerk decision.

'I decided I just wanted to leave the country and not go back. I told my family, "I'm going, and you won't see me again."'

Once again, Karim ran away. Once again, he carried his hurt with him.

Would he ever be free?

'I came to Europe in the 1980s, and some amazing things happened.'

AMAZING GRACE

I knew something must have happened to have produced the radiant man I saw before me, but nothing about Karim's story so far had revealed any hint of happiness, even when he made it as a musician. But, in Europe, he had an unexpected conversation that changed the trajectory of his thinking.

'It was actually a former Muslim who had met Jesus and told me about Jesus.'

When this man tried to talk to Karim about Jesus, initially he wasn't ready to listen. Like Reza, he'd left faith behind when he came to Europe, and he had no interest in talking to fellow Arabs, whether they were Christians or Muslims. The irony was that, while he'd buried his faith in God, his religious prejudice was as strong as ever.

'I found it very frustrating that it was a Muslim who was telling me about Jesus, because I thought, "I am the Christian."'

Karim assumed that it was impossible to change your religion – it wasn't a choice; it was just what you were born into. He came from a Christian family, and Jesus was 'his thing'. But his conviction was challenged by the presence of this new friend.

Eventually, curiosity overcame him.

'I told this person, "I need to hear about Jesus from you."'

But to justify himself, he added, 'I'm ready to die for Jesus.'

Given his past, that wasn't an entirely unfounded statement, but his new friend saw things differently.

'My former-Muslim friend said to me, "You're ready to die for religion, but Jesus died for you."'

That caught Karim off guard. He'd never known why Jesus died; nobody had really explained it to him, and he'd never asked.

'This guy showed me the Bible; it was the first time I'd seen it with my own eyes.'

For the first time, Karim read the Gospels.

'He showed me the words of John's Gospel . . . the joy was unbelievable.'

Karim went home, read everything and then raced round to his friend's house.

'I went and knocked on his door and said, "Tell me more." He told me that Jesus wanted to give me a new life.'

Karim decided to leave his religious tribalism behind and pursue something, or perhaps someone, new.

'I don't call myself a Christian,' he said, 'just a follower of Jesus.'

But letting go of the pain and prejudice of his youth was easier said than done. His new lease of life didn't make all those traumatic memories evaporate overnight; he still carried a lot of hurt and he wasn't quite ready to face the ghosts of his past. Not yet.

'I said to my friend, "Please don't put me among Arabs," because I still had a lot of pain and trauma about what had happened to me. So he sent me instead to a church with British pastors, and I was baptised there.'

For a time, Karim was the happiest man alive.

'I used to lead the worship and the music, and I started to learn the language and forget my Arabic. I also started working as an electrician in renewable energy, and I met Mya, who became my wife.'

I later tracked down those British pastors, Steve and Karen, who are now back in the UK. I had dinner with them one evening, and they filled me in on the day they met Karim.

'He was so full of joy,' Steve told me. 'You know what he's like – full of energy, full of life.'

Karim described his time at Steve and Karen's church as one of the best of his life. He would jam with anyone; music became his universal language. It was a diverse church with Greeks, Brits, Albanians, Ghanaians, all worshipping God together, and Karim loved it. He even taught Steve and Karen's three-year-old son how to play the drums.

'He's now a professional drummer,' Karen told me with a laugh. 'That's the impact Karim had on him, he was so charismatic.'

All the time he was there, Karim spoke Greek and refused to engage with anyone in Arabic.

'Through that whole period, I didn't speak any Arabic,' he told me. 'I hated the Arabs.'

Steve and Karen knew that Karim would never find peace while he harboured such bitterness, and they gently tried to show him that following Jesus was about forgiveness, not resentment. Karim knew they were right, but he wasn't ready – it was too painful. Running away was always easier, mentally and physically.

But there came a time when running away was no longer an option. As Greece found itself at the centre of a global economic recession, Karim started to look for work further afield.

'In my work, I was given an electrical project in Qatar.'

The Gulf states are culturally very different to life in Syria, and he reasoned that if he spoke Greek with his colleagues and went to an English-speaking international church, he could continue to avoid Arabic and continue to run away from his past life, even in Qatar.

That didn't last long.

When he arrived in Qatar, he found a church with South African pastors and prepared to lose himself in the music. But when Arab Christians came and befriended him, he suddenly remembered his mother tongue.

'It was a big shock for me . . . I had rejected Arabic and locked it away, never to be touched.'

The Arab Christians in Qatar treated him with such love and dignity, he started to realise that he couldn't harbour his resentment forever. With the help of his new friends, he started to process the trauma of his early years, to forgive the people who had hurt him and to find freedom from the anxiety he had buried when he had moved to Greece all those years earlier.

His new friends were exactly what he needed. They helped him find peace, not by running away from conflict, but by choosing forgiveness and mercy instead. And he didn't just find freedom from his past, he also began to discover a new love for the Arab world, a love he believed God was rekindling for a purpose.

Something was brewing on the horizon.

DREAMS AND VISIONS

Karim loved Qatar, he loved the job, he loved his new friends and he had everything he could want. He started making plans to bring his wife and children over and even began looking at schools. But as they all started to get excited about this new life, Karim had a strange and powerful vision, which caught him completely off guard.

'I had a vision of the Middle East with inter-connected circles. There were four circles over Turkey and one circle over Greece, and in that circle over Greece there was an arrow that was going to be fired into Europe.'

He had no idea what it meant, but he knew from experience that mass migrations out of the Middle East are usually a bad sign. The situation in Syria had been escalating for some time, but at that point few people were leaving. Most Syrians thought their country was too stable to completely implode and it would only be a matter of time before the conflict would be resolved, like it had been in Tunisia at the outset of the Arab Spring. Karim's vision seemed to suggest otherwise. He started to fear for his homeland, his people, his family. What should he do? How could he warn people? Would they take him seriously? He didn't even know if he took the vision seriously himself.

He decided to take a short break and return to Greece to talk it through with the one person he trusted more than anyone: Mya.

'I shared my vision with my wife and told her that I felt I needed to stay in Greece, but it was very difficult because it was leaving all the certainty and stability of Qatar.'

They were at a crossroads. They could escape to Qatar and live a life of luxury before the refugee crisis really kicked off, or Karim could quit his job in Qatar and move back to Greece, and they could all roll their sleeves up and prepare for a mass migration.

But how would they provide for their family?

Mya was nervous. She was raising their young children and without Karim's well-paid job in Qatar they were on thin ice. She saw it as a test of faith and, despite her fears, she believed if God had given Karim a vision, God would provide the resources; they just had to be obedient.

'God told us, "I will take care of everything,"' Karim told us confidently.

He moved back to Greece full-time and took on work as an electrician. It wasn't the prestigious job he had had in Qatar, but they were surviving.

Then the phone started to ring.

People in boats on the Mediterranean began calling Karim in a panic, often as they were taking on water and starting to sink. Karim would work out their location while Mya would be next to him with a map, finding the nearest island and calling the Greek coastguard. When people got to the mainland, Karim and Mya would take them in and help get them back on their feet.

As Karim explained the situation, I couldn't help but wonder where people got his number.

Mya explained: 'There was a guy who we helped in the early days of the war; he was a friend of ours. When the refugee crisis really escalated, he set up a Facebook page in Arabic with instructions to fellow Syrians saying, "When you get to Greece, call this guy. He is a Syrian living in Greece. He can help you."'

He put Karim's number on the Facebook page, but for some reason he forgot to tell Karim and Mya. They were none the wiser.

The phone continued to ring.

'These are Syrians. They're relational people; they want to talk to someone they trust,' she explained. 'There is a lot of fear.'

It's easy for people in the UK to think that in an emergency we'd phone 999, but we're not fleeing a war zone where the authorities that are supposedly there to protect us are part of the problem. When you don't know who to trust, who do you turn to? When a former refugee who has made it to Greece says, 'Call this guy. He's Syrian. He can help you,' that's exactly what any sane person would do.

But, unlike Reza, Karim wasn't qualified to deal with the complexities of emergency rescues or mass migration. His skill set was as an electrician and his background was in music. Many churches in Greece opened their doors and became points of shelter for refugees and they were a lifeline to people like Reza and Zain, but Karim wasn't sure that working for a church was his calling.

'I had no plan, and I knew that I didn't want to become the pastor of a church. I'm happiest as a musician, just worshipping God, playing music.'

He decided that if playing music was what had brought him comfort in his darkest hour, then music would be the thing he'd bring to other people in theirs. He started visiting refugees in their squats and settlements with nothing but a meal and his guitar.

'I used to go to the supermarket, buy some food, take my guitar and just visit a family.'

He went wherever he felt God leading him and reached out to whoever was put before him.

'I would just play music, as that seemed to bring a sense of peace and joy to people.'

On one occasion, he went to visit a couple of Syrian guys. Mya had cooked some food for him to take for them. When he arrived, there were more than twenty people in the house. They were chatting about their situation, and they invited Karim to join in the conversation and then play some music. As he strummed his guitar, the mood lifted and people started to sing. One guy was out that night, but halfway through the evening he walked in and said something nobody was expecting.

Karim explained, 'One person called Ahmed came in and said to me, "Do you know about Jesus?"'

Karim hadn't been talking about religion. None of his new friends knew anything about his faith.

'I said, "Yes, of course," and he said, "Can you tell me?" I was surprised, but gently and tentatively I shared about my faith, and Ahmed said, "Can you pray with me?"'

Mya later filled me in on Ahmed's story. He had been searching for God for some time, but nobody seemed willing or able to tell him about Jesus, even in the Orthodox churches. It was the same experience Zain had had. One evening, while Ahmed was out having a coffee, he felt an overwhelming urge to go home.

'He felt within himself that he had to go home right then,' Mya told me.

When he walked in and saw Karim, he felt immediately, 'That man knows Jesus.' He had never met Karim before and there was nothing about him that signalled his faith – he wasn't singing Christian music or wearing a giant cross around his neck. But something prompted Ahmed to ask. Karim quietly shared his story of freedom and healing through faith in Jesus, and Ahmed was gripped.

'Ahmed is now going to a church in Sweden,' Karim said, with a laugh.

It wasn't that Karim became a preacher – far from it; he was a musician, not a priest. He never forced his faith on others, nor did he get sucked into heated arguments – that was the very thing he'd left behind in his youth. He simply loved people, and when they wanted to know the reason for the hope inside him, or when, like Ahmed, people had a strange conviction that he had something they needed to know, he was happy to share his story.

'Many, many times, I've had people asking me about faith and wanting to believe before I even approach them. There are many people all across Europe who came to know Jesus.'

The more he got to know people, the more he wanted to help them, but playing music and sharing his story wasn't going to help them find a place to live. Karim had another string to his bow that was desperately needed by the authorities in Greece: he could translate between Greek and Arabic.

After years of running away from his mother tongue, now he found it was the very thing he could offer. He comforted refugees who'd just arrived, he liaised with the Greek authorities to help people with their resettlement applications and, often, he was simply a shoulder to cry on, someone willing and able to listen.

Mya was more gifted than Karim in logistics and business and she also spoke English, so between them they were quite a team. They gave out emergency meals, winter clothing, language lessons, specialist care for refugees with disabilities – whatever was needed. They soon attracted funding from donors and organisations who wanted to help but needed people on the ground they could trust. Before they knew it, Karim and Mya were running an organisation.

Karim had to leave all his work as an electrician to run the centre full-time and, as he did so, the funds and resources flowed in like never before.

The more people came to them, the more they needed to expand, but rather than building a big business with five-year plans and slick marketing campaigns, they decided to employ refugees whom they'd previously helped, to reach out to the next wave.

The rescued became the rescuers.

'Everyone comes with different wounds. Here you see people from different Arab countries, crying together, praying together ... it's amazing.'

Some have suffered at the hands of soldiers; others were the soldiers, even as children.

'One of the guys here was forced to fight, to carry weapons and to shoot. He hated it; he never wanted to do it, but he was forced to.'

Even though Karim's centre has people who have come from opposite sides of multiple conflicts, it felt like one of the safest places I've ever visited. It's impossible to overstate the significance of this. Enemies don't become friends just like that. Hatred and hurt don't disappear without something quite extraordinary taking their place.

'It just seems like we're a big family,' he said, looking for a way to capture the movement. 'We have a team of employees, all former refugees from Syria, Iran and Kurdistan, who are helping people to resettle.'

Having such a competent team frees Karim up to do what he does best – to listen to people as they pour their heart out.

'We first need to listen to them, listen to all their pain and all their troubles, and then embrace them.'

He wrapped his arms around himself, closed his eyes and smiled, as if we needed to be reminded of the simple power of a hug.

'I tell them that God is love.'

That was more than a throwaway comment; people saw it in him.

I saw it in him.

While we chatted in the corner of the meeting room, there was a constant stream of people stopping to see Karim and to receive the same fatherly affection that he'd shown us. I've never heard so much laughter from so many people. There were young and old, Muslims and Christians, men and women from nations all over the world, many of them previously at war with each other. There were no rivals in Karim's meetings, just translators. Even the smallest of gatherings often had four or more languages being translated at a time.

It was slow going, but nobody was in a hurry. The more time people spent with Karim, the more they seemed to catch his uncrushable joy.

He lives the original mandate of a peacemaker – not someone who negotiates agreements between warring parties, but someone who *makes* peace, who brings a deep healing and wholeness into people's lives, until old feelings of hatred are overwhelmed by new desires to love.

For me, not speaking the language of the people I interview is almost always a disadvantage, but occasionally it can give a fresh perspective. Until Karim's words were translated, I watched his body language and tuned in to the unspoken atmosphere around the people he met. As I observed him interacting with everyone around him, I had a profound realisation. One of the saddest lessons I've learned in situations of trauma is that, often, hurt people hurt people. The bullied become the next bullies.

But in my encounter with Karim, I realised that the opposite is also true.

Healed people heal people.

Free people free people.

It's beautiful to behold.

Karim had found healing and freedom from the scars of his past and he wanted to help others find the same. Even the external scars from the burning seemed to have faded and, looking at his beaming face, you'd never know.

Unless you knew.

But he isn't entirely without a reminder.

He stretched out his leg as he chatted to Dan, our translator, and without thinking, I leaned over to look. Karim thought I was leaning over to physically touch his leg, but to be honest, I didn't really know what I was doing. I was just curious. Dan filled me in.

'He said that the scars on his legs remain and he needs to put cream on every day, even all these years later.'

I didn't know what to say. Karim grinned.

'It's OK,' he said in English. 'You can touch.'

I leaned down, a little awkwardly, and touched the skin on his leg. The back of his knee was hard and leathery, like a lizard. Decades after that fateful day, he had a daily reminder of that moment of madness. He looked serious for a second and patted his leg.

'I feel that God has said to me, "I allowed these scars to remain so that you can convince people of what you have been through."'

Then he grinned and stretched his fingers out over his face. '"But I've brought healing to your face," he said, "so you can show them that nothing is impossible."'

He laughed and, seeing the solemn look on Dan's face, leaned across the table and squeezed his arm reassuringly.

The scars on his legs might remain, but the inner pain that he had carried for years has long since evaporated. There wasn't a sniff of bitterness about him. Only laughter. Constantly.

Never have I met someone who has found such joy after such trauma. And he hasn't kept it to himself. Countless others have found their peace through meeting Karim.

Free people free people.

It's just what they do.

8

THE TWENTY-ONE

ONE OF THE threads running through all my interviews was the desire people had for me to share their story. I'd set out on this journey thinking that I would have to politely ask whether people would mind me recording their words, and offer quick reassurance that I would change names and disguise any distinguishing details, but most of them were far less anxious than I was. While I was worried about who I might offend, my new Middle Eastern friends weren't inhibited by political correctness; they just wanted to get their stories out there. They saw themselves as witnesses with testimonies that needed to be heard.

I guess that's what they are.

In a court of law, there are many people with different roles, arguing one way or another. Some are presenting a case; others are defending a person or company; the jury has to discuss the evidence and decide on a verdict; the judge has to listen to everyone and work out the sentence. It's all very stressful (or exciting, if you like courtroom dramas).

But the witnesses don't have to worry about any of that; they are simply asked to share their story. All they need to do is tell the truth, the whole truth and nothing but the truth, and what people do with the evidence, well, that's out of their hands. It's the exact commission that Jesus gave to his first followers.

His parting words to his early team were, 'You will be my witnesses in Jerusalem, and in all Judea and Samaria, and to the ends of the earth.'[1]

It must have sounded far-fetched to the first followers, that ragtag bunch of fishermen with no oratory skills, no legal qualifications and no idea how they would get to 'the ends of the earth'.

But, as history has shown, that's precisely what happened. The early Jesus movement grew and flourished with almost no resources and under intense persecution. And it really did reach the ends of the earth.

I would know.

The only reason I heard about Jesus in my homeland was because once upon a time, some brave souls from the Middle East took a perilous journey to a muddy island in the North Atlantic, learned the language of these strange farmers and told one of my ancestors that there was more to life than turnips and tribal warfare.

The archaeological record of pagan Britain paints a grim picture of mass murder and cannibalism.[2] When Roman historians first set foot on British soil, they found the inhabitants wading through swamps naked,[3] polygamous to the point of utter confusion, obsessed with dyeing their entire bodies blue,[4] highly superstitious and extremely savage.[5]

It seems we were a bit weird.

Thank God those Middle Eastern Christians stopped by.

They must have been brave.

Being a witness, then as now, is dangerous work. There's a reason why witnesses in significant court cases need protection. But Jesus' witnesses don't always have 'protection'; he never promised that they would. If you want to represent a Messiah who was beaten and killed, there must be at least the possibility that you'll meet the same fate. In the original language of the New Testament, the word we translated as 'witness' is a word most of us already know.

Martyr.

The fact that we think of a martyr as someone who has died for their faith shows how far the earliest witnesses were prepared to go.

The same is true today.

In February 2015, twenty-one Christians were beheaded on a Libyan beach by ISIS fighters. The grisly event was filmed and posted on social media, and the image of these men in orange jumpsuits kneeling in front of soldiers dressed in black haunted people's screens right across the world.

The newspapers reported them as victims, but in Egypt that's not how they are remembered.

They were martyrs.

None of those twenty-one men was a helpless victim. If they had renounced their faith, there is a strong possibility that they would have been set free. They didn't.

Two years after their execution, the German writer Martin Mosebach travelled to a remote corner of Egypt to interview their families. What he encountered was not grieving relatives, but forgiving parents and emboldened partners, honoured that their husbands and brothers and sons had passed the ultimate test of the witness and refused to cave in at the final moment.

Mosebach explained, 'All the houses I visited shared one common feature: the household was not in mourning. Condolences and expressions of sympathy seemed out of place. Each family seemed to me to be elevated to a higher plane.'[6]

When he later heard people referring to them as victims, Mosebach was indignant: 'I found it repugnant when the Twenty-One were referred to as "victims of terrorism." The word "victim" seemed too passive to me . . . they had audibly professed their faith in Jesus Christ just before and even during their decapitation.'[7]

Few martyrs are ever given a fair trial, not even Jesus. His own trial was so shamelessly rigged, it was embarrassing. The unjust execution of the twenty-one seems especially unfair given that they were being punished by ISIS for an association with religious and political battles they had nothing to do with. The hooded soldier who ordered the executions made a passionate speech inciting Rome and incriminating America, with a stream of visual cues to reinforce his point.

But none of these men was connected to any of that; they were Egyptian Copts.

The Copts are not bound to Europe or America; they played no part in the Crusades or the invasion of Iraq. Their long history speaks more of quiet endurance than violent retribution.

Far from being a curse to the Middle East and North Africa, they have more often been a blessing, running everything from Cairo's rubbish collection to state-of-the-art hospitals in Upper Egypt. Despite the institutionalised racism that has plagued them for centuries, most Egyptians admire the Copts. Some even seek them out in times of need, for the prayers of the Copts seem to invite mercy on every people group. And when persecution does come, by the minority who oppose them, they tend to fight fire not with fire but with forgiveness. Endurance. Even love.

How is it that twenty-one men, after loving their neighbours so flawlessly, could be rounded up and executed for their perceived connection to an international battle that they were never part of? Perhaps they were in the wrong place at the wrong time.

But, as Mosebach discovered, the men knew exactly what dangers lay ahead when they travelled to Libya in search of work. And still they went. As impoverished farmers, the wages they earned as migrant workers would enable them to provide for their families far better than if they were to stay at home. As good husbands and fathers, they were willing to take the risk to provide for the ones they loved.

But they also vowed that if they were captured, they would not and could not recant their faith. Mosebach explained, 'The Christians' concept of truth is neither formula nor doctrine – it is a person, Jesus Christ . . . The secret behind the religion's expansion are the people who, from the very start, were ready to die for their love of Jesus: martyrs.'[8]

Of the twenty-one martyrs, twenty were Egyptian. Only one was not: Matthew was Ghanaian.

Of all of those captured, Matthew would have found it easiest, in theory, to escape. The others had known each other from childhood and would have supported one another to the final hour, representing their shared Coptic heritage and standing in a long line of brave martyrs who are now revered as saints. But Matthew was not part of that. He was even reportedly offered to be set free, to deny his connection to 'the nation of the cross' and hit the road.

He did nothing of the sort.

He may not have been a Coptic Egyptian, but as a fellow follower of Jesus he was considered a brother to the other twenty, a saint in the Egyptian church and a martyr on the beach of Libya. In the gory film released by ISIS, Matthew's posture was tall and defiant; he held his head high, unswerving in his faith, as Issam, one of his Coptic brothers, whispered a word of encouragement to strengthen his soul. Their last words. At least in this life.

STRONGER THAN REVENGE

If this was a Hollywood film and the execution of the twenty-one formed the opening scene, the rest of the film would probably be an action-packed revenge plot, culminating in a bloody shoot-out, where the families finally get their 'justice'. For a world increasingly indoctrinated by formulaic movies, the families of the twenty-one speak a truth that is better than any revenge story.

Their desire not to cave in to bitterness or revenge should not be misinterpreted as weakness or denial. Far from it. Both the martyrs and their families went through hell, and they were deeply honest about their pain, raw with tears. But as the dust settled on their desert town, all were adamant that grief would not have the last word.

'ISIS thought they would break our hearts. They did not,' the wife of twenty-six-year-old Milad Makin declared with quiet conviction. 'Milad is a hero now and an inspiration for the whole world.'

Perhaps the mother of Abanoub Ayiad found the greatest strength of all. 'May God forgive ISIS for the pain and suffering we have been through,' she said, just days after their execution.[9]

Forgiveness does not mean passivity, and some commended the Egyptian President's immediate decision to attack ISIS strongholds in Libya. But such praise was driven more by a desire to protect other minorities from the same fate than a hunger for personal payback.

Mosebach himself witnessed, 'In the many conversations I had, never once did anyone call for retribution or revenge, not even for the murderers to be punished . . . because the martyrs' sheer splendour outshone them . . . The martyrs had "fought the good fight," "finished the race," and "kept the faith," as the apostle Paul writes, in a line all of them would have known well.'[10]

Revenge wasn't absent only from the lips of the families; it was also absent from the final words of the men themselves. In their last moments on earth, they didn't plead for mercy or incite war. They did not behave like victims or enemies, for ultimately they were neither. They were not desperate or fearful or angry or despairing, but calm, collected, assured and confident. With their dying breath, they simply offered the name of their Saviour with gentle, unbreakable conviction.

'Ya Rabbi Yassou!' 'Oh, my Lord Jesus!'[11]

Two thousand years may have passed between the earthly lives of the twenty-one and their hero, but their lives and legacies are not so different. Jesus' dying prayer as he hung from the cross was, 'Father, forgive them, for they do not know what they are doing.'[12] Those words must have echoed in the soldiers' ears long after they hammered the nails into his wrists, for they soon realised the full force of what they had done.

'And when the centurion, who stood there in front of Jesus, saw how he died, he said, "Surely this man was the Son of God!"'[13]

He wasn't the last centurion to make such a confession, and nor was Jesus the last to die. The first disciple to meet a similar fate was Stephen, 'a man full of God's grace and power',[14] who, on completion of a powerful witness statement, was subject to a public stoning by the religious elite. With his dying breath, he echoed the same words as his hero: 'Lord, do not hold this sin against them.'[15]

Few stop to realise that Stephen's dying prayer was answered. The murderer, Saul of Tarsus, who was overseeing the execution, was later converted, and he travelled the world witnessing to the mercy of Jesus, the mercy he had first witnessed in the martyr, Stephen.

Two thousand years later, the revolution continues. As fresh blood soaks into the desert sands of North Africa, the wildfire of forgiven souls spreads once again through the dying prayers and courageous mercy of the martyrs. I wonder if we owe these martyrs more than we realise, for if nobody had refused to bow the knee to Caesar, perhaps we would still be ruled by Rome.

Only the brave resisted, but then, as now, when someone makes a stand, 'the spines of others are strengthened'.[16] And refusing to recant your faith when you have a sword pressed against your neck really is making a stand.

Of course, that's not true just in the Middle East. For hundreds of years, being a follower of Jesus in Europe could have got you into serious trouble from the government and even from the medieval church. What went wrong there?

The same pattern continues all over the world today. I have interviewed people in the persecuted church on every continent, people who imitate the life of the peaceful revolutionary and who refuse to deny him, however much they suffer for the privilege.

The irony is that, all over the world, as Christians are treated with suspicion, some killed and others rounded up and thrown into prison, their captors rarely realise that these Christians pose no threat to the state at all. Jesus taught his followers to love their neighbours, to defend the poor, to respect those in authority, to pay their taxes and to pray for those who persecute them.[17]

When paranoid dictators throw Christians to the lions, they're shooting themselves in the foot.

I recently interviewed an Eritrean doctor, a man wanted by the Eritrean authorities for daring to expose the way they treat their Christians. Thousands of Christians in Eritrea have been detained indefinitely with no trial and for no charge other than because the government just doesn't like Christians unless they're in churches that are controlled by the state. Prisoners are given the option of signing a form to recant their faith or staying in prison.

Some have signed it. Some have refused.

The refusers are still in prison – those who have survived, that is.

The doctor told me about one young girl, a teenager when she was arrested. She refused to sign the form to recant her faith. She's now in her twenties and is still in prison.

She's not alone. Eritrea is by no means the only government that acts in this way.

Some 3,711 Christians were thrown into prison last year by authoritarian regimes right across the world.[18] I wonder who is crazier – the paranoid nationalists who throw innocent believers into jail, or the die-hard faithful who refuse to give in? I asked my Eritrean friend why that young lady wouldn't sign the form. His answer still rings in my ears: 'She is brave.'

A similar story unfolded in West Africa when the extremist group Boko Haram abducted 110 schoolgirls on 19 February 2018. Many escaped, but Leah Sharibu stayed with a sick classmate and was captured. It was typical of Leah, as fellow classmate Affodia Andrawus recalled: 'If anyone is sick . . . Leah is always the first to go and greet and pray for that person.'

A month later, all the surviving girls were released. Except one.

One of Leah's fellow prisoners explained that before they boarded the truck home, they were told to deny their faith. Leah refused.

'Never.'

So they kept her in captivity.

'No matter how much Leah is mistreated or insulted . . . she will never retaliate,' her friend said. 'Instead, Leah will look for a way to make peace with everyone.'[19]

She is a peacemaker, never retaliating, yet never denying her faith.

She is brave.

Before she watched the truck disappear, Leah scribbled a note to her mother and pressed it into the hand of a classmate:

I know it is not easy missing me, but I want to assure you that I am fine where I am. My God, whom we have been praying to with you, is showing Himself mighty in my trying moment. I know your words to me during our morning devotions that God is very close to people in pain. I am witnessing this now. I am confident that one day, I shall see your face again. If not here, then there at the bosom of our Lord Jesus Christ.[20]

Leah is no victim; she is a witness to the true Jesus revolution, a community built on courageous faith, servant-hearted compassion and unbreakable peace. In many ways, her life is a window into the purity of the early Jesus movement.

PIONEERS

For three centuries, the early Jesus movement expanded in number and potency despite all the persecutions the ancient world could muster. The early Christians were kinder, braver and happier than anyone else on earth. Despite having what appeared to be the hardest lives imaginable, they had a deep joy that Rome simply couldn't extinguish. No tortures could threaten them, no temptations could dissuade them and no treasures could seduce them. They were unbreakable. And people from every segment of society joined their communities.

But then something happened that nobody expected.

Christianity became fashionable.

The Emperor Constantine declared Christianity to be the official state religion, and the movement that couldn't be quenched by three centuries of persecution lost its way at the hands of political popularity.[21] Comfort quenched the passion that oppression never could.

With Constantine's 'help', Jesus' radical movement of peace and love became just another man-made institution with buildings and budgets, violence and politics.

That's popularity for you.

The supposedly Christian state grew in power and influence, while the followers of Jesus – those who actually behaved like him – took the movement underground. European powers continued to wage war on the rest of the world, getting further and further from the God they claimed to worship, but the Jesus movement continued, below the radar, quietly building schools and hospitals while the powers-that-be were more interested in building forts and stealing resources. At times, the state ignored the Jesus movement, but when the movement threatened the state's power, the believers were found hanging from the gallows. Teachers and doctors, missionaries and pastors had a habit of disappearing when they spoke out against injustice.

But while power corrupts, persecution tends to purify.

Perhaps this explains the timeless paradox at the heart of the current rise in persecution. While religious oppression has increased almost universally worldwide, while eight Christians die for their faith every day, and while thousands more are being thrown into prison and driven from their homes, the movement they are part of is *growing*.

How can this be?

Surely, if so many Christians are being exiled, imprisoned and executed, their faith should be shrinking?

The reality is that while Christians are leaving Africa and the Middle East in their millions, others are finding Jesus in their wake, some of them the very oppressors who were persecuting the Christians who have just left. I recently met an Iraqi man who was raised to hate Christians more than any other people group, until a vision of Jesus in the middle of the night led him to become a secret disciple of the faith he once sought to destroy. These aren't just stories from the ancient past. I met this man. I shook his hand. We laughed and chatted and drank coffee together. He is a brother, one of the countless new believers in a revolution that is as unstoppable as it is unpredictable.

In many ways, all the people in these chapters are martyrs.

There are those, like the twenty-one, who have paid the ultimate price, and others, like the faithful in prison, whose living sacrifices are a witness to their fellow inmates and their prison guards and will one day be a witness, I hope, to the world. Then there are the Middle Eastern believers whom I've had the privilege of meeting at the end of their tumultuous journeys across mountains and oceans and whose witness statements I've heard with my own ears. Their stories point far beyond the religious bickering of leaders and politicians, to the raw power of a life lived in relationship with a loving God.

But for all the trials and tribulations of the martyrs, the thing that inspired me most about all of them was not their endurance, but their joy. It is something I haven't witnessed anywhere else, not even in the comfortable West.

It's not the deluded happiness of people living in denial, for these martyrs are well aware of their predicament, and they don't take kindly to it. But there is a deeper contentment in their souls, a fire in their belly that cannot be quenched, despite all the persecutions that any extremist can muster.

Perhaps one of the greatest testaments to the joy of the witness comes from those who have escaped a war zone, who have endured a journey of unimaginable trauma, who have waited for months or even years in a refugee camp, who finally get the paperwork to settle in the comfort of another country . . . and have turned it down.

Why would anyone do that?

All three of my Syrian friends – Zain, Reza and Karim – turned down health, wealth and prosperity, from lucrative jobs in Qatar to saunas in Finland, for the higher joy of being the heart and hands of Jesus to those who need their love and support more than ever.

That's real witness.

Part Three
COMMUNITY

9.

HEAVEN'S HOOLIGANS

AS MY GAZE shifted back to my own culture, I wondered how I could carry the lessons I'd learned from the Middle East into the world that I live in. Can love and freedom overcome fear and division in the West? Where are the peacemakers in my nation?

Compared to the Middle East, I didn't think the UK had such distinct 'us and them' divisions. We don't need to 'love our enemies'; most of us don't really have enemies. Or do we? Is the United Kingdom really that united? How about the United States – one big happy family, right?

The term 'united' is becoming a bit stretched.

Political debates and border disputes have a habit of rekindling old prejudices. Perhaps now, more than ever, we need to learn how to love the other communities in our nation, or perhaps the other nations in our communities. Some prejudices are easy to spot, but others are more subtle, like political allegiances and opinions.

I've heard people on both the left and the right accusing *everyone* on the other side of being judgemental or intolerant. How ironic. The tragedy of both pride and prejudice is that they are so easy to spot . . . in others. But can I learn to love the neighbours in my community, and in the process conquer the pride and prejudice in my own heart?

If there's one person who has helped me answer that question, it's Dave.

In every English city, perhaps every European city, there is a tribal tendency that echoes through football stadiums on either side of town. Everyone knows the score: you're either north or south, red or blue,

Celtic or Rangers. The only thing that can unite people across such divides is even bigger divides: France vs Germany, Spain vs Portugal, England vs anyone.

I remember the first time I saw Tottenham play at White Hart Lane. It was intense. If an Arsenal fan had found themselves in the wrong stand, they'd probably have been safer in a war zone.[1]

Bristol has one of the least sophisticated rivalries in the country. There's literally a river dividing the city. If you're south, you're City; if you're north, you're Rovers.

The Bristol City supporters had a rather zealous wing known as the City Service Firm.

Rovers fans are officially known as 'The Pirates', but within this motley crew a more executive gang started to form: the Young Executives. They didn't attend matches to sing songs; they went to meet the City Service Firm.

And those meetings meant business.

My first glimpse into the world of football hooliganism came when I least expected it, during a school assembly. I was standing at the back with the other geography teachers in our crumpled Gore-Tex® jackets, looking like we were about to take off on a field trip. After some rapturous applause for the house that won Sports Day, everyone settled down to hear a short talk from our guest speaker, the Rev. Dave Jeal, chaplain to Bristol Rovers.

It's fair to say, nobody was quite prepared for what came next. It's not every day you meet a Pirate hooligan. Thousands of ears hung on his every word as I struggled to reconcile his history of violence with the quiet peace that seemed to surround him as he spoke. If his path had been mapped out by a careers advisor, it would have looked like this:

One: Start by terrorising your rival football club.

Two: Graduate to international street fights with fascist gangs in Sweden.

Three: Become a vicar.

How did that Dave become this Dave?

I recruited former student Zac Crawley, now running his own film-making business in London, and we hiked over to Dave's estate on a windy summer's morning to capture an unbarred account of his story.

We were about to discover one of the most unlikely friendships in hooligan history.

WILD CHILD

The paradox of a life of violence is that for those immersed in that world, it takes greater strength to fight for peace than it does to knock someone out. Raising a fist is second nature; turning the other cheek takes real courage.

When we met Dave that morning, it was clear he had found that courage somewhere. As we followed him through the labyrinth of church corridors, shuffling round the mums and tots and chatting to the staff in the kitchen, there was an unmistakable lightness in the air.

When you trust someone implicitly and feel safe in their presence, it shows in a thousand subconscious signs. Dave is that man for many in his neighbourhood. We could see it in the way people spoke to him that morning, and we saw it in their faces as we walked the streets later in the day.

It's as if the intensity he once possessed to damage people, he now exercises in loving them. He has the same zeal, just for good rather than evil.

It's not that people didn't know the past Dave; they knew his story, and they knew his history of violence. But they had also witnessed the transformation. As we slumped down on the moth-eaten IKEA sofas at the back of the church kitchen, I asked Dave where it all started. I wanted to know the whole story: the good, the bad and the ugly.

For Dave, life had turned ugly at an early age.

'My parents had split up and I was living with my nan . . . I was expelled from school for stabbing someone in the face with a pencil.'

He was five years old.

'That was pretty bad.'

A fair assessment.

By the time he left school at fifteen, Dave had honed the art of aggression all through his childhood.

'Growing up, I never felt happy. I just felt anger and resentment towards anyone and anything.'

When he started going to football matches, he met the Young Executives. It was a match made in heaven.

'The whole football violence thing is that you are angry.'

It was a good summary for beginners.

'Happy people don't wanna hurt people.'

That makes sense.

'It takes over your life . . . Whenever I was in the car, I would be lairy with people. If I was walking along the street and I thought someone was being a bit unpleasant, I would have a go back. I was . . .' He paused for a second, searching for the right phrase. 'I was bristling with unpleasantness.'

Dave's rivalry with the City Service Firm grew into mass brawls that seemed to bring the whole city to a standstill.

'They hated us, and we hated them. There were areas of town you could go to on a Friday or Saturday night and areas you couldn't, 'cos they'd be City pubs and these would be Rovers' pubs. When we crossed over . . .'

He hesitated.

'When we crossed over, it wasn't nice.'

We got the idea.

I couldn't help but wonder what happened when rivals met at work or in the supermarket? Surely the entire city couldn't be red or blue? There are plenty in Bristol who are neither. The Bristol Rugby supporters are rather courteous in my experience, and minor cricket rivalries tend to boil over into a polite 'tut' rather than a fight to the death. Surely the entire city wouldn't tolerate this inane violence?

Dave explained how it worked when they were off duty.

'There were sort of cross-overs. If you were on a building site and you knew someone, you'd be kind of like, "Alright, mate." They'd know you were Rovers, and you'd know they were City. There were friend-ships, but it couldn't be sort of open.'

He laughed. 'Especially on a Saturday, all that went out the window.'

It seemed bizarre that when forced to get on, they could manage it. In the cold light of day they could forget their differences and work semi-harmoniously together. It made it even more ridiculous that on match day they could switch off their brains and turn into mortal enemies.

It's something teachers see the world over. One to one, even the most disruptive teenagers can be positively endearing, but when they're with their mates, mob rule can take over. Maybe that's what football hooligans are – just big teenagers.

But the culture isn't entirely without morals; there were unwritten rules they all abided by.

'People with hats and shirts and the rest of it, they're not involved; you leave them alone.'

The City Service Firm abided by the same code. One of their leaders was Mark Saunders, Divvy to his mates. He was one of the big players in Bristol's football violence with up to a thousand men under his command in match-day clashes.

Dave and Divvy didn't get on, to put it mildly.

But they both abided by the same code. Divvy described it like this: 'Nobody with a scarf or a hat on got hit, no one who didn't wanna have a fight had a fight.'

This wasn't the last time that Dave and Divvy would agree on some-thing.

The 'rules' made me think these men weren't as unhinged as I had first thought. They were just guys who enjoyed fighting and were happy to keep it among themselves. Even fight clubs have rules.

But to say he 'enjoyed' fighting seems like a slightly twisted way of putting it. Joy didn't feature very highly in his early days.

'Happy people don't wanna hurt people.'

INTERNATIONAL MAN OF MYSTERY

It wasn't long before Dave was itching for something bigger. The weekly scraps in Bristol were becoming too familiar. He'd been banned from the Rovers' stadium for five years – not that he stopped going. 'They didn't have cameras in those days,' he said with a smirk.

At one point, he did a runner from the country and ended up in Thailand.

'I wanted to become a hippy,' he said, then added with a modest chuckle, 'but I was a bit too lairy to be a hippy.'

Things went from bad to worse.

'My unpleasantness got me to the point where the girl I was living with left me, I lost my job through the football violence because the bosses had seen me on the television doing stuff and I had nowhere to live . . . I hated my life.'

He'd reached rock bottom.

'I think with any kind of addiction, or whatever it is, you've got to get to the stage where you hit rock bottom.'

You'd think that this would be the place where he'd start to question what he was doing, but if anything, he got worse.

'I'd gone to Sweden for the European championships, and it all kicked off with these Swedish fans . . . I punched this lad, and he went down, and I kicked him. We went off up the road and looted a petrol station. As we came back down the road, the guy was on the ground, and he was unconscious, and there were people jumping on him, up and down on his head.'

Something shifted in Dave.

'I went over, and I was like, "What you doing?" and they said, "He's Swedish," and I said, "Flippin leave him, you're gonna kill him." I just felt sickened, the way he kind of moved, or didn't move on the ground, and the blood . . . it was just horrible.'

For the first time, Dave started to react to what he was part of, to defend the supposed enemy, although admittedly he was the one who had put the guy on the floor in the first place. He decided to call on the only person he knew who had any sense.

'My mum had become a Christian, so I phoned her and said, "Could you do one of your prayers?" She said, "Listen, I don't want anything else to do with you . . . we've seen what you've done and the police are after you in Sweden."'

Dave's family had seen footage of him on the news. Not at his best.

If he'd thought he was hitting rock bottom before, now there was no doubt. His voice quietened as he continued. 'Not only was I pretty upset by my family not wanting anything to do with me, but I was in a foreign country and wanted.'

Despite reaching out to his mum and asking for prayer in that moment of madness, Dave wasn't exactly open to religion.

'I gotta say, I was looking for something, but I wasn't looking for God. And the last thing I was looking for was Jesus because I absolutely hated Christians.'

Dave's mum was clearly the lucky exception.

'I just thought they were the most judgemental, unpleasant people I had ever met in my life . . . ' He laughed. '. . . until I met some.'

I'M NOT SCARED OF ANYTHING

When Val, Dave's mum, said she didn't want any more to do with him, evidently she didn't entirely mean it. That's the thing with some Christians – they just keep on forgiving.

'My mum had become a Christian and set up a homeless project, so I went to that because I needed some references for court.'

Dave wasn't exactly the model volunteer, but Val was willing to give him a chance. Maybe it was the unending loyalty of a mother, or perhaps it was the belief that Dave could still change. Whatever it was, Val took Dave into her project, and while he was there he met someone who told him a few home truths.

'I met a girl there who was a Christian – she was quite nice actually – and I said to her, "Do you fancy going for a beer?" She said, "Not really, I'm a Christian."'

Not an ideal confession in the present company.

'I said, "That's alright, so am I."'

What? That's a surprising claim for someone who claimed to hate Christians.

She wasn't convinced. 'I don't think you are.'

'I said, "Yeah, I am. You're born in England, you're Church of England – that's how it works."'

He laughed at how ridiculous he must have sounded, thinking he had made it because he flew the St George's flag on match day.

His new friend spelt it out for him: 'You have to make a decision to be a Christian.'

Dave didn't really understand. 'But I kind of went along with it because I wanted to get to know her a little bit better.'

He tried unsuccessfully to hide a smirk.

'She said, "OK, I'll go for a drink with you if you come to church with me."'

It was an odd deal, but Dave was happy to take a risk to 'get to know her'. All he had to do was sit through a boring service, then he would have the rest of the evening to work his charm.

It's fair to say, his first experience of her church wasn't exactly positive.

'It was quite happy and quite clappy, and I really didn't like it. I felt very threatened.'

For a man who could hold his own in a riot, it was strange to hear him feeling threatened, but when he explained why, it made even less sense: 'I didn't like the people; they were just so friendly and nice to me.'

How petrifying.

'I just wanted to be away from them, so I was particularly prickly that night, but they were just so lovely to me,' he said sheepishly.

They started singing.

'I don't really like singing,' he said, and to be fair, he'd never sung much in the football stands, so church wasn't the place to start.

Then came the talk. 'This guy started speaking, and it was as if he was speaking to me. Everything he was saying I thought, "Flip me, that's my life."'

His eyes widened as he recalled the moment he couldn't take it any more.

'It pressed buttons inside me, and I just felt absolutely terrified. I felt something was going on inside me, and I had to get out of there.'

Just like that, he was gone.

'There was a rough cider pub across the road, so I went in and had a few pints of cider, a few cigarettes, calmed myself down and went home.'

I wondered what happened to his new friend.

'Later that night the girl turned up and knocked on the door and said, "What happened to you? I thought we were going for a drink." I said, "I don't like your church. I don't wanna go to your church. I'm not interested," and she said, "Well, do you still wanna go for this drink?"'

Silly question.

Then came the right hook.

'"Great, let's go tomorrow night. We've got another thing on at church. Come to that and we can go afterwards."'

Dave wasn't going to be so easily persuaded this time.

'"Not a chance."'

'She said, "What are you scared of?" I said, "I'm not scared of anything," so she said, "Well, I'll see you tomorrow then."'

He sighed as he recalled being outwitted and said, with a guilty expression, 'So, I went, and the same thing happened. I was particularly unpleasant.'

He shook his head as if quietly despairing of his own behaviour. 'This time I was in the middle of a row and I couldn't get out.'

Of course, he could have if he'd wanted to, but he didn't want to draw attention to himself.

'I felt all these emotions coming over me, and I thought, "I'm gonna flippin' cry in a minute, and I don't want these mugs to see me upset . . . I can't get out because they're gonna see."'

He laughed with his typical self-deprecating honesty. We were laughing too. The irony was, it was pride, supposedly the deadliest of sins, that had brought him back to church to show this girl that he wasn't scared, and it was also pride that kept him from leaving to avoid letting people see him upset. In his desperate attempt to maintain a macho image, he came up with a plan.

'I thought, "I know what I'll do. I'll shut my eyes, I'll stick my hands together and I'll pretend I'm praying."'

By now Dave was royally taking the mick out of himself, mimicking how a man who doesn't pray pretends to be praying.

'I didn't have a clue. I didn't know what prayer was, but I thought they'd just leave me alone if I did that. I was biting my lip and thinking, "Hold it together."'

Dave's acting hadn't convinced everyone. As the service ended, two guys came up to him and asked him if he was okay.

'Yeah, I'm fine,' he replied, using the universal British response to any situation.

'They said, "Can we pray with you?" so I was like, "You can do what you want."'

Dave wasn't going to make life easy for anyone.

'One of them asked, "What do *you* want?" and I said, "Nothing that you've got."'

They started to get a little bolder,

'One of the guys said, "Why are you upset?" I thought, "I'm gonna knock you out, mate."'

I couldn't help but wonder if the guys continued in courage or naivety; they clearly hadn't met Dave in Sweden.

'The other guy said to me, "If you call on the name of Jesus, it'll all change; your life will change," and I said, "What are you on about, call on Jesus?"'

In a rare moment of vulnerability, Dave dropped his guard for a second. 'What do I have to do?' he asked them.

The guy kept it simple. 'Just talk to him as if he's here now.'

'I said, "Alright, I want all the hate and all the anger and all the pain in my life to go, and I want to be different."'

A few seconds later, Dave was lying on the floor, although for once nobody had knocked him out.

'The weird thing was, I fell over, but it wasn't as if anyone pushed me over and it wasn't as though I had to fall over. I just ended up on the ground. I ended up . . .' He paused for what seemed like an eternity. '. . . I ended up . . . different.'

He was searching for words to try to unpack an experience that he still didn't entirely understand.

'I can't explain quite how, but when I got up, it was as if the rucksack I had been carrying around my whole life, just full of crap and hate and pain, had been taken off me, and I didn't have to be that person any more.'

It was difficult to believe that an entire lifetime of anger could be rewritten in a momentary spiritual encounter, but it seems that really is what happened. And for Dave, it was only the start.

10.

THE LIONS' DEN

DAVE WASN'T JUST trying to be different; he *was* different. A new man with new desires, new ambitions and, for once in his life, the strength to change. He'd tried to reform himself many times in the past, but it had never worked.

'I couldn't commit to anything. I'd say, "This is it; I'm not getting involved in any more trouble." It never lasted very long.'

But after Dave's 'Damascus Road experience',[1] he wasn't just mustering up the willpower to be a bit nicer; he was utterly transformed, and his deepest desire was to make good all the things he'd previously made bad.

When he got back to his flat, he saw all the idols that he'd brought back from Thailand while he'd been on the run from the police.

'I had collected all these "god" things, and one of the first things that I knew I had to do was to get rid of them all out of my flat, so I went out into the car park with a lump hammer . . .'

Next came the contents of his flat. It was all stuff that had been stolen.

'I went to this guy in the church and said, "Look I've got all this stuff. It's robbed, but I can't have it, 'cos I'm a Christian now."'

The minister explained, a little nervously, that they couldn't accept stolen goods, but Dave insisted, 'Surely there are poor people in your church? Don't think I'm going to the Old Bill.'

It was an awkward position for a minister to be in, but there weren't many options. Dave couldn't prove the items were nicked – the guys who'd lifted them from the warehouse didn't exactly give receipts, and he wasn't going to grass anyone up. Short of wandering around the nearest shopping centre with an out-of-date washing machine, trying to give it back, there wasn't an obvious solution.

Eventually, he found a home for the stuff through various organisations in Bristol who help vulnerable people, and before long he was replacing everything he'd once stolen through good, honest hard work, and the help of some kind friends.

He stopped fighting, stopped getting drunk, even stopped swearing, but it wasn't enough. He didn't want to just quit bad behaviour; he wanted to live for the opposite, to channel his aggression into fighting *for* people instead of against them.

'As soon as I became a Christian, I knew I had to serve God with my whole life. That was it – there were no other options for me, because . . .' He chuckled to himself as he found a way to describe why he had to serve God. '. . . because I'd almost been serving the devil for so many years.'

The irony is, having spent years dodging prison, after leaving his life of crime, prison was one of the first places he went to. He wanted to see other young lads who'd got onto the wrong path turn their life around and find the same kind of freedom that he'd found, so he asked if he could volunteer and chat to the lads about Jesus.

The governor of the prison soon saw the difference Dave was making in the inmates, so he asked him to stay and work full-time as the prison chaplain. Before long, hundreds of men were experiencing the same freedom that Dave had experienced – the permission to be different, the ability to let go of hatred and anger. Dave showed them a God who loved, forgave and delighted in them even if everyone else had dismissed them.

You might think it unlikely that lads in prison would want to be studying the Bible, but they quickly discovered that much of the Bible was written in prison, by guys not unlike themselves, men with eventful pasts.

Despite having been twice banned from the Rovers' stadium, it wasn't long before Dave was serving as a chaplain to the club.

'I had a meeting with the old chairman and owner and said, "Look,

I really appreciate you offering me this, but I've been banned," and they said, "Yeah, we know all about you."'

Dave was precisely the kind of person they were looking for – someone who could show others that it's possible to change. He trained with the first team on Thursday evenings, and he was there for players who needed a broad shoulder to lean on.

'That's what God is in the business of doing: he redeems things, he makes things better than they ever were . . . Now I get to go training with the team . . .' He interrupted himself with a laugh. 'When I say I train, I collect balls. I'm the oldest ball boy in the game.'

He soon discovered that the church in the middle of the estate was empty, and he immediately felt that this was what he'd been born to do: to reopen the church for the local people. He was honest with us about how it happened, refusing to take any credit and deflecting the kudos to God and those around him, especially his wife.

'Without Nikki, there would be no church,' he said. 'She's amazing.'

Dave became an ordained vicar in the Church of England and began to run the church with Nikki and to shepherd the young congregation. People flocked from all over Bristol to see a guy who had once spent his days shouting obscenities at City fans, now standing up in the middle of the estate, preaching about love.

'We've been open twelve years this last weekend,' he said, looking for a way to sum it all up. 'It's been hard, but it's been worthwhile. We share what we have with our community, and that's what it's all about. It's about loving people and looking out for them.'

His voice quietened a little as his emotion became tangible. 'These are my people, they're my community, they're people that I love and want to look after.'

The compassion Dave has shown for his community over the last twenty years is as profound as the violence he previously unleashed in his wild youth. But it's one thing showing love for *your own* people; it's quite another to reach out to someone from the *other* estate. It wasn't long before Dave's compassion reserves were tested further than he dared imagine.

RIVALS

Most people with a rough history will tell you that, however glorious your new redeemed life is, it's only so long before the ghosts of your past come back to haunt you.

It was one of those phone calls that blind-sides you on a Friday morning and, however good the person on the other end is at 'breaking the news', it's still a sickening shock.

'Your son's in hospital.'

Dave's stepson had been in a motorbike accident. Nikki is a consultant at the hospital and she knew what this could mean, so when they rushed in, they were relieved to see him alive and responsive, albeit with some serious injuries. The doctors gave him a good prognosis, but it was going to take a long time.

Dave spent the next few weeks in and out of the hospital, sitting with his son, chatting, praying, sometimes just being present with him as he slowly recovered.

Then he saw Divvy.

Lying on the other side of the ward was one of the leaders of the City Service Firm, whom Dave had once fought against with the Young Executives.

'Divvy was a big player,' he explained. 'We didn't like one another, that was for sure.'

Since Dave was no longer terrorising the streets of Bristol, it had been a while since he'd seen Divvy. But in an instant, all those memories came flooding back.

'I'm not here to get involved in anything to do with him. I'm gonna concentrate on my son,' he told himself. But as the hours wore on, it became more and more awkward, sitting opposite a major rival, pretending to ignore each other. For football hooligans, few places are sacred ground; even a hospital could be a dangerous place to meet, although an ideal location if either of them got injured.

Finally, Dave wandered over and broke the silence. 'I know you.'

Not a bad start; factual at least.

'Yeah, you know you know me,' Divvy replied.

It was tense. Dave could see that Divvy was barely moving, for he'd had a tumour removed and was in a lot of pain, so he wasn't really a threat. Unbeknown to Divvy, the Rev. Dave was no longer a threat to him either.

The tension eased a little as Dave started talking to him like he was another human being, rather than just an enemy. Divvy responded well. In the choice between fight or flight, he could do neither, so he humoured Dave and they started chatting.

A few minutes went past, then an hour. Something was shifting. Divvy was trying to work it out. Was this a game? Why was a rival thug from the Young Executives chatting to him, a gang leader from the City Service Firm, as if they were mates?

Then Dave slipped in a curveball. 'I'm a vicar now.'

Divvy laughed, despite the pain of the tumour; he couldn't help himself. Dave? A vicar? 'Get on your bike.'

If Dave had told him he'd ridden to the hospital on a unicorn, Divvy would have been less surprised. The tension evaporated. This was now safe ground – utterly unexpected ground, but safe. The former rivals who'd spent years chasing each other around town were now chatting, laughing, opening up their hearts, sharing their hopes and fears, showing each other an ounce of respect across the invisible divide.

Divvy started talking about his health. He'd just lost his brother to lung cancer, and he feared he would be next. Dave did what vicars do. He offered to pray. Divvy welcomed it.

'Yeah, please do.'

But Dave didn't mean back at church on his knees; he meant there and then in the hospital.

What happened next took them both by surprise.

As soon as he started praying, the same power that had hit Dave in church seemed to come in full force for Divvy, and he lay there, motionless, as a wave of peace swept over him. In a later interview, he likened it to the first conviction of love he'd ever known. 'I've got two experiences in my life I can't explain to anybody. The first was the day I met my wife, and I had a feeling in 'ere to know that she was the right one for me. People say that doesn't happen, but let me tell you it does . . .'

After three decades of marriage, Divvy could silence the doubters, and he drew parallels with the moment Dave prayed for him. 'I don't care what anyone thinks of me, or what anyone says, it happened, and that's all there is to it. I had the most glorious warm feeling come over my body, to let me know the Lord had come into my body, the same way as when I met my wife, thirty-one years ago, that she was the one for me . . . They're the two best experiences of my life.'

Like Dave's, Divvy's spiritual experience wasn't just a flash in the pan; it was a game changer. He saw something in his new mate, and he wanted to know it for himself. Dave talked him through the same steps that he'd taken in becoming a Christian and leaving his old life behind. They prayed together, Divvy laying down his life to follow Jesus, and within a few weeks, he was preparing to get baptised.

The baptismal service was powerful for many reasons. Aside from the remarkable transformation in Divvy, mirrored in the life of his rival, there was the knowledge in the back of their minds that Divvy's new life might be cut short. He'd just been diagnosed with asbestos-related lung cancer and given six to eight weeks to live.

Dave was there for him and his family during the whole ordeal, reaching out to a family he'd once considered nothing but a bunch of people in the wrong-coloured shirts. He even went to a Bristol City match with Divvy, out of solidarity for his unlikely friendship. 'In the lions' den,' as Divvy described it.

Divvy put up a sterling fight, stretching the six-week prognosis for six months, but the following September he breathed his last.

Dave led the funeral, as Divvy had requested, and at the following City match, thousands of supporters stood to cheer their club hero, as shouts of 'MARK DIVVY SAUNDERS' rattled round the stands and rapturous applause rose into the cold Bristol air.

For Dave, it was a privilege to stand by one of his closest friends, dignifying his final hours and being there for him, against all previous instincts, out of solidarity and love. To be a prison chaplain, a football chaplain and a vicar on an estate is to give your life to standing with bereaved and broken people, friends and rivals, the poor and marginalised, speaking hope into every situation.

A year or so after I met Dave and made the film, his adventures took him in a new direction. The prison chaplain who became a football chaplain is now a Royal Navy chaplain. The trauma of war can paralyse even the toughest of men. Nothing quite compares to the solidarity of serving alongside a reformed 'tough guy' who has spent his life mentoring other tough guys through their dark night of the soul. Dave is more than qualified.

As I reflected on my conversations with Dave, I wondered if his friendship with Divvy is exactly what our nation needs to hear about in this hour. For some, it can be easy to think none of this applies to us; few are running around town looking to have a fight with someone simply because they identify with either the red team or the blue team. But the vehement division between supporters of opposing political parties, both red and blue, is cutting through our nation like never before. Aggression channelled through social media might not be accompanied by an actual physical fight, but is the heart behind it really that different?

Most of us identify with a political view that comes out of our values, but isn't it ironic when those very values are jeopardised by the way we defend them?

Hating half the nation because 'they' voted differently from 'us' and 'we' have the moral high ground is something of a paradox.

Many are content to see everything as 'their fault', passing the blame to someone else, but perhaps that exact reaction is what's so illuminating. Perhaps Dave and Divvy have something to teach all of us, whichever tribe we identify with. Dave may have been more extreme in his anger than most, but he also went on to become more extreme in his compassion. Extremism can be a wonderful force if it's channelled for good, which is why Jesus chose so many extremists to pioneer his early movement of love. He seems to specialise in using the most unlikely of people.

The most prolific writer in the New Testament, the man who penned some of the most beautiful words in all of Scripture was a terrorist. He was literally on his way to kill Christians in Syria when he encountered Jesus.

To say it was unexpected is something of an understatement.

That man was Saul of Tarsus, the one who had overseen the stoning of Stephen, the first martyr. Saul was knocked to the ground on the road to Damascus by a spiritual vision of Jesus, not unlike the way Dave Jeal was knocked to the ground by a spiritual encounter in Bristol. When Saul got up, he was a changed man, and was later known by the name Paul. He spent his final years travelling the known world, healing the sick, preaching love, collecting offerings for the poor and starving in Judea, and responding with compassion and mercy to the very people who beat him up and threw him in prison in the process. He would later write to the church in Rome, 'Do not be overcome by evil, but overcome evil with good.'[2]

Those weren't empty words; he lived them. As far as Dave is concerned, following Jesus doesn't just mean you stop doing bad things and live a mild life of inoffensive niceness. It means you become like him: courageous, compassionate, at war with anything that hurts people. In the words of Martin Luther King Jr, 'Jesus Christ was an extremist for love, truth and goodness.'[3]

It's not extremism that God opposes; it's evil. People are extremists for good – well, we could do with a few more of those, people who will risk everything to reach out in love to their neighbour, even their enemy.

What would the world look like with a few more of those extremists?

11.

COMMUNITY HOUSE

IT'S EASY TO see now how powerful it can be to harness someone's 'extremism for good', but one of the critical details in Dave's story is another Dave, the behind-the-scenes Dave.

With many glorious second-chance stories, there is an unsung hero in the background who believed in the rebel before anyone else did. I remember hearing Raheem Sterling, in an interview with BBC Sport, thanking his mum and sister for believing in him, and crediting his mentor, Clive Ellington, for turning his life around. Mo Farah said the same about his PE teacher, Alan Watkinson, who took an unruly teenager and turned him into a disciplined athlete.

These are the champions behind the champions, the friends who never gave up on them.

For Dave Jeal, one of those friends was Dave Mitchell.

Everyone seems to know the Mitchells in Bristol – it's like *EastEnders*. The oldest son, Robin Mitchell, gigs all over Bristol, and I got to know Joey Mitchell, the school chaplain, through Friday night staff football. Dave Mitchell leads Woodlands Church in Bristol, where Dave Jeal first found faith, and when he left his life of violence, the Mitchells invited him to live with them.

That's real community.

The Mitchells' house was the fresh start Dave needed, a place to call home, where people looked out for him, and he looked out for them.

Not everyone would invite a football hooligan into their home. Some would think it a risk to their own family, but, if anything, they were all safer with Dave Jeal living there. If a petty thief were ever to have broken in, Dave Jeal would have defended the Mitchell kids with his life.

The Mitchells saw something in Dave that was more than his past; they saw his potential. They saw a man who had been given a second chance and they wanted to nurture that. Perhaps that's what real community is – seeing the potential in others and investing in it, forgiving the moments of frustration and celebrating the breakthroughs.

And they're not the only ones.

The Mitchells' place is known in Bristol as a 'community house', a place where people have a shared vision to bless their neighbourhood in whatever way they can. The network of community houses that the Mitchells pioneered has grown into something of a movement, as others have followed their lead.

I'm one of them.

THIS IS PERSONAL

I remember chatting on the phone about these community houses with my sister, Emma, who lived in London with her husband Chris. As I shared stories of people like the Mitchells who were opening up their home to help others, she interrupted with a game changer.

'We're thinking of moving to Bristol.'

'Really?'

'Let's start one of these community houses ourselves.'

Chris grew up in a house with a similar vision. His parents hosted international students throughout his childhood, so before Chris had finished school, he'd lived with people from all over the world. You can see it in the way he interacts with people – he's at home with anyone, finding common ground across every culture.

We pooled all our savings with a mutual friend, Anna, a farmer from Guernsey who was living in Bristol as a sports massage therapist, and we set about trying to convince a bank to split a mortgage four ways. Our plan was to find somewhere big enough to house several people so we could take up the 'community house' vision and serve our neighbourhood together. We were on a tight budget, but if we found somewhere that needed extensive renovation and did it up ourselves, it was possible. Maybe. Hopefully.

The night came when I found myself at an auction in the conference room of Bristol Zoo, armed with the life savings of four people, to bid on a giant derelict house in the inner city that had long been boarded up and left to crumble.

Auctions like these attract big-money buyers from housing developers looking to turn old inner-city properties into small, sweaty flats to let out to indebted students at inflated prices. I was competing with these guys to buy a house with my family, to actually live in. Audacious.

The four of us agreed in advance the limit for me to stop at, and the frantic bidding began. We never expected to get it even for our maximum price, for when we pooled our money, we still had much less than the house was worth, but we reasoned that if the good Lord really wanted us to have it, we'd get it for a steal.

We prayed.

I went.

As the bidding started, I hovered nervously at the back, my heart thumping as I nodded my head at the auctioneer, trying to look composed in jeans and a T-shirt, surrounded by professionals in pinstriped suits. For some reason, possibly because the house was a dilapidated den of rotten floors, broken windows, a leaking roof and a mouldy basement with no running water, electricity or gas, we got it for less than we expected.

It was a steal.

I phoned Em and Chris.

'Whatever.'

I insisted, 'I'm not joking; we got the house.'

There was a pause.

'Now what?'

The following weekend they came down to see what I had got them into. They hadn't even seen it before I went to the auction. That's trust for you.

Anna was upbeat – she's an optimist. Emma was positive, if a little tearful – she's a realist. Chris offered some practical words: 'It needs a lot of work.'

Well done, Sherlock.

The next two years were hard. Em and I grew up in the rolling green hills of the West Country, in a village that looked more like the Shire in *The Lord of the Rings* than the inner city. We were more familiar with hooting owls than screaming sirens.

It was a steep learning curve.

We were burgled on our first night. Someone climbed the scaffolding, took the tiles off, punched through the felt and went down through the house, grabbing whatever valuables they could find. There weren't many.

Welcome to the neighbourhood.

The roof had been leaking for so long, most of the wooden joists were rotten. We needed to dry out the brickwork, replace the floors, put in windows and doors, replumb and wire the entire house and build a kitchen and a bathroom.

On the plus side, we had walls.

Another community house kindly gave us a survey they'd done on it, and a builder in my church helped us get the ball rolling. For the next couple of years, we spent our evenings and weekends hauling rubble around, balancing precariously on ladders and making endless trips to the DIY store.

The house was in a notorious crime hotspot, and we saw a lot of suspicious activity. We weren't there to join in, but nor were we going to grass anyone up, so we kept our heads down and tried to be friendly to everyone we met.

Some returned our smiles; others looked at us like we were complete idiots.

A fair assessment.

I was still teaching, and exam classes were swelling as austerity forced class sizes to breaking point. I would come home after an exhausting week, with a stack of essays to mark, to a house of chaos and a list of jobs that was growing faster than we were getting anything done.

Then we ran out of money.

In those long months, I wrestled with anxiety like never before. It seemed as if there was no escape. We had started out with a vision of building a community house to bless our neighbourhood, but what did that even mean?

What could we possibly offer people?

I wasn't even holding it together myself.

Why should anyone trust us?

Some people thought we were a cult, and a rumour started that I was an undercover cop. Most people just wondered who these weirdos were, moving into the inner city and ambling around, smiling at people inanely.

Em and Chris were convinced that this is where we were meant to be, but none of us really knew why.

We decided to pray.

We prayed for each other, we prayed for our street and we prayed for the community.

One of our neighbours came around one morning, and she had tinnitus. We put our hands on her ear and prayed.

It stopped immediately.

We were all a little shocked, although we really shouldn't have been. If you pray in faith, you're supposed to actually believe it might happen. Our faith was small, evidently, but maybe even the tiniest seed of faith is where it starts.

We kept praying.

We were soon joined by our Northern Irish friends, Louise, the physics teacher who had come to Chile with Ross and me, and our mutual friend Catherine, another Northern Irish lass. They moved into a house across the road, joined our little community and gave our prayers a new lease of life.

Little by little, the atmosphere started to change. People eventually let go of the rumour that I was an undercover cop because I evidently had no idea what was going on most the time. As the occasional student wandering past said, 'Alright sir,' with a vintage Bristol accent, people realised the geography teacher 'cover story' must actually be the truth.

As we got to know more people in the neighbourhood, barriers started to come down.

Louise helped one of our neighbours with his maths homework, and my sister volunteered for a local charity, One25, which had been started by Val, Dave Jeal's mum, to care for Bristol's street sex workers, who have been forced into their situation after fleeing situations of abuse.

We spent Christmas in the nearby homeless shelter, and on nights off we went for a drink with our Jamaican neighbours in the local pub and played dominoes.

We have a spare room in the house and over the last few years we've kept it as a bolthole for all sorts of people – international students, someone on the run from an abusive ex-boyfriend, more often than not people who are simply lonely and need a bit of compassion. That's all of us at some point in life.

It's not that we've transformed our community; far from it. Nor do we see ourselves as heroes – quite the opposite. Our neighbours are far more of a blessing to us than the other way around. They were there for us in the early days, lending a hand, making a brew, sometimes just sitting on the doorstep chatting about the neighbourhood or cooking us some curried goat.

Even the supposed 'bad guys' looked out for us.

One night, Chris lit a chiminea in the back yard. I didn't know what a chiminea was at first, but it turns out it's like a firepit with a chimney, invented for city folk to toast marshmallows (I assume). We'd sawn up all the old timbers for firewood, but some of them were still damp, and the chiminea was kicking out some serious smoke. Within seconds the lads hanging around outside were about to break the door down to come and rescue us. We came out to see what the commotion was, and they were shouting, 'Your house is on fire!'

Emma thanked them for their kindness and reassured them that it was a chiminea and, after a brief explanation of what that was, they wandered off, relieved that nobody was burning to death.

If we'd lived in the 'safer' suburbs, I wonder how long it would have taken for someone to break down our door to rescue us from a burning building? Here, it took seconds.

Perhaps there's beauty in the inner city that you only see when you move in.

SWEDISH HOUSE MANIA

One weekend, Em and Chris organised a DIY SOS event where people from churches all over the city volunteered to do some decorating or gardening for people in our communities, to practically demonstrate that 'loving our neighbours' is more than a cliché. Our house became the launch pad for projects all over Bristol, and before long, well-meaning people were pouring into the house carrying dirt-clad gardening forks and tins of paint (and happily depositing debris from both all over the floor).

On the Friday night, as the storm was brewing, I received an odd phone call. 'How do you feel about taking in a travelling Swedish folk musician for the weekend?'

'I thought you'd never ask.'

'Great.'

'Wait . . . what?'

A young Swedish musician called Daniel Abrahamsson had been travelling around Britain, busking in different cities and raising awareness for the anti-human-trafficking organisation, Stop the Traffik.[1] He'd turned up in Bristol, tired and lonely, and decided to phone around some churches to see if someone could put him up. He got through to my friend Olivia in the City Church office, and she said, 'I know a guy.'

Of all the weekends to host a complete stranger, this was not the one. I ran the idea past the rest of the house, and they agreed, providing he was entirely my responsibility.

For some reason (I still don't really know why), I accepted.

When I called him back, he was sitting on a park bench praying, 'Please, Lord, find me someone nice to stay with.'

Poor guy, I'm not sure we were what he pictured.

Within half an hour, there was a knock at the door, and I was greeted by the most stereotypically Swedish man I have ever met. He had a neat trilby, the sort of small circular thinking-man spectacles that only a Scandinavian would wear, and he was clutching a guitar to balance out his enormous backpack. He grinned at me through blonde stubble and said with a loud and unavoidably Nordic lisp, 'Hello, I am Daniel.'

I ushered him in and introduced him to the rest of the house, and we sat down to dinner.

I apologised for the chaos around us and explained that we might not be able to spend much time with him this weekend, that it wasn't personal and that he was still very welcome.

'I can help,' he said, still wearing the unshakable grin that he'd maintained since I'd found him on the pavement.

'Oh . . . are you sure?'

It felt slightly poor form to invite in a travelling musician and immediately send him out to do some DIY, but he seemed so delighted by the idea, it would have been ruder not to let him join us.

On Saturday morning, we all discovered that taking in Swedish Daniel was one of the best decisions we've ever made. While he'd planned to spend the day busking, what he actually did was spend the entire weekend painting other people's houses.

He loved it. I've never met a man more willing to serve. Our friend next door invented the name Swe-Dan, to differentiate between the two of us, and it quickly stuck.

Swe-Dan was a hit with everyone. He got the kids singing while he painted a large attic bedroom, treated our neighbours like they'd been friends for life, and he was still touching up edges when everyone else had grown tired and given up.

On the Sunday night, he played a gig in our back garden and broadcast it on Facebook Live. It was a strange feeling knowing that people all over the world were watching a gig taking place in our back garden. The actual live audience was considerably smaller: Louise and Catherine, our Northern Irish neighbours and their friends, various kids from across the neighbourhood, a smattering of volunteers from around the city and three former homeless guys whom we'd recently befriended.

As Swe-Dan's deep rolling tones ricocheted around our back yard, people started gathering in from the street, curious to see what sounded like a Scandinavian Johnny Cash.

The families we met that weekend are still close friends. The kids go to school together, the girls sing karaoke on Saturday nights, and they all go camping in Devon every summer. I wonder if we'd have bonded that quickly without a travelling Swedish musician to break the ice.

Swe-Dan left his mark on us. It wouldn't be the last time our paths were to cross on this journey.

It seems we left our mark on him too.

When he arrived back in Sweden, he got to work, saved up some money and started a community house like ours with two refugees who'd recently fled from Iran. It was the place of rest and healing they needed after the trauma they'd narrowly escaped.

Back in Bristol, the network of community houses continues to grow as more people have caught the vision. The Mitchell family became good friends of ours, along with Greg and Clare Thompson, who have pioneered community living for decades, and we learned much from them in those early days. Many of the community houses now come together to share ideas and support one another through an enterprise called 'Love Bristol' that Greg and Clare set up.[2]

Some of the houses have twenty or more people in them; others are simply a family who have decided to be a stopgap for one person who needs a stable home for a season. Some have taken in asylum seekers who have fled war zones all over the world. Writing #refugeeswelcome on your social media status is a start, but people also need those who will welcome them into their home in real life. Others have even gone beyond the houses to start businesses that help vulnerable people to get back on their feet.

Who knows where this movement will end?

Nobody in these homes sees themselves as a hero, for we all have seasons when we can offer support to another, and there are other seasons when we're the one needing help. The roles can switch overnight. That's community. Nor is this unique to Christians – there are selfless volunteers from every faith background in Bristol. I have worked with almost every group I can think of over the years: Christians showing compassion, Muslims practising zakat and humanists looking out for fellow humans. Kindness doesn't have boundaries. We need each other.

When the Covid-19 pandemic hit in 2020, the position of our home, in the middle of the hustle and bustle of the community, meant that we became one of the go-to points for emergency food and medicine in lockdown. Compared to countless key workers, our efforts were comparatively small, but we knew families in the neighbourhood who needed support and we also knew people who were willing and able to give it. We simply had the privilege of joining the dots.

My sister, Emma, coordinated everything through that tried and tested powerhouse of communication, the local mums' WhatsApp group, and I followed whatever instructions I was given. Many a day some local hero would appear at the door with a delivery of food, and later in the evening we would wander the streets (at a social distance), dropping parcels on particular doorsteps, ringing the bell and running away, in what felt like a strange, legally enforced game of Knock, Knock, Ginger.

We weren't alone. The same thing was happening in thousands of streets across the nation. A survey conducted by King's College London found that 60 per cent of people in the UK offered help to friends, family and neighbours during the pandemic, and 47 per cent said they had experienced such help.[3]

While the crisis unlocked a wave of compassion in communities across the world (dubbed 'care-mongering' in Canada), many people began to ask why looking out for their neighbours with such good-natured intentionality shouldn't become the norm, even after the crisis had ended. Surely we need each other in every season, not only in a global pandemic? Perhaps 2020 will be remembered as a watershed year, a cultural shift – the moment care-mongering became the new normal.

Of course, these stories make this sort of community sound very ideal, and the day-to-day reality isn't always so glorious, especially when you live with people who don't see the world like you do. I often get asked, 'What if you end up living with someone really annoying?'

It's a good question. I always offer the same response: 'Oh, that definitely happens.'

Everyone is annoying when you get to know them, especially me. But when I learn to get over myself and love people anyway (and enjoy the mercy of people doing the same for me), well, that makes for a beautiful world. It's not exactly rocket science, but it can be hard to carry this vision out in a society that has focused on individual rights and comforts far and above loving the other.

For the network of community houses pioneered by the Mitchells, the concept of community was built on the team that Jesus forged, and it was no small feat for him either. If you flip open a children's Bible, you'll probably see a picture of Jesus standing on a grassy hill teaching a crowd of infeasibly cheerful peasants to 'love one another'. More than likely, they'll be smiling, clean-shaven individuals, giving the thumbs-up to his sermon. But these child-friendly images don't always capture the challenge behind Jesus' words, and the Gospel writers were painfully honest about the flaws in Jesus' community. They were continually misunderstanding him, they rebuked each other for wasting money and they had sharp disagreements over who was in charge.

In Jesus' final hour, one friend doubted him, another betrayed him and his closest friend denied he even existed. The rest just ran away.

Cheers, lads.

How did Jesus cope with such a bunch of dropouts?

His formula was simple – he loved them, even (and especially) when they least deserved it. Perhaps love is at its purest when it's undeserved.

Before the fated hour when they abandoned him, he knelt and washed their feet, the dirtiest and most humble task imaginable in his culture. He was modelling the kind of servant-heartedness he wanted them to continue after he left.

Having mopped their toes with the towel around his waist, he said, 'As I have loved you, so you must love one another.'[4]

It's the same vision he has for us.

And just in case people misunderstood him (which they always did and probably always will), he showed us that 'loving your neighbour' is not just about the people we like, but also (and especially) the people we'd rather avoid.

That's real love.

12.

ROBBER OF THE CRUEL STREETS

MY JOURNEY INTO the community house movement was inspired by those who went before me, like the Mitchells and the Thompsons, but who inspired them? Deep within Bristol's dark history there is a shining light: the German immigrant who 'robbed the cruel streets of the thousands of victims, the jails of thousands of felons, and the workhouses of thousands of helpless waifs'.[1]

In the 1830s, George Müller came to Bristol to lead a small church and noticed thousands of orphaned children on the streets, starving to death. When he asked who took care of them, he got the same answer from everyone: 'Nobody.'

Orphans were left to beg, borrow and steal. If the workhouse didn't get them, the rats would. End of story.

Müller decided to rewrite the script.

His legacy is personal to me because I have taught kids who are descended from Müller orphans – young people who wouldn't be here if a German preacher hadn't turned up in Bristol more than a century ago.

Throughout his ministry, Müller took more than ten thousand orphans into his homes to be fed, housed and educated. For free. His work caught the attention of the Victorian novelist Charles Dickens, who paid Müller a surprise visit following suspicions regarding the living conditions. Müller gave him the keys, told him to look anywhere he liked and invited him to speak to any student he could find. The children were unanimous in their praise for Müller; there were no skeletons in the closet. Instead, Dickens found countless children who'd been left to die by everyone else, yet had been rescued by the one person who saw them, not as the scum of the streets, but rather as fellow human beings.

If Müller was criticised for anything, it was that he educated the orphans 'above their social status'. The state-school teacher in me rather likes that.

Dickens didn't share Müller's faith, yet he was quick to defend him. He publicly testified that, in Müller's homes, 'all prospered', a feat which he claimed should earn Müller the 'respect of all good men, whatever may be the form of their religious faith'.[2]

Perhaps the most striking phenomenon of George Müller was not his compassion, but his methods. He built his entire ministry on prayer.

Müller never asked for money, nor did he give any indication of what he or the children needed. In the privacy of his own study, he gave everything to Jesus in prayer and kept detailed records as the goods fortuitously arrived.

One of his first homes was on Wilson Street, just around the corner from where I live today. There was a particularly low moment when the food reserves ran out in the home and, with no money left in the pot, they were stuck. And starving.

Rather than send out a desperate plea through the Victorian equivalent of a Facebook post, he simply gathered the children for breakfast, thanked God for the 'food', and waited in faith.

They hadn't waited long when there was a knock at the door, and Müller was greeted by a local baker who claimed that God had woken him up in the middle of the night and he couldn't get back to sleep. Acting on a conviction he couldn't describe, he baked an extra batch of bread for Müller and the children, for free, and brought it over that morning.

Müller smirked and thanked him. It wasn't over yet.

As he was taking the bread upstairs, a milk wagon broke down just outside. The milkman complained that he couldn't finish his delivery and asked Müller and the kids to drink all the milk to remove the weight, so he could fix the wagon.

Müller thanked him, passed round the milk and returned to his study to thank God and update his records. These stories are not one-offs, nor are they unsupported. Müller's stories are well documented, even by the secular press, which was as quick to discredit a religious role model then as it can be today.

On Müller's death at the age of ninety-two, the entire city stopped working and lined the streets for his funeral in a manner unknown in the city's history.

Inspired by the difference he made to thousands of orphans, his life of prayer and his practice of community, people continue to run some of Müller's homes to reach out to people in the city today. We have fewer orphans than we did in the nineteenth century, thankfully, but we are not without loneliness.

One of the families who took on a Müller home were the Mitchells, who took in Dave Jeal. Perhaps Müller's legacy and his methods still have a role to play in this generation.

EYEWITNESS

As my journey into Bristol's secret history of miracles continued, I discovered that these stories were not merely confined to the past. There are glimpses of divine mercy woven into the fabric of the city today.

When the Samoan International, Pat Lam, took over as Head Coach of Bristol Bears Rugby Team in 2017, the team rocketed to the top of the Championship to secure a hard-earned promotion. By 2020 they were third in the Premier League and Champions of the European Challenge Cup. When asked about the secret of their success, Pat had one word: 'Vision'.

When the players and coaching staff had a shared vision, when they knew what they were fighting for and how to get there, everything else fell into place.

But Pat's family had learned the importance of vision long before they got onto the pitch.

Pat's wife, Steph, was visiting Storehouse one day (a clothing bank run by Severn Vineyard Church), and joined a team sorting through donations. I happened to be working in the office that day and I got chatting to the team during the break. When I shared a bit about the Chilean miners, Steph quietly mentioned that she loved hearing stories of healing and that God had really opened her eyes to the miraculous. I assumed this was a metaphor for something she'd witnessed in New Zealand, but it turns out she meant it literally.

She once was blind.

'We were turning our garage into an extra play area for the children, and I was trying out some different paints on the wall. I had a plastic bowl of paint stripper to clean the brushes, and when I went to clean a brush, the pot had disintegrated and the bottom of the plastic container was stuck to the floor.'

Paint stripper is essentially a corrosive acid.

'I was leaning over that bowl, trying to unstick it from the floor with a knife, when it just popped up, flicking the acid into my left eye.'

That sounded nasty.

I had no idea.

'I've given birth naturally, with no pain relief, to five children, but when that acid went in my eye, it was the most excruciating pain I've ever experienced. It was like someone had stuck a knife in my eye.'

When a woman mentions the pain of childbirth, I've learned that there's literally nothing a man can say that will sound remotely reasonable, so I just clenched my teeth in the universal sign of pain-empathy and kept listening.

'I was blind in my left eye.'

A few months before the accident, the Lams had taken in one of Steph's nieces from Samoa to live with them (maybe they got the community house idea before we did). As Steph frantically washed her eye under the running water of the laundry tap, the acid soaked in deeper, but in her moment of anguish, Steph's eight-year-old niece appeared and said, 'Auntie, do you want me to pray to Jesus.'

Despite the pain, Steph held it together enough to give her a muffled response: 'Yes please, Tori.'

Steph didn't want to panic her niece, and she was doing her best to put on a brave face, but it seemed that Tori was the one who had the calm assurance. As she prayed, Steph had a strange sense that something special was going to happen.

Pat was at work in the city, an hour's drive away, but thankfully one of his cousins was visiting, so she drove Steph and the children to the local A&E, where they rushed her in and flushed the eye. The doctors soon realised this was more than a minor incident, and she was referred to Auckland Hospital Eye Clinic, which was another hour's drive.

In true understated style, she didn't phone Pat in a panic, demand an ambulance or ask for painkillers. She just calmly asked Pat's cousin if she could look after the children for the afternoon, called their local pastor and his wife and asked for a lift to Auckland.

If there's one thing in the rugby world tougher than a number eight, it's his wife.

She was rushed straight into the eye clinic, but when the doctor peered into her eye, the scar tissue was so extensive that there was very little they could do; the damage was already done.

They flushed the left eye again and finally gave her some pain relief.

The next day, when she was wheeled in to see the eye doctor again, they undid her bandages to test her vision and cemented the news she had dreaded. All she could see out of her left eye was a white blur. The surface of the eye, the cornea, is a beautifully smooth plane, a thin organic lens, the sort photographers could only dream of. But when the cornea is scarred irreparably, it's like a camera lens being smashed and painted at the same time.

For the first few days, she couldn't see at all, for they had had to bandage both eyes. The muscles in the eyes are so interlinked and so sensitive that even the slightest movement in one eye can cause agony in the other.

Every day they would take off the bandages, flush the left eye, check the scar tissue, ask if there was any change in pain or sight, then bandage her up again.

'It was such a surreal experience going from normal sight to blind; it was amazing to find my other senses tuning in to compensate for my lack of sight.'

Ever the optimist, Steph reflected on the silver lining in the dark cloud hanging over her. 'I could really hear the kindness or unkindness in someone's voice. I could even sense by their footsteps which one of my children was entering the room. Everything felt so intricate to the touch.'

I closed my eyes for a second and tried to imagine it. Just darkness. I felt so vulnerable.

'It was a different world,' Steph continued, 'but I had peace in the waiting. I still believed God was going to do something.'

For three days, there was no improvement, just a lot of pain and a milky blur. Day four was a Sunday, so Steph asked the doctors if she could miss the treatment for twenty-four hours and go to church.

Not a chance. They thought she was joking.

Steph is a determined soul. After a resolute discussion, she eventually assured them with her sheer positivity that her church was the safest place in the world and that she would come back immediately to resume treatment on Monday.

Her family led her to the front of the service and everyone present gathered round her, laying their hands on her head and shoulders, praying and believing for a miracle.

On the Monday morning she returned to the hospital. Her bandages were gently peeled off and the eye doctor peered through his little instrument. He jumped back, wide-eyed. 'There's no scar tissue.'

Her left eye had become as clear as her right. Overnight.

As she peered around the room, she realised that for the first time there was no pain.

'I knew Jesus was going to do something!' she told the doctor.

He looked rather awkward and mumbled something about a medical phenomenon, somewhat unwilling to credit a miracle, but equally unable to explain the rather peculiar evidence.

'What does this mean?' she asked.

Doctors aren't really trained for this sort of thing, so he defaulted to some practical advice. 'Well, you can drive yourself home if you like.'

She thanked the doctor repeatedly and drove home.

It took some time for the shock to settle, and her family were equally in awe, but even now, years later, there's still a sense of wonder when they look back on that day.

I invited Steph and Pat over for tea so they could share their story with my community house, and everyone was gripped. Pat shook his head as she talked about the pot of paint stripper and added, 'I remember looking at that plastic pot, melted and mangled by the acid, the same acid that went in my wife's eye.'

It takes a lot to frighten a rugby player.

But he's not frightened any more.

'God's been guiding us the whole way,' he said with an air of calm confidence.

Like Steph, Pat hadn't started out in life as a strong believer, but while he was playing for Newcastle years before, they both had a change of heart and put their faith in Jesus.

Every rugby team Pat has played for or coached can witness the depth of his faith. He's not ashamed to share it, even in the secular world of sport. It's not that he's delivering sermons, for his job is to talk tactics, but off the pitch or in the bar, in quiet moments of friendship and reflection, he offers the gentle confession of a man who is grateful for the hand of God in the life of his family.

For Steph, that was the first of many testimonies of God's providence in her life. It's no small feat to raise five children, ferry them around to different rugby matches and throw herself into whatever voluntary work she can find in whatever city she ends up in.

But if she ever forgets, even for a second, how God responds to her prayers, she can close her left eye, pause for a few seconds, open it and remember.

FREEDOM FIGHTERS

It seems there are divine fingerprints in the toughest of communities, from rugby families and football gangs to inner-city estates. Sometimes they appear in signs and wonders, but perhaps these are no more significant than the miracle of a safe home for someone fleeing persecution or an unlikely friendship between two former hooligans. When all these threads are woven together into a tapestry of mercies and miracles, they form something larger than the sum of their parts: they become a movement.

That's when cities are transformed.

Few cities have a more sinister history than Bristol, a city built on the wealth of the global slave trade. Even the bricks themselves were often laid by the young, the orphaned and the vulnerable. There was exploitation at every stage.

Perhaps the key to redeeming the past lies in championing the heroes rather than the villains.

Throughout its shameful past, Bristol has always had those who fought back, from the abolitionist Hannah More[3] to the father of thousands, George Müller, to the 'mother of black British culture', Delores Campbell, who fostered thirty children and is celebrated as one of the Seven Saints of St Pauls.[4] These are the lives we can follow. The future of Bristol, like any city, depends on the courageous actions of unsung heroes like these brave souls who will fight the forces of evil with a thousand acts of sacrifice and love.

Perhaps that shift is already taking place, for glimmers of such a revolution are starting to show. Bristol was recently declared Britain's kindest city, based on an independent survey of the collective action of individuals supporting vulnerable people in our streets.[5] Since 2011, Bristol has officially become a City of Sanctuary for thousands of hurting people from all over the world. I've interviewed many of Bristol's refugees while working for local charity Bridges for Communities, and I've had the privilege of seeing people redeeming their futures in the city I call home.

But I'd be fooling myself if I thought that we'd now made it, for despite some encouraging signs, the inequality gap between the rich and the poor is still more pronounced in Bristol than in almost any other city in the UK. And despite the best efforts of a thousand kind people, slavery still exists, even today, even on the streets of our supposedly generous city.

Every generation needs those who, like George Müller, will continue to 'rob the cruel streets' of its victims. Every generation needs freedom fighters who will take up the cause of another.

Just as there were role models of the past who rolled back the darkness, so there are unsung heroes in this generation who are fighting with every bone in their body to set people free. I recently met a young lady who rescues and mentors victims of human trafficking in Bristol. She spoke candidly about both the dangers she faces and the joy of seeing another human being set free. Can there be a greater cause to fight for?

It's the leadership of these quiet heroes that inspired the final stage of my journey.

Part Four
DESERT TRAILS

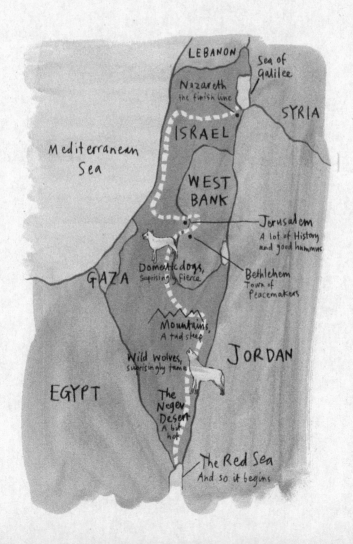

13.

DIRT TRACKS

ONE OF THE most important principles I've learned from all the peace-makers I've encountered on my journey is that true peace isn't merely an absence of conflict; it's a state of complete wholeness, of human flourishing. Peace at the deepest level seems to exude a pure, unquenchable joy that overcomes the toughest circumstances and the hardest of hearts.

How did José Henríquez maintain such calmness, such faith, such uncrushable hope in the chaos of the San José mine disaster? How did Karim find such an overwhelming love for the people he had feared and resented for so long? How did a violent football hooligan become as zealous for love as he had previously been for hatred?

It seemed more than mind over matter, or the ability to be a bit nicer, or try harder. As Dave Jeal openly confessed, 'I'd tried that; it never lasted. I was too weak.'

Whatever it was that happened when he was overwhelmed by a sublime spiritual peace, it changed him immeasurably more than will-power ever had. In fact, years later, when he prayed for Divvy, his arch-rival, Divvy described the same transforming peace, a tangible warmth flowing through his body like electricity.

What is this immeasurable peace they speak of?

From the miners of Chile to the secret believers of the Middle East to the community houses of Bristol, everyone I interviewed pointed to the carpenter from Nazareth as the source of their greatest peace. But what does that mean? Were they simply inspired by his story? Encouraged by his teaching?

As I discovered in my interviews with Middle Eastern believers, there's more to following Jesus than simply wearing the label 'Christian'. Not everyone who has identified with the Christian religion over the centuries has been peaceful. Some people, ironically, seem about as far from the peaceful life of Jesus as possible, yet claim to be his followers. There's a paradox. Dave believed he was a Christian while waging war on rival gangs in Sweden, and he even tried (unsuccessfully) to convince a young lady of his faith.

'You're born in England, you're Church of England – that's how it works.'

Apparently not.

When he eventually did join the Church of England, as a vicar, he had become someone who knew more about Jesus than as a vague figure in a supposed national religion. It's not even that he started to learn *about* Jesus; there was more to it than head knowledge.

I've spent my life studying the historical sources about Jesus, both the first-century texts and the latest archaeological excavations. But in the lives of the peacemakers I met on my journey, I became increasingly convinced that there are mysteries to his leadership that can't be gleaned from study alone.

Some things have to be experienced to be believed.

Who was this man they called the 'Prince of Peace'?

The world he was born into was hardly peaceful, despite centuries of European airbrushing. He might have given us some of the most famous tenets of peaceful society – 'Blessed are the peacemakers . . . love your neighbour . . . turn the other cheek' – but wherever he got those ideas, it can't have been from the Greco-Roman world around him, as historian Tom Holland demonstrated in his landmark work, *Dominion*.[1]

Whatever started in Bethlehem two millennia ago, it was something entirely new, and unpicking the truth requires the careful removal of all the rubbish that European history has added to it. The nativity scenes that adorn our Christmas cards portray a happy baby on a clean bed of straw surrounded by pristine animals and unnervingly glowing Europeans. The more historically accurate picture would be of a Middle Eastern

Jewish teenager giving birth under suspicious circumstances, in a spare room, stinking of animal faeces, in an insignificant town under military occupation, surrounded by the most humble and impoverished members of society.

Not many Christmas cards paint that picture.

But even a historically accurate nativity scene wouldn't capture Jesus' own first memories. All of us, including Jesus, begin to form lasting memories from around the age of two, a phenomenon psychologists call 'childhood amnesia'. For Jesus, this could only mean one thing – his earliest memories would not have been as a child in Bethlehem, but as a refugee in Africa.

Before Jesus was two years old, his family fled to Egypt in the dead of night to escape the bloodthirsty reign of King Herod, who had heard that another potential king had been born in Bethlehem. After Herod died in 4 BC, Jesus' parents returned all the way from Egypt to the town of Nazareth in the northern region of Galilee.

Some have questioned the story in Matthew's Gospel, but if you study first-century Palestine, it's tragically in keeping with what we know of the geography and politics of the time. The bloodthirsty reign of the Herods is well documented by historians, and the sizeable Jewish community in Egypt would have been the obvious place to escape Herod's latest massacre.

At the age when most kids would be starting school, Jesus walked hundreds of miles on desert trails and dirt tracks through a wasteland devoid of life apart from a few savage animals and the odd band of merciless bandits.

How could a child forget something like that?

How did he even make it?

How does a young couple protect their child on such a perilous road, in the knowledge that he could potentially be the next king?

No pressure.

If I really wanted to know something about this humble peacemaker, then perhaps I should *literally* walk in his footsteps, on his journey from Egypt to Nazareth, where his first human memories were formed.

Perhaps I could experience something of the peace he has instilled in the people I have interviewed by stepping into his shoes?

The thought occurred to me when I was visiting friends in Toronto, Canada, and as I shared it one morning as a vague, plan-on-the-back-of-an-envelope idea, in a sea of other suggestions that were floating around, one of my new friends, an American called Sean, stopped everyone.

'You've got to do this. God is calling you to make this journey.'

A bit dramatic.

Everyone present started to join in, affirming me in this bizarre quest and praying into the journey. It all seemed a bit overwhelming and my British reserve was rather challenged, so at the time I just smiled and nodded. But later on, when the dust had settled and everyone had left, I started to wonder if his encouragement was the thing I needed to rescue me from years of procrastinating over a one-day-in-the-future idea? Ideas are more fun when they're years in the future, but when you're actually close to carrying them out, that's when the fear sets in. If I was going to do this, I had to do it soon before I changed my mind.

I booked an EasyJet flight to Tel Aviv and a bus to the border with Egypt, bought a guidebook for hikers in Israel and planned a vague route on some wilderness trails, dropping pins on Google Maps where I could fill up with water in the remote towns nestled in the vast expanses of the desert.

My aim was simple: by going back to Jesus' earliest earthly memories and by walking the road he walked, I hoped to learn something about his life that history books alone couldn't communicate – to get into the mind of the original peacemaker.

I didn't just want to read about his formative years in the wilderness; I wanted to experience them. I picked up a Hebrew phrase book and took an evening class in Arabic in preparation for when I crossed into the West Bank. Given that I struggled to pick up any Spanish in Chile, I'm not sure why I thought Arabic would be easier, but after ten weeks I could confidently say, 'Marhaba' (Hello) and 'Ma'salama' (Goodbye). That was about it. Hebrew was a shade easier, for '*Shalom*' is both hello and goodbye. Even I can handle that.

Both *shalom* and *salam* mean 'peace'. How nice. Two people groups living side by side, continually greeting each other with peace. Ideal.

There was a vague trail through the desert from Egypt to Nazareth. I doubt it was the exact route that Jesus followed, but it was about five hundred miles long, and I figured that would be enough to experience something of the perils he would have encountered when crossing a Middle Eastern desert.

There's a sort of unwritten rule in British culture that if you suffer enough, you're allowed to ask people for money. A sponsored walk might generate a few pennies, but a sponsored 'I might actually die' gets people digging a bit deeper. If I was going to be walking in the footsteps of the world's most famous refugee, I figured I might as well raise support for refugees in the current generation.

In the wake of the Arab Spring, some sinister entrepreneurs took advantage of the complete breakdown of law and order, and human trafficking flourished as millions of refugees found themselves in the hands of traffickers who were there to 'help'. Vulnerable girls fleeing war zones across the region were tricked and trafficked into an even darker world than the one they had left behind.

Who would run a trade like that?

Who would fight back?

As Desmond Tutu famously argued, freedom and liberty are lost when good people are not vigilant. If you are neutral in a situation of injustice, you have chosen the side of the oppressor.[2]

One of my great heroes is the Australian activist Christine Caine. I remember taking a road trip one weekend in the car my friend Anna had kindly lent me – a small, purple VW Polo. There was no music, no audiobooks, no digital radio, just three CDs from a women's conference that Caine had spoken at. I looked at the box, realised that I was about to learn how to be a strong, confident woman and put on the first CD.

I have never forgotten what I heard on that drive.

To this day, I can't remember where I was even going, or what I did there. But I remember those three CDs because they changed my life.

In 2007, Christine Caine was on her way to Thessaloniki in Greece to speak at a women's conference. She'd travelled from Sydney, Australia, where she was a pastor, and she recalls waiting in the airport for her delayed baggage and spotting posters of missing children plastered across a wall. She wandered over for a closer look, and in the middle was an image of Madeleine McCann.

'I looked back at Madeleine's picture and thought of her parents, waking up to discover that their child was no longer in the bed into which they had tucked her and watched her fall into an innocent sleep. The word *missing* beneath her picture gripped my heart.'[3]

There were lots of pictures, all of sweet, smiling children juxtaposed against the cold figures of case numbers, a contact number to call if they were spotted, and the word 'Missing'.

Christine's hosts arrived, grabbed her bags and whisked her off to meet new friends over a hearty meal in a Greek restaurant, but as the evening wore on, she couldn't shake the thought of those missing girls. She asked her host, Maria, about them.

'Why are there so many missing children and young women?'

Maria spelled it out. 'It's suspected that they were kidnapped, which seems to happen frequently these days.'[4]

That night, as jetlag took its toll, Caine found herself reading the story of the Good Samaritan in the early hours.[5] It's a story that is familiar to millions: a Jewish man, beaten half to death by bandits, abandoned at the side of the road. Two good Jewish leaders scurry past, but a Samaritan, a mortal enemy of the Jews, goes over to him, puts him on his donkey and takes him to an inn, where he pays for his treatment. It's a powerful story, perhaps Jesus' most famous, and one that Caine was going to preach on at the conference. In that moment, though she'd heard it a hundred times, she felt a new awareness of the line, 'He went to him.'

The Good Samaritan didn't wait until his Jewish brother showed up at his door; he went to him when he needed it most.

Returning to Sydney the following week, still captivated by those words and haunted by the photos of the missing children in Thessaloniki, Christine shared the story with her husband Nick. After months of research into the global trade in human beings, they made a bold move.

They went.

Laying down the comfort and security of their jobs in Australia, they returned to Greece to set up an organisation to rescue people who had been kidnapped and trafficked around the region – the Middle East, North Africa, Eastern Europe, the Stans. Greece is surrounded by an underground trade in human beings.

They hired a team of professionals to help them set up, and the advice was unanimous: this is too hard; there are too many obstacles; you can't succeed.

Undeterred and without the money, skills or resources to tackle what has become a global trade, they pressed on with prayer and stubborn-hearted compassion. Within a year, against all the odds, they had a safe house, a rescue team and the beginnings of a multinational organisation. A21 was born, which stands for 'Abolitionists in the twenty-first century'. At the time of writing they are in twelve countries and still growing.

A few years later, the Middle East was turned upside down and millions of refugees flooded into Europe. Human traffickers were ready and waiting, but so too were the A21 teams, who had been prepared for the Arab Spring before any of them even knew it was coming.

A21 now has multiple safe houses where rescued girls are learning to be free again, and there are traffickers behind bars right now thanks to its work. For years I have followed its progress and championed its cause. Every new academic year, I taught young geography students about the modern slave trade and implored them to be the generation that fights it. Now, years later, it was my time to walk the talk. I don't have the skills, language or experience to rescue trafficked people in the darkest corners of the globe, but I can support those who do.

If I was going to be journeying along the fringe of the Mediterranean, it made sense to back the efforts of those more qualified than me to rescue people from its shores.

I set up an online fundraiser, made a vow to walk 500 miles in support of A21, packed my bags and got on the plane.

LIFE ON MARS

The Hebrew language has a little play on words about the desert that I learned from Chief Rabbi Lord Jonathan Sacks. The word for 'wilderness' is roughly the same as the word for 'speaking', so the fourth book of the Bible is a sort of Hebrew pun, the words that God 'spoke' in the 'wilderness'.[6] It's not a laugh-out-loud joke, but I would need whatever encouragement I could find to survive the 500-mile slog to Nazareth.

I wondered if God was still speaking in this wilderness.

My greatest blessing in those first fragile days was that Pete, a sterling friend and fellow Cornish brother, had taken a week off work to join me on the first ascent.

I'd planned this journey to start in January because that was Israel's winter, the 'rainy season' which I thought would ease the searing heat of the Negev. The Judean hills further north are quite fresh in January, and I'd packed extra layers to ward off the cold, but the desert seemed to ignore the forecast like a rebellious teenager doing their own thing.

As soon as the sun appeared over Jordan, it became unbearably hot. Reassurance from a lady by the Red Sea that 'it's much worse in July' didn't really help. While my thick leather walking boots were the perfect match for a wet Scottish mountain, I soon realised that they were an object of torture in the desert. My pack was more than double the recommended weight, and within an hour the mesh straps had bitten a red honeycomb pattern into my hips, and it was growing deeper with every step.

Like any optimistic traveller packing their bag in a hurry a few hours before leaving to catch a flight, I'd thrown in a ton of unnecessary tat, happily telling myself, 'I'll be needing this.'

How wrong I was.

We'd stayed the night in a half-built hostel in the nearby town of Eilat, six miles from the start of a rugged desert trail, and hiking to the shore of the Red Sea that morning was a rude awakening.

We stopped at the start of the trail, and I unlaced my sweaty boots to tend to a fizzy spot on my sole, the sure promise of an approaching blister. I arrived at the depressing realisation that I was already struggling, and we hadn't even started. I mean, we literally hadn't started. The short hike from the hostel to the start of the trail didn't count in our planning.

It counted for my feet.

I looked up into the looming red mountains. It felt like the Negev was mocking me, belly laughing from its giant creases at the audacious Brit who thought he could defy the vast Martian wilderness of the desert, dressed like a muppet on a geography field trip.

We stopped for one last coffee in an isolated roadside shop before leaving civilisation. I'm still not sure why I wanted a hot drink to help me cope with unbearable heat. That's delirium for you. We tentatively approached the first hill.

'Only 500 miles to go,' I whispered, embracing the mockery. If you can't beat the wilderness, you might as well join it.

As we summited the first peak, chasing the gentle comfort of a sea breeze, the hazy horizon greeted us with endless mountains, bigger and darker, stretching out into the unknown. Anxiety engulfed me like the giant nothingness of the road ahead, and I reasoned, rather logically, that if I was struggling now, the chances of me making it to the end were slim.

We stopped after an hour to rehydrate and looked proudly back at the view of the Red Sea. When you've suffered to accomplish something, the victory is a million times sweeter than if it were handed to you on a plate. I imagined the glistening waters of the Sea of Galilee on the final day of my journey, hundreds of miles to the north.

If I ever made it, that would be a sweet sight.

I took a sip of now warm water and we ploughed on. I'd arranged for a driver in the previous town to drop some water at our first night camp, which wasn't far from the main desert road, so we were on a deadline. After that, we would be nowhere near the road and there would be nowhere to get water until the desert oasis of Timna, three days' walk away.

As the hours ticked on and the exhaustion set in, I started to process the weeks ahead as the fear marinated in my stomach. I had told people back home that I would be 'walking in the footsteps of the world's most famous refugee to raise money for refugees in this generation', which sounded neat at the time, but here I was on day one, faced with the strong possibility that I might not make it.

How unbelievably lame.

If I failed, would people still donate anything to A21?

I could almost taste the guilt.

If I didn't make it, I also had to come to terms with the fact that I'd failed on a journey that had been completed a couple of millennia previously by a child. Admittedly, that child was Jesus, but that didn't mean it had been easier. He took no short cuts.

When an insurmountable hurdle is set before you, I'd heard it's best to break it down into smaller chunks and just deal with the task in front of you. If I could just focus on making it into camp every day, those days would add up. That was my plan.

As the sun dipped below the shifting sands of Egypt and the desert switched from unbearable heat to lifeless cold, we rolled into our night camp, dropped our bags and collapsed in the dirt. I wanted to lie there for hours, but with darkness setting in and the cold wrapping itself around us like an icy blanket, we had to get the tent up and the stove on for dinner. I called our contact and told him we were ready for the water. We were in for a rude shock.

The guy's wife answered the phone and casually informed us, 'He is out of the country.' I explained that I'd spoken to him the previous day, but she was adamant. 'He's not here.'

I told Pete.

'Oh.'

This had been Pete's only real concern for the expedition – how would we get water? He even offered to help research the options.

'Don't worry,' I told him, 'I've got it sorted.'

Awkward.

People often turn to prayer as a last resort, but when you have literally zero other options, it ends up being your first resort. I echoed the prayer that José had taught the men in the San José mine, below another barren desert, the prayer that I'd since used countless times on my journey: 'Lord, I'm not the best of men, but have mercy on us.'

As we stretched the tent over the thankless bedrock of the night camp and built a feeble stone wall around it to ease the icy breeze, two young Israeli women wandered in. We were soon catching up on the day's adventures and raving about the beautiful views while I pretended that it had all been utter fun and not remotely painful.

'What are you doing for water?' they asked.

Pete casually mentioned that we were running low but were hoping to make it to the Timna Oasis. After a brief discussion in Hebrew, the girls offered some words that were as refreshing as the promise they held: 'We've got a friend who can help.'

Those young ladies literally rescued us. The funny thing is that they shouldn't have even been there: Israelis rarely hike so early in the year. It's widely agreed that the winter months are too cold at night and the risk of flash floods makes the sun-baked wadis a potential deathtrap. Later in February, as the cold eases and the rains subside, hikers from all over the country start to emerge, but to find a couple of friends out in the desert at the beginning of January is not standard practice. For some reason, they'd decided to buck the trend and hike into the desert for a random, one-off expedition that night.

Their friend was a chap who was planning to hike the trail later in the season, and he'd buried a load of water bottles in preparation. It's the way most desert hikers survive the Negev: they drive into the remotest parts in 4x4s laden with water bottles, bury their liquid lifelines in secret stashes along the route and then set off from the start of the trail with a handmade treasure map. My plan was different: we would carry all our water on our backs and fill up in desert towns every couple of days.

Such an amateur.

In my calculations, the only time we needed a drop-off was on the first night. It was a solid plan. Until it failed. On day one.

The mystery friend texted the location of his buried treasure to the Israeli women, and we paid him over WhatsApp – the wonders of modern technology. We built a fire and chatted to our new friends late into the night about life in Israel, for they were curious to know why we were there and even more surprised to discover that we were walking in Jesus' footsteps. It was news to them that he ever went to Egypt. Israelis aren't taught much about Jesus, other than to be wary of anyone who claims to be one of his followers. The supposedly 'Christian' Europe doesn't have a great history when it comes to supporting the Jews, and that's not just Germany. Thirteenth-century England, fourteenth-century France and fifteenth-century Spain all have blood on their hands. Pete explained that we personally didn't support the prejudices of European history and that Jesus himself was Jewish, and we respected his people.

When we woke early the following morning, they were gone. But not without trace. As we peered out into the half-light of dawn, there were six litres of water waiting outside our tent.

It's a story you rarely hear in the land, the simple kindness of ordinary people. In the weeks that followed, we experienced the same life-saving generosity from every tribe and tongue – Israelis and Palestinians, Christians, Muslims and Jews. Despite the extreme views that I was peppered with before I left, as the weeks went on it became harder and harder to subscribe to the polarised political rhetoric that any people group is inherently good or evil. It seems there are secret mercies and unsung heroes in every society, once you get off the beaten track.

As we pressed on, deeper into the Negev, our spirits lifted. We had survived the first day of almost constant ascent, we had enough water for two days, and we even met a friendly German called Eric to walk with us until the oasis. His feet were suffering like mine, so we discussed our various approaches to blister management along the path and tested different ways of rearranging our bags to make them magically lighter (to no avail).

As I limped through the desert, cut and torn, whining like a cat on hot coals, Pete, who had opted for a pair of lightweight trainers and a smaller pack, was dancing along the rocky trails like a mountain goat. Good job we're mates. He graciously packed some of my gear around his bursting rucksack and cheered me on with relentless optimism and the promise of dried fruit with semi-melted chocolate.

As the days went on and we slowly chomped up the miles of ridges and ravines, the pain started to ease. Or maybe I just learned to toughen up.

As we set up camp in the tiny oasis of Timna, a few days into the desert, I paused and pondered what this journey must have been like for a young child two thousand years ago. Pete was balancing his phone precariously on a rock and attempting to catch a time-lapse of the setting sun, while I sat down with a sewing needle, a bottle of iodine (for the foot) and a hip flask (for the soul).

For all my moaning about blisters and bruises, I had to face up to the fact that I'm a grown man, with the latest gear, some fine single malt and many years of experience in the outdoors – although, granted, you wouldn't think it from my many rookie errors. Jesus would have made this journey as a child, without a decent rucksack, a three-man tent or Italian walking boots.

Two thousand years feels like an unimaginably long time, but the realisation that I was physically in the place where he walked, knowing that his little feet really did scuff these dusty roads, seemed to evaporate the centuries between us.

However long ago it was, it still happened, and all the mod cons that have come along since that time only reinforce the fact that it would have been unimaginably harder for him.

Would he have fared better in sandals?

Did he even have sandals?

Finding new shoes for a growing boy in a foreign nation every time his feet jumped a size wouldn't have been easy. The boy Jesus may even have walked the razor-like ridges of the desert barefoot.

Although we don't know their exact route, they would likely have walked further west than me, along the shores of the Mediterranean. Did this child bathe his blistered feet in the sea he had created?

There's a paradox.

Unlike many world leaders in our generation, nobody can say that Jesus had it easy. For millions of refugee children on perilous journeys along dirt tracks and desert trails all over the world, Jesus can say, 'I know your trials; I've been there too.'

As Pete mixed a can of tuna into our pasta pesto over a roaring gas stove, I realised I knew little of the ordeal that this young exile from Egypt faced two thousand years ago, yet, as an adult, he never looked back and complained of his humble start in life – far from it.

Has there ever been a man of greater *shalom*?

Like the vast tapestry of stars in the desert sky, that night I counted my blessings.

14.

THE LONELIEST PLACE ON EARTH

A BURDEN SHARED is a burden halved. Apparently. Researchers at the Marshall Business School in California have even put this to the test. They could have just joined me in the desert.[1] For a week, Pete and I shared one other's burdens. Sometimes literally, when the tent was split between our backpacks; at other times emotionally, as we discussed the trials and challenges of life. We laughed about the mishaps of the journey, compared our photos of desert landscapes and spent hours endlessly tweaking our rather bland pasta dinner to make it marginally tastier with various Middle Eastern spices that we picked up in desert towns en route.

Pete worked for the Physics Department at Bristol University and couldn't take a long holiday in the middle of the academic year. After a week of blazing through the desert, he veered east towards the main desert road to catch a ride north, leaving me to fend for myself.

I had seen this point on the horizon since we had set off. It was the moment I'd dreaded most.

I was planning to meet friends in Jerusalem, just over halfway, but that was still one hundred and eighty miles away.

Which is a long way to walk alone.

I remember a few months before the trip, Caroline, a lady from my church in Bristol, had a message for me. She caught me after a service one morning and told me that while she'd been praying, a picture had flashed into her mind's eye of me, dressed as an explorer, trekking through the desert, and she sensed that God was calling me to be brave. She tentatively asked whether that meant anything. Perhaps I was going through a 'desert stage' in life?

I explained that it wasn't a metaphor; I really was about to cross a desert, and I really would need to dig deep and find some courage. Caroline knew nothing about my trip at that time, but her mysteriously accurate message became a timely encouragement on the morning Pete left.

I thought about the lady from Mendoza who had shared a prophetic word with José Henríquez's family while he was buried in the mine. I've heard it said that sometimes an insight like this comes before a real trial, a stronghold of hope to propel you through the challenges ahead. I would need it.

I vividly remember the first night I spent by myself in the wilderness. I had hiked the trail westward, out of the Jordan Valley and into the mountains where the air was cooler. I pitched up as it was getting dark in a small ravine at the top of a ridge, thinking I would get phone signal higher up to call home.

I was wrong.

Even when I was physically without company, I could usually still phone my family. Israel is obsessively well connected, and while it was a constant challenge to find water, phone signal was easy to come by.

But not this night.

I put the tent up in a hurry. It was harder pitching it alone, and rocks that had been slowly hardening for a million years weren't going to surrender to a set of flimsy tent pegs without a fight.

As the sun set over Egypt, the night pounced out of the shadows.

The ravine was pitch dark, and the quietness was tangible. It's rare to find complete and utter silence these days, especially in the inner-city world I call home.

There was not a whisper of life up there on the ridge. No gentle hum of traffic, nobody laughing downstairs, no music coming from a car outside.

Just silence.

I remember thinking, 'Is this the loneliest place on earth?'

Three weeks suddenly seemed like a long time.

I felt like Mark Watney in the film *The Martian*, at the moment he realised he'd been left on Mars, surrounded by nothing but an inhospitable wasteland of red rocks.

I lay down in my tent and fired up the gas stove by the open door. I realised that my feeling of intense isolation out in the desert mirrored a broader phenomenon that is plaguing this generation. We may be the most well-connected people in history, but many are lonelier than ever.

For me, the ironies didn't end there. I later learned that my first night alone in the wilderness was the same night the UK government announced it was launching a new operation to tackle loneliness. As the moon rose over the measureless sands of the Negev, the Prime Minister was hosting a crowded reception, three thousand miles north in central London, to lay out plans to tackle the 'loneliness epidemic'. That felt a little close to home.

The report highlighted some stark findings: more than nine million people 'always or often feel lonely', while the proportion of young disabled adults experiencing loneliness is 85 per cent. In the older generation, there are 200,000 people 'who have not had a conversation with a friend or relative in more than a month'.[2]

A month?

I'd barely gone twenty-four hours, and it was killing me.

It's not just in the UK where the alarm bells are sounding. In 2018, former US Surgeon General Vivek Murthy described loneliness as a profound public health crisis and likened it to smoking 15 cigarettes a day.[3] Mother Teresa described it as 'the most terrible poverty'.[4]

The deafening silence of the desert night wakened me to the daily reality for millions all over the world. I thought about this a great deal over the following weeks. I had the time to, after all.

Is there any way out of our endemic loneliness?

The desert became the laboratory where I tested this question, although, to be more accurate, it was the desert that was testing me.

The current pantomime villain fuelling our anxious loneliness is social media, but I've started to wonder whether that's too simple a conclusion, as if losing Facebook tomorrow would make us all happier and more sociable. For some people, it might be a good idea, but I doubt it's the ultimate cure for isolation. What if our increasing use of social media is less the problem and more a symptom of the deeper issue, a cry for connection in an increasingly fragmented world?

For many people, the latest technology has connected them to loved ones, where previous generations have known even more isolation. For someone working on a ship in the middle of the ocean, being able to videocall their kids on their birthday is a lifeline, and there are thousands of comparable examples like this. Out in the desert, I was one of them.

I celebrate the good that social media has brought to our fragmented world, but in those long days under the desert sun, I started to view it the same way I saw a snack: it feeds your appetite and keeps you going, but in the long run it can't replace a sit-down meal with friends and family. We are wired for genuine, unhurried human contact, the way we need real home-made meals, and if we only supply our souls with digital 'snack connections' we are left socially undernourished and starved of real community.

Perhaps the greatest danger of social media is not its prevalence or even its usefulness, but its distortion of reality, for in the words of my friend, James Lee, 'Real friendship, real community, real family is being sidelined and replaced with connectivity that lacks authenticity.'[5]

People are often more audacious (or more aggressive) on social media than in real life because the buffer of not actually being present with the people we're interacting with can give us false confidence. But words (and images) that are shared with false confidence can come back to haunt us. Even the most innocent of contributions can lack a small degree of integrity, for nobody posts pictures of themselves at their worst on Instagram. Sometimes, without even realising it, by offering the world an artificially upcycled version of ourselves, we end up tempting each other into a painful cycle of endless comparison.

But I still wonder whether it's too easy to blame technology for everything, even as a teacher whose greatest temptation is to say, 'Kids these days . . .'

Having a smartphone (and giant power bank) in the desert helped to digitally medicate the loneliness. There were tracks on my Spotify playlist that put words to the emotions I couldn't articulate in the dark valleys and lofty mountains. Every morning I listened to 'Blinded by Your Grace' by Stormzy and felt like it had been written for me. I pondered on podcasts from Tim and Jon at The Bible Project, gleaning insights about events that had happened in the very desert I was crossing. I could email ahead to contacts in Bethlehem, setting up interviews for the following month, and every few days I put that timeless message on the family WhatsApp group: 'Hey everyone! I'm still alive.'

It's not even just on a personal basis that technology has helped. While social media has fuelled many great evils in our generation, it has also been used to fight them. The prevalence of the charity A21 on social media means that people have been able to tip it off to human trafficking rings. This has led to successful operations to catch the criminals and set victims free all over the world.

In recent years, nations have changed, even whole regions have been transformed, through social media, and vast injustices have been finally brought into the light. Thanks to smartphones, it's getting harder for those in authority to hide acts of brutality. That's as true in the Middle East as it is in the West. The Black Lives Matter protests that unfolded around the world in the wake of George Floyd's murder were only possible because someone caught the incident on camera. As actor Will Smith previously pointed out, 'Racism isn't getting worse; it's getting filmed.'[6]

The first step in tackling any injustice is bringing the truth into the light, letting people know what's really going on. Knowledge is power. Social media, when harnessed for good, is an immense tool in this generation. The issue is how we use it.

For me, the secret to celebrating its virtues while avoiding its vices lies in understanding its limitations. For some people, screen time has so engulfed their minute-to-minute activity that they've lost the very thing that social media was supposed to promote: connection.

FaceTime is a useful tool when you can't physically be with someone, but it can't replace actual presence. My face is not a three-inch, two-dimensional blur, and nor is anyone else's. When I want real face time with someone I love, I switch off my phone, put the kettle on and focus on the real thing.

For the long weeks of lockdown during the coronavirus pandemic, people were forced to communicate with family members through phones and laptops, and while the technology was a gift that helped us to endure the isolation, it was only ever a stopgap. As lockdown eased, and we were finally safe to see loved ones, people rediscovered the simple joy of meeting another human in real life.

I have found there's something irreplaceable about the ability to look into the whites of someone's eyes, to detect the tiny creases around their smile, to listen to their stories without google-checking every fact, laughing when they laugh, crying when they cry, just listening when I have nothing to add, which is most of the time. All of us need times to be present with another beating heart, even without speaking, to enjoy their company in a level of HD that no screen can replicate.

The lack of human contact in those first lonely days in the desert brought this home to me like never before, but my personal insights are only a dim reflection of the evidence that has already come to light.

The Commission for Loneliness launched by the UK government was steered by a report from the Red Cross and the Co-op, which found, 'People . . . are wary of the ability for digital-only support to fully meet their need for human engagement.' Across the board, 'face-to-face support is vastly preferred'.[7]

The benefits of the community I had left behind were magnified in the realisation that I missed it. I missed them. As I reflected on the last few years of my life, it occurred to me that the network of community houses in Bristol, which have meant so much to me personally, could hold some keys to the broader loneliness epidemic.

I can but wonder.

For some, the default recipe for making 'community' is to find a soul mate, settle down, buy a house, have kids, hold down a job, release those kids into civilisation, retire somewhere nice and die happy and content that they have followed the script.

As if life were that straightforward.

For many people, who haven't found the job, partner or pay cheque they want, they cannot follow the script, and that hurts. But for others who have walked the expected path, ticked all the relevant boxes and lived up to all societal expectations . . . they're still lonely.

What are we missing?

JUST LOVE

On those long days stumbling through desert ravines, I began to realise it wasn't just having people around that I missed, for loneliness is more than just an absence of people. Ironically, some of the most crowded places on the planet are also the loneliest.

In the words of Mother Teresa, 'We can cure physical diseases with medicine, but the only cure for loneliness . . . is love.'[8]

We need loving, honouring, meaningful relationships, but the current of western culture has been subtly teaching us to prioritise selfish needs over collective compassion. Maybe the loneliness epidemic is a symptom of the myth that the path to happiness lies in selfishness. As a generation, we are more aware of our individual rights than ever before, more able to customise our lifestyles to our preferred parameters, and more technologically tuned in to our own specific tastes. While this can be nice to an extent, have we swung so far into the realms of an obsessive, self-orientated pursuit of happiness that we've forgotten the person next to us?

Maybe the solution to loneliness is to reach out to someone else, even someone we're a bit uncomfortable with, to take the first step, to make someone else's life a little bit better, rather than worrying about our own. What if, deep down, we're actually hard-wired for compassion, and all our fluffy material interests have smothered that innate desire to prioritise the other?

As I reflect on the heroes I have met on this journey, the people who have inspired me the most are not those with the newest ideas or the most profound theories, but those who have demonstrated compassion and built community at every cost to themselves.

Pete is one of those. He lives in a community house at the other end of the neighbourhood to me. In our first week in the desert, as we chatted around the fire, he shared how his house had recently taken in a pregnant asylum seeker who was homeless.

I asked him why.

'Because she needed somewhere to live.'

You can't argue with that.

I can't share the full story, but suffice it to say that Pete's house is clearly a place with its eyes and heart open. I wonder if Dave Jeal would be where he is today if it weren't for the Mitchells taking him into their community house.

For me, some of the most inspiring communities in Bristol are the smallest ones – places where a family has simply taken in one person – an adopted child, a refugee fleeing persecution, a recovering addict – and invested everything they've got in that one person. If every household focused on one person in need, we could change the nation.

It's not that every story has a happy ending, but what if people were 'loved anyway', regardless of the outcome?[9]

I'm not suggesting that I've mastered this; indeed, I must confess to having daily battles with my own selfishness and the constant frustration of living with people who are not like me.

The battle is never entirely won, but it's always worth fighting, and I've found role models from every walk of life who are leading the way and showing us how to love the other.

The Commission to tackle loneliness in the UK was inspired by the work of the late Jo Cox, MP for Batley and Spen, who was murdered in 2016. She worked tirelessly with vulnerable and isolated people in West Yorkshire, and those closest to her determined that her legacy should continue what she started, to wake people up to the raw power of compassion.

Inspired by the Jo Cox Foundation's The Great Get Together, and similar programmes such as The Feast youth project in Birmingham, I joined the Bristol charity Bridges for Communities who help connect isolated people living in our city who are from different cultures. We developed a programme called 'Peace Feast' which brings people together from different cultures and faiths for a hearty meal and the opportunity to build new friendships. I spoke to Kim Leadbeater, Jo Cox's sister, while we were running Peace Feasts online during the lockdown in 2020 to get some advice on how to help people overcome isolation.[10]

It's the collective action of all these creative ideas that is needed to roll back the tide of loneliness. And we have our work cut out. For some, the feeling of loneliness is just the tip of the iceberg, the symptom of a far greater tragedy, for there are forty million slaves in the world today. More than half are women. One in four is a child.[11]

For young girls forced into the underground sex trade and 'visited' by dozens of men every day, the loneliness of their situation is a tragic irony. They don't suffer for lack of contact, but for lack of compassion. A few nights alone in the wilderness can never compare to that level of isolated exploitation.

Maybe that is the loneliest place on earth.

While many of us can feel overwhelmed by human crises like these, some people have refused to be neutralised by despair. You have to start somewhere. Right now, a growing army of abolitionists, like the teams from A21, are tracking down thousands of trafficked people – sons and daughters with friends and families, gifts and talents, hopes and dreams, equally deserving of a loving home like mine. Right now, there are rescued girls in community houses of sanctuary and redemption, far from danger, who can dare to dream again.

If my lonely trek does nothing but draw people's attention to those who need it far more than me, then I will have no regrets.

On my first night alone in the desert, I watched the stars twinkling in the night sky and rejoiced for those individuals who have given their lives to fighting these unimaginable evils.

Up there in that desert ravine, I couldn't have been further from another human being if I'd tried. Sometimes hardship can be a blessing in disguise; it shows us what really matters.

15.

ANGELS AND WOLVES

MY PHONE VIBRATED violently next to my head, piercing the silence before dawn. Leaving the warm embrace of my sleeping bag for the icy nothingness of the desert felt like the worst idea in history, but I needed to be moving before the heat of the day set in.

I pressed snooze.

Five minutes later, I went through the same emotions.

If I didn't suffer now, I would suffer later.

I rolled out into the merciless face-slap of the morning air and got a saucepan of water boiling for a cup of tea, still slightly greasy from my dinner of tuna-pasta-pesto the night before. As a few golden beads of olive oil danced on the surface of the water, I packed the tent up slowly and clumsily.

By the time I set off, the horizon was glowing, and I scolded myself for faffing so much. Despite the cruel cold of dawn and the dread of the miles ahead, I felt a small dose of elation rising within me as the first shards of light flexed over the mountains of Jordan, tickling the furrows of the desert.

I had made it.

I had lived through my first night alone in the wilderness, and I was alive.

I listened to 'Shadows of the Dawn' by The Gray Havens, and soon discovered the surprising number of songs on Spotify about being 'in the wilderness'. Although they were mostly metaphorical, I felt a smug sense of satisfaction that I was living the metaphor.

It wasn't long before exhaustion evaporated my smugness like the morning dew. The isolation of the desert had woken me up to the value of the community I'd left behind, and for that I rejoice. But it didn't change the fact that I still had to walk another 180 miles, through a desert, by myself.

Ironically, my greatest fear turned out to be the realisation that I wasn't alone after all.

Two days later, I crawled from my sleeping bag, reached for a bag of granola and munched on the overly sweetened clusters of oats, spilling flecks of grain on the ground like an animal.

'This should keep the wolf from the door,' I muttered, rubbing the sleep from my eyes and ignoring what people say about the insanity of talking to yourself.

A minute later, as I finished my morning brew and watered the desert sand with that first satisfying pee of the day, I saw a flash of grey-brown whistle past me.

A lone wolf.

It was gone in a matter of seconds, but I stood there, paralysed, for ages. It was somehow frightening and beautiful at the same time – bounding across the valley, gliding over the rocks with untameable elegance. Whatever it was running from, or after, it was consumed by the chase.

As I eventually snapped into gear and turned onto the trail, I chuckled about the timing of my 'wolf from the door' comment and offered a prayer of thanks that it really had stayed away from my flimsy tent door that past night.[1]

As the day tracked on, the thought seemed to prowl around my head.

Was it really a wolf?

Maybe I'd just seen a jackal or a runaway German Shepherd from a desert farm.

As I scoffed down another fistful of raisins, I did something I should never have done.

I googled it.

I had three bars of signal; it was too tempting.

One of the first hits was a *Guardian* article from four months earlier entitled, 'Campers in Israel warned after series of wolf attacks'.[2]

My imagination ran wild.

Until recently, it transpired, no wolf attacks had been reported in Israel since 2008. But in the summer of 2017, there was an unprecedented rise from one in ten years to ten in one year.

Good to know.

I read on. It transpired that a few individual wolves were adapting to proximity with humans, losing their instinctive fear and looking for opportunities to steal a camper's dinner. Or child.

Little Red Riding Hood just got real.

One woman ran out of her tent to discover a wolf red-handed with its fangs in her daughter, trying to drag her away. It didn't get very far. You don't mess with mother bear.

Fortunately, none of the attacks were fatal, thanks to the swift action and furious love of their parents pouncing to the rescue. But the scars were more than just teeth marks.

A few nights later, as I set up camp in a natural amphitheatre nestled on a hilltop by the edge of the Makhtesh Katan crater, I discovered I had company. There were a few smashed-up wooden pallets left by a previous group of campers, so I made a roaring fire and cooked dinner over the embers, a welcome break from my piddly gas stove.

I was settling down in the darkness, glued to 'nature's TV' as the flames rose into the night, when I was suddenly brought to my senses by the thunder of feet sweeping across the desert behind me.

In the dim light of my head torch, I saw two great shadows galloping past me, snorting and snarling. With my heart racing and adrenaline coursing through my arteries, I grabbed a flaming log from the fire and chased after them, launching rocks hot on their tail. As I slowly retreated to the comfort of the fire, I felt a renewed courage.

No wolf would be coming near my door that night.

When I eventually calmed down and slipped into my tent, I flashed my torch into the darkness one final time and saw two little eyes staring back at me.

Freaky.

It can't have been a large animal – the eyes were small and close together – maybe a fox or a wild cat, nothing to fear. Camp spots attract no small amount of wildlife. In the barren wasteland of the desert, the possibility of stealing someone else's dinner is a treat that attracts many paws.

It's fair to say I didn't sleep much that night. It's a weird feeling trying to doze off in the wild, knowing that you're not entirely alone. As the dawn slowly conquered the night on the crown of the mountain, I emerged from my tent to survey the scene.

Something about the previous night didn't feel right.

I thought about the thunder of feet galloping across the camp, the sound amplified in the natural bowl-shape of the mountain-top crater.

Wolves don't thunder; they creep.

They are masters of stealth, not stampeding.

Come to think of it, the sound was more like hooves than paws. The noise they made was more of a snort than a snarl and certainly not a howl. The shadowy beasts were big, that's for sure, but perhaps too big for the stealthy frame of a wolf. And why were there two, anyway? So far, I had only seen a lone wolf, and that was a few days earlier. But ibex, the sure-footed mountain goats of the Negev, well, I had seen a family scaling the rocky peak only half an hour before setting up camp.

Suddenly I didn't feel so impressive. Last night, I had prepared myself to see off a pack of wolves with a flaming log, like that scene in *The Bourne Legacy*. But in the cold light of day, it dawned on me that I had probably just chased after a couple of harmless goats with a smouldering stick.

It was wildly unimpressive.

I did see a wolf again, later in the trek, sniffing through some garbage outside a quarry, but it ran away when it saw me, silently. It was thin, scruffy and rather underwhelming.

As I reflect on these brushes with beasts, deep in the desert, I feel slightly embarrassed. For all my fears, they turned out to be rather innocuous. In fact, a desert rescue volunteer in the town of Arad laughed when I told him about the wolves and said something that, roughly translated was, 'Wolves? Ha! They won't hurt you. Don't be a pansy.'

Cheers.

The only creatures that did come close to attacking me were three guard dogs outside a village on a valley path north of the desert. They surrounded me on all sides, barking and snapping as I circled and side-stepped along the path but, being fiercely territorial, once I was out of their patch, they lost interest and left me alone.

A Jewish lawyer in the next town told me that the last hiker who was due to come through had been rushed to hospital after being bitten by dogs. I really did have a lucky escape.

It turns out, the only dangerous animals on my journey were the supposedly domesticated ones. There's a lesson in there somewhere.

While my anxiety of wolves subsided, I realised that it's one thing to defend yourself as a full-grown adult in the clear light of day, but it's quite another to protect a flock of lambs at night, while hungry opportunists lurk in the shadows. The wolf might not attack me, but it would happily take my dinner given half a chance.

There are some sentences in Scripture that I will never look at in the same way again.

When Jesus was alone in the Judean wilderness, Mark records that he was 'with the wild animals'.[3] No kidding.

When he was born in Bethlehem, there were shepherds out in fields nearby, 'keeping watch over their flocks at night'.[4]

I now know why.

In the days of destitute poverty when farmers struggled to pay savage taxes to the violent Roman Empire, keeping your flock intact was a matter of life and death.

I met a young Bedouin shepherd in a narrow ravine, the morning after I saw that wolf, and shared my semi-melted chocolate with him. I wonder how much sleep he got the night before.

When Jesus taught his followers that he is the 'gate',[5] he used the image of a shepherd lying in the gateway to a stone-walled pen, so that wolves would have to cross him to get to the flock. A 'hired hand' would abandon the flock in a wolf attack, but the good shepherd would literally lay down his life for the sheep. Jesus spoke metaphorically; we are no sheep (although the parallels are uncanny), but not long after he shared this teaching, he really did lay down his life.

'I am the good shepherd,' he said. 'The good shepherd lays down his life for the sheep.'[6]

I guess he really meant it.

I thought back to his early years, far from Jerusalem, when he would have hiked these dirt tracks as a young boy with two dusty feet, leaving child-sized footprints in the vast shifting sands of the desert.

Perhaps death wasn't so far from his door, even back then. If a wolf would attack a child in the twenty-first century, would it not go for one in the first century? I hardly think wolves have become more civilised over time.

When Joseph and Mary brought their toddler home from Egypt through many a wilderness mile, they had far more cause for fear than I did all those years later.

Did they lie awake under the stars, taking it in turns to defend their child through the early hours? Did they stoke the fire all night to keep the wolf from . . . ? Well, there was no door.

Perhaps Jesus was sandwiched between them for warmth and safety, much like any young child sneaks into their parents' bed at night.

Probably all of the above.

But for all the challenges of life in the desert, there was one enormous blessing that was as true in the first century as it is now. It would have saved Jesus' family in the wilderness, and it saved me too.

THE KINDNESS OF STRANGERS

Before I left the UK, I had a coffee with an old friend, Ben, as the anxiety of the approaching expedition seemed overwhelming. He gave me some wise advice as we parted: 'Before Pete leaves, make a plan for how you'll deal with the challenge of loneliness before it arrives.' He was right. It's good to prepare for a season of darkness while it's still light.

As I pored over maps and plotted my route in the weeks before the trip, I took note of the desert towns along the way. The trail has a feature that became my saving grace on this journey.

Trail angels.

A wide range of people living in the outposts of the Negev, known as 'angels', offer to host weary travellers for a night or two, to give moral support and much-needed encouragement, not to mention a comfy bed, a hot shower and a hearty meal for the restless wanderer.

I found the forum online where trail angels post their availability, and every couple of days I would text ahead and arrange a visit.

I remember my first night as a guest. I rolled into the small pepper-growing village of Paran in the heart of the Negev. Noam, my host, willingly surrendered his room – I couldn't stop him – and he stayed next door with a friend while I had my first shower in five days and the first night of sleeping through till dawn since starting the expedition.

It was heavenly.

In the morning, he came back from his early shift on the farm to cook a magnificent *shakshuka*, a North African dish of tomatoes and eggs from where his family hails from, complete with a host of local trimmings – salty sardines, sweet dates and fresh olives.

While my laundry was flapping gently on the line in the sunshine, we chatted about life and faith late into the day, and as the heat of noon waned into the cool of the late afternoon, I set off again into the desert, clean, well fed, restocked with supplies and ready to take on the world.

This pattern was repeated over the coming weeks, time and again. I would stumble into a village after a couple of days in the wild – broken, exhausted and starving – and a trail angel would take me in, treat me like family and renew my strength for the path ahead. Some were religious, others secular; there were families and singles, young and old, those from European descent and others from North Africa and the Middle East. There were doctors and teachers, farmers and builders, scientists and lawyers. Some were keen to see my photos of the wilderness, others were fascinated by my faith (Christians are a minority in this land), and others just wanted to share trekking stories or hear about life in the UK.

Every moment was dignified with openness and respect, every shared meal was marinated in grace, everyone I met lived up to the title of 'trail angel'.

Some people weren't even on the trail angel list, but they greeted me with mercy on the spur of the moment. I met a group of Jewish scouts on the edge of the Makhtesh Katan crater who gave me a giant piece of *halvah* for energy (a rich dough of tahini and sugar). Then there were the scientists from Tel Aviv who made me a coffee on a hilltop. And I will never forget the two Israeli women on the first night who found water for Pete and me, when we were on our last dregs.

The manager of Philip Farm near Tel Keshet greeted me with a strong coffee, a heap of Bedouin flatbread and a selection of soft cheeses with ripe green olive oil. A lawyer in Meitar offered to drive my tent to Jerusalem to save me carrying it, and a lemon farmer insisted I take his walking pole to ease the strain on my knees. I'd never gone for walking poles before, but after narrowly escaping the trio of vicious dogs, I found myself gripping it tightly every time I heard a bark in the distance. It stayed with me until Jerusalem, where I left it with another trail angel who had lost hers.

I had left my community in the UK but found one in the wilderness. Having taken people into our home in Bristol, I now felt what it was like to be on the receiving end. Maybe that's what happens when you live in a hospitality culture, everyone just 'pays it forward'.

Who knows how far it goes?

It occurred to me just how utterly redeeming an act of kindness can be. No matter how challenging the trials of the previous day were, they were frequently eclipsed by a glorious evening with new friends. I recall a quote from one of my favourite childhood authors, Roald Dahl: 'Kindness is my number one attribute in a human being. I'll put it before any of the things like courage or bravery or generosity or anything else . . . To be kind – it covers everything.'[7]

As the trail wound north, I took a detour into the West Bank to visit a Palestinian family and experienced the same warm embrace of trust and friendship. I stayed with them for three nights as I wrote up the journey so far. Every evening we drank fragrant, bittersweet Arabic coffee, laughed as their kids sang and danced their way around the living room, and chatted late into the night about their hopes and dreams for peace.

For all the stories of conflict and division that are sprayed across our newspapers like shrapnel, the vast majority of encounters I made in the land demonstrated the often-unreported fact that not all Israelis and Palestinians are as dangerous as some politicians claim.

The aggressive minority steal the headlines in a media that is obsessed with marketing fear, but they don't tell the whole story. When I left the tourist trail and crossed the desert, I discovered a different world – a world of people whose generosity far outweighed that of their leaders in the limelight.

I wonder if Jesus' young family experienced the same blessings that I encountered in this place. He would have needed the kindness of strangers, as a child out there in the wilderness, far more than I did.

Did he meet any unsung heroes on his own path?

Perhaps he did.

For one, his teaching is littered with stories of precisely this sort of hospitality. There are frequent parables about banquets, where the poor, the lame and the outcasts are invited in for a feast they could never repay. Then there's the parable of a man who wakes his neighbour in the middle of the night to borrow bread for a visiting companion who has turned up unannounced.

These stories are Jesus' rallying cry to a new, inclusive movement, the cornerstones of compassion that defined the culture he created. But I wonder whether the examples he chose were more than hypothetical. As a refugee child on a mammoth journey home from Egypt, he would have relied on the kindness of strangers to care for him on the road. Did the man who demonstrated such wild generosity as an adult catch a glimpse of it as a child?

Perhaps some wise men could answer that question.

For Jesus, showing unconditional love to strangers was standard procedure, even to those sent to kill him. When the time came for him to lay down his life, he showed mercy even to those employed in his execution, healing the soldier in the garden whom Peter had sliced up with a sword, reassuring the rebel who was crucified next to him, even forgiving the very killers who drove nails into his wrists.

For me, the life of Jesus – not to mention the acts of mercy shown to me by the 'angels' on my trail – shows that the words of Roald Dahl ring true in every generation.

'To be kind – it covers everything.'

16.

PRESENCE

MY WEEKS IN the desert taught me the immeasurable value of the community I had left at home while opening my eyes to the under-reported kindness of people in the Middle East. But I still had one last lesson to learn in the loneliness laboratory of the Negev.

There are times in life, desert stages in the soul, when people testify to having everything they want and all the friends they could dream of and yet they still yearn for something deeper. In the words of British journalist Bernard Levin:

> Countries like ours are full of people who have all the material comforts they desire, together with such non-material blessings as a happy family, and yet lead lives of quiet and, at times, noisy desperation, understanding nothing but the fact that there is a hole inside them. And however much food and drink they pour into it, however many motorcars and television sets they stuff it with, however many well-balanced children and loyal friends they parade around the edges of it, it aches.[1]

Is there a place inside us that even human connection can't satisfy?

Has the creed of western secularism seduced us into denying anything we can't see? This question had lain in the back of my mind since I had heard the Chilean miners speak of a divine 'presence' in the mine.

In the materialistic culture in which I was brought up, any talk of 'divine presence' is often written off as a warm feeling which people of faith naively attribute to the existence of God. But for me, the evidence I have encountered on my journey has called this assumption into question. It's often in the most unlikely places that people experience this subversive peace, from José's calm reassurance of God's grace when the Chilean mine first collapsed, to the strange sense of divine favour that Steph felt in the initial agony of being blinded by an acid spill in New Zealand.

For me, what really caught my attention were the signs that accompanied the stories, the gentle breeze that brought healing to Omar and the scar tissue that vanished from Steph's eye.

A warm fuzzy feeling is easy to explain away, but these sorts of miracles are on another level.

Does God really show up when we seek him?

Is the divine presence really available to us in the here and now?

As I set off on this foolhardy expedition, back in Bristol a few friends decided to pray for me. Catherine, my Northern Irish neighbour, recorded their prayers on her phone and sent me the audio message.

One of the most 'out there' prayers came from Grace, who co-leads an evening school at the Love Bristol community. She said that God would be so close to me, I would literally feel him telling me when to go right or left. While I was encouraged by her support, I couldn't help but think it was a bit too far. I was happy that God spoke to people; I've seen the evidence. But for me to be navigating through the desert with a sort of God-satnav – well, it felt a bit unnecessary.

I had maps; I was fine.

One night, as I was poring over the guidebook in the warmth of the tent, jotting down a plan for the route ahead, I made a slightly unnerving discovery.

I wasn't going to make it.

I had arranged to get to Jerusalem before friends from home arrived to join me. Louise, the physics teacher who'd joined me in Chile, was flying over with history teacher Dan Coe, in their half-term holiday. I had interviews set up for when they arrived, and I was on a deadline. I had to get to Jerusalem by early February, on foot, and I wasn't going to cave in to the temptation to hike down to the road and hitch a ride north. That was never an option for Jesus and, while everything else about my journey had been far more manageable than his had been, I wasn't going to betray the only thing that we had in common, which was walking on our own two feet.

But with the distance I had to cover, on the trail I was walking, in the time I had, I wouldn't make it. I went back to the map. Surely there was another way.

On the edge of a mountainous ridge in the Negev, the Shvil trail turns west and winds its way to the desert city of Mitzpe Ramon before continuing north and east in a giant horseshoe into a series of giant craters known as Makhtesh.

This was my chance.

I worked out that if I were to drop off to the east and hike up the Jordan Valley for a day, I could get up to the fringe of the craters on the second day, doing the climb in one big ascent and bypassing Mitzpe Ramon.

It would save me about a week.

There was just one problem: it dropped off the edge of my map, and I didn't have time to detour to a desert town in search of another one. I could plot the route roughly on Google Maps, but the resolution was too low to navigate accurately, and, in the valleys, signal tended to vanish anyway.

I could see the start of another rough path leading up to the ridge, so I reasoned if I followed it carefully, I could join the dots. It was a risk, but it meant I would make it into Jerusalem, on foot, just in time to meet my fellow teachers.

Worth it.

But leaving the trail meant leaving the trail angels too. If I were to take this short cut, I really would be on my own.

The desert suddenly felt a bit bigger.

The first day worked out better than expected. I'd stayed with a trail angel the night before, and a thunderstorm had swept through in the night. Who knows what I might have encountered if I'd camped in the valley? From the sound of rain on the tin roof, the flash-flood rumours are to be taken seriously.

The following morning I set off early, straight up the Jordan Valley next to the road. This was the easy part. In the middle of the afternoon it became bizarrely windy and grit was whipping against the back of my legs like a belt-sander. I took refuge in a service station and feasted out, restocked for the coming days and then hiked up to the edge of the valley ready to climb back onto the ridge.

It was the following morning that I saw that first wolf. After an hour or two of hiking uphill, I came to a sign that read 'sea level'. Turns out I'd spent the previous night in the lowest valley on earth. Not the best plan when you're aiming for the top of a mountain. Let's make this as hard as possible.

I paused at the brow of a hill to take some paracetamol. I was feeling the strain, and I'd barely left the valley. In the distance, I could see the ridge stretching up into the sky. I tended to my feet, sipped some warm water, ate a handful of peanuts and paused for a few minutes. That was the moment I googled 'Wolves in the Negev' and regretted it. I was tired, my feet hurt, the biggest climb of the journey lay before me, and I was about to branch off the road and drop off the map. To add to the almost comical misfortune of the day, I had just discovered that I was surrounded by wolves who were apparently no longer afraid of people.

It felt like a good time to pray.

What happened next, I still cannot explain.

As I set off into the most dangerous and lonely stage of the entire journey, I felt an overwhelming joy descend upon me and I found myself dancing, almost involuntarily, as I walked down the road. That's not like me. I'm British. I don't usually dance unless it's dark, I'm at a wedding disco, I'm in a good mood and I've had a couple of drinks. In the cold light of day, feeling miserable, lonely and tired, this was vastly out of character. There was something odd in the atmosphere; it was as if the whole valley was saturated in a wave of deep peace and I couldn't escape it.

The surreal joy stayed with me for the rest of the day; I just couldn't shake it off. None of my circumstances had changed – if anything I should have been getting more tired and miserable – but for hours the trail seemed to just disappear beneath me.

I have considered various physiological explanations: oxygen starvation to the brain, dehydration and delusion, the subconscious acceptance of death and the consequent excitement of heaven, perhaps? I even checked my paracetamol on the off-chance that it had been laced with something, but when I took some later in the journey there was no such joy.

What happened in that place?

The only thing I can think is that I had asked God to help me and he answered.

Is that really so surprising?

It wasn't a complicated prayer, just the one I learned from José that had got me thus far on the journey: 'Lord, I'm not the best of men, but have mercy on me.'

Perhaps he responded, not by shrinking the mountain or removing the wolves or even by making my pack lighter, but simply by turning up and being present with me on the journey. And just when I could have dismissed the entire thing as a psychological moment of self-induced madness, it started to get specific.

I'd been climbing gradually all day, and the valleys were getting narrower and narrower as I neared the final ascent. As I came to the apex of the last valley, I hit a dead end.

Not good.

The rock in front of me was stretching up vertically, like a cliff face. This was the final ascent, the ridge I had aimed for between the two craters. But this destination seemed a mockery to me at that moment, for in that dark ravine there was no way up onto the ridge, just a polished slab of rock smooth as a giant pebble, no doubt carved out by a thousand flash floods. While its natural sheen was quite striking, its beauty was deceptive. There was no climbing it, certainly not with a pack more than one-third of my bodyweight.

I was stuck.

It was late afternoon by this point, and as the sun left the valley, a coolness that had crouched in the shade rolled out to engulf the narrow ravine. Time was of the essence. It was too late to turn back, but the bottom of the abyss, the very epicentre of a flash flood, was no place to set up camp. Besides, I had to get to the top, for there was a small weather station on the crater edge where I could refill my water which, as always, was running out. I didn't have the luxury of waiting another day. I needed to keep going, but how was I going to get up a mountain that presented me with nothing but a sheer cliff face?

I started to plot my route up the side, picking a line around the edge of the polished slab. It would be a risky climb, but I had no other option. I started towards the left of the rock face.

'Go back.'

What? I stopped in my tracks.

'Go back.'

In an unexpected moment, I experienced such a strange conviction that I was going the wrong way that I voiced it out loud.

I stood for a moment and wrestled with the urge to turn around.

The panic was starting to set in, and the peace that had wrapped itself around me earlier in the day seemed to fade a little. I was desperate to get going, and daylight was fading. I needed to find a way up, and going back would be nothing but a waste of time and an acceptance of defeat. I hadn't turned back for a hundred miles.

There is always a way, I reasoned. Turning back is never it.

I took a step forward. My feet felt like cement. I couldn't do it. It was worse than a bad idea; it actually felt like pure disobedience. There was no audible voice, just a deep conviction for reasons that I couldn't articulate that something was telling me to turn around, and as soon as I did, I felt a wonderful reassurance. It wasn't a test of willpower as much as an invitation, as if God was saying, 'Trust me.'

I went back.

I snaked across the valley and, as it widened out from that polished slab, I felt strongly drawn to the left. About ten minutes later, I stumbled upon a narrow path out of the ravine.

There was a tiny black and white symbol painted onto a rock, marking the route, only visible from the place where I was standing. I could never have seen it the first time I walked up the valley for I had been on the other side. It pointed to a narrow track that branched right, climbed up the side of the ravine and then looped left at the end of the valley like a natural bridge over the giant slab – a slab which, moments before, I was foolishly planning to climb.

I had no phone signal in the valley; I was off the edge of the map and nobody knew I was there. If I had fallen, it might have been a long time before anyone found me. I didn't have water for more than a day, and the cold would have got me at night if I had lain unconscious for long. I thought through all the scenarios and felt an immense relief that I had turned back rather than tried to climb that slab. Even if I'd made it, I would have had to keep going off-piste the whole way, scaling the cliff for miles. The chances of me making it to the top without a fall would have been very slim.

A year later, when I shared this story with my friend Elisa, who illustrated this book, she told me that her parents had taken a similar trip into the Negev when they were younger. It ended rather traumatically when they found a decomposed body in a remote ravine. The victim was only later identified from his belt buckle.

Could I have ended up the same way?

As I finally summited onto the top of the ridge with night setting in, I found that stack of pallets that had been left by a previous group. It felt like a reward, the sweet taste of victory. There was a dirt road leading up from the other side of the ridge to the weather station, a hint of civilisation on the top of the world to lift my spirits.

Presumably this was how most people got up there, for you certainly couldn't drive the route I had taken. I had completed my two-day shortcut, thanks to a strange dose of euphoria and a sort of spiritual navigation method.

I always question experiences like this and test out the natural explanations, which is why I came around to thinking that the 'wolves' in my night camp had probably just been harmless goats.

But the way I got up that ridge was not a figment of my imagination.

The strange conviction I had in the ravine – this way, that way, left, right – guided me directly to a narrow, hidden path, and the deep peace I experienced throughout much of the day was as alien to me as the environment I was in. Up until that point, left to my own devices, I had produced nothing but fear and anxiety. The sudden change was more than human courage; I had lacked that for the last 200 miles.

I realised that possibly the most famous psalm of all was as true for me then as it had been for David, singing these lyrics three thousand years previously, camped out in the same land:

> The LORD is my shepherd, I shall not want.
> He makes me lie down in green pastures.
> He leads me beside still waters.
> He restores my soul.
> He leads me in paths of righteousness
> for his name's sake.
> Even though I walk through the valley of the shadow of death,
> I will fear no evil,
> for you are with me.[2]

I thought back to the prayer Grace had sent me in Catherine's WhatsApp message. Though I doubted at the time that God would literally guide me along the right paths, I might not have made it if he hadn't.

I can't pretend that everything was super easy from that moment onwards. There were many challenges ahead, and there wasn't a sublime peace in all of them. I didn't always navigate perfectly either, although the times I got lost were generally the times when I stopped praying and just ploughed on under my own initiative. There's a lesson in there somewhere.

The experience in my 'valley of the shadow of death' made me wonder whether there's a place of connection, a deep part of our soul, that not even friends or family can reach.

While new expressions of community and selfless acts of compassion are establishing themselves as cornerstones in the modern battle against loneliness, I wonder whether the deepest longings of our hearts find their peace in a higher love.

I'm not the first to ask this question. In the fourth century, the North African philosopher Augustine famously prayed, 'Our hearts are restless until they find their rest in you.'[3]

In my own journey, paradoxically it was in the place of most profound isolation, when all other contact was stripped away, that I felt most at peace, not in a human sense, for that day had started with exhaustion and fear, but in the moment when I sought the presence of God . . . and, it seems, he showed up.

Despite the challenges of that journey, I would not trade it for all the comforts in the world.

Part Five
TAUGHT TO LOVE

We refuse
to be
enemies

17.

JERUSALEM

ANOTHER HUNDRED MILES after that fated valley, I rolled into the Old City of Jerusalem after three weeks in the wilderness, and the relief was overwhelming. I had faced many a trial: from wolves and wild dogs to searing heat and driving rain, with tired shoulders and bleeding feet, but I had made it, with a lot of help from friends old and new, and Jerusalem felt like heaven, the light at the end of the tunnel.

There were stalls of freshly squeezed pomegranate juice blended with root ginger, hot Arabic coffee roasted with cardamom, and oven-baked trays of fragrant cheese pastries known as *kanafeh*, a Middle Eastern rocket fuel for weary travellers.

Above all, there were the beautiful faces. Fellow humans. Old men with smile lines carved into their olive skin and patient mothers herding giggling schoolchildren through ancient streets with cries of, '*Yalla, yalla,*' which loosely means, 'Come on, let's go!' in both Arabic and Hebrew street talk.

The intensity of being in a city that the whole world is watching was a surreal experience after the solitude of the desert.

I made the complex five-mile journey into the West Bank to spend a few days with old Palestinian friends and wrote up the journey so far in the comfort of their family home. The oldest son is a Juventus fan, and while I was there Tottenham were playing Juventus in the second leg of the Champions League (with a two-goal lead). There was endless pre-match speculation over a dinner of fresh fish – a strong biblical meal if ever there was one. Never mind the outcome of the match. We caught up on stories from my previous visit and cheered on the youngest son as he played the piano for us and dreamed of starring in the Arabic series of *The Voice Kids*.

I uploaded some blog posts from the desert stage, confirmed my interviews for the following week and headed back to Jerusalem to meet Louise. It was good to see a friend from home. To be able to share stories from the desert with someone who'd started this journey with me in another desert in Chile, three years previously, was just what I needed.

She filled me in on news from our little community back in Bristol, and we found the only Irish bar in Jerusalem to watch Ireland play France in the Six Nations. A couple of days later, we were joined by our mutual friend Dan Coe, a history teacher from Bristol with a bushy ginger beard and an infectious grin. The party was complete – almost.

I hadn't seen Swe-Dan since the day he had turned up on the spur of the moment at our house in Bristol. Given the random nature of that first encounter, I figured it would be entirely in keeping with our friendship if I returned the favour and invited him to the Holy Land, out of the blue, a couple of years later. I dropped him a message on Facebook, he booked flights and our final member of the gang touched down in Jerusalem.

Three Dans and a Louise. We sounded like an Indie folk band. Our Palestinian friends told us of an Arab proverb where finding three of the same thing leads you to treasure, which they decided was Louise. She rather liked that. Swe-Dan was looking blonder, burlier and more Viking than ever. With that and Dan Coe's hipster beard, we looked like a gang of vagabonds from the fringes of Europe, a little out of place in the bustling heart of Jerusalem's busy avenues. We clearly weren't locals, but then we weren't there to be tourists either. There was someone I wanted them to meet.

SAMI AWAD

Perched in a small rooftop café on the steep slopes of Bethlehem, we gazed out over the Judean wilderness, as a patchwork of high-rise apartments petered out into the desert.

I had met Sami twice before, and he greeted me that day like an old friend returning from battle. The previous time he had been in Bristol, I had shared my tentative plan to walk from Egypt to Nazareth in pursuit of Jesus' refugee route, and he gave me no end of encouragement, for his own journey had started with a similarly wild desert pilgrimage. I promised I'd stop in Bethlehem halfway and bring some friends, and Sami treated them all like honoured guests.

He ordered us a strong coffee and a water-pipe of lemon, while Louise sipped a breakfast tea and the Dans rummaged around for pencil and paper. As the air filled with the sweet smell of shisha, Sami walked us through his journey as an Arab Christian living in a semi-autonomous region of occupied Palestine, under an Israeli government.

'My grandmother lived in Jerusalem with her husband and seven children in 1948, in a neighbourhood where Jews, Christians and Muslims lived together as good neighbours. I mean really, really good neighbours.'

It was a different story from the one I'm used to hearing.

'The Christians and the Muslims would go into the Jewish homes . . . and do the things that the Jews couldn't do during Shabbat, even turning on and off the lights for them and cooking for them.'

The witness of Sami's grandmother is mirrored in many similar memoirs of Jews and Arabs writing of peaceful co-existence pre-1948, which have now been brought to light.[1] Of course, there are accounts of conflict as well; British Palestine was no utopia, but the story of Sami's family shows that harmonious communities of Jews and Arabs aren't just a naive pipe dream. For many it was usual practice, once upon a time.

What changed?

'My grandfather was killed in 1948 and my grandmother and her seven children became refugees. They were kicked out from their home.'

1948 was the 'Year of Independence' for Israel, the birth of its modern state. Palestinians refer to it as the *Nakba*, the catastrophe. Thousands of Palestinians were forced from their homes; others, like Sami's grandfather, were shot dead.

'He was killed as a civilian. He wasn't involved in the combat; he was shot by a sniper.'

I wondered how I would have reacted if I had been Sami's grandmother, recently widowed with seven children, now a refugee in her own country.

'The reason why I do what I do is my grandmother, who from her faith always insisted, "We will never seek revenge or retaliation, but we will also never remain silent in the face of violence and injustice. We will seek peace and reconciliation with those who have done this to us."'

The mandate of peace and reconciliation that Sami's grandmother pioneered in that moment built a legacy in Sami's family that would span the generations.

As Sami explained the inspiration of his grandparents, I came to a rather haunting realisation. My own grandfather, Bernard 'Sam' Gwyther, was in Jerusalem in the 1940s with the British Palestine Police Force. I wonder if he would have seen Sami's grandparents going into the homes of their Jewish neighbours to cook for them during Shabbat.

The conversation became strangely personal.

The British had promised the Arabs an independent state in 1915, following the McMahon–Hussein Correspondence in which the Arabs fought with the British against the Ottomans,[2] although the exact boundaries have long since been debated. A couple of years later, in 1917, the British proposed that they favoured 'the establishment in Palestine of a National Home for the Jewish People'.

It wasn't initially clear how Britain envisioned an independent state for two separate people groups in the same area, so Balfour concluded, 'Nothing shall be done which may prejudice the civil and religious rights of existing non-Jewish communities in Palestine, or the rights and political status enjoyed by Jews in any other country.'[3]

Easier said than done.

Having made promises they couldn't keep to friends on all sides, the British started to face increasing opposition from factions of Arab and

Jewish organisations alike. So, after careful thought, they made the rather undignified move of abandoning ship in 1948 and watching from a distance as a war unfolded behind them. Fortunately, all responsibility had been unceremoniously transferred to the UN.

How convenient.

My grandfather never spoke about his time in Palestine, but in recent years I have found myself badgering my gran for stories over endless cups of tea and riffling through his old black-and-white photos. All I have been able to glean was that he loved Palestine and he didn't want to leave, especially when he saw what was brewing, but when orders came to move out, he had no choice.

I wonder how he felt about what unfolded in his wake.

He died when I was eighteen. I wish I'd known then how valuable his insights would have been for my own journey, here and now.

I asked my gran what he had been doing out there.

'Keeping the peace.'

I'm not sure that worked.

Two generations later, I was still looking for the same thing.

Peace seems to be that elusive quality, that eternal prize that everyone speaks about and nobody seems to find, especially the British.

But I wasn't there to study my own history; I wanted to hear from the people of the land itself, and Sami had learned peacemaking, not from political leaders or national agendas, but from the front line.

'Living in the Holy Land, living in the midst of conflict, we believe that the answer to peace and justice in this land is engaging the communities in the peacemaking process.'

As national peace agreements failed and violence continued year after year, Sami felt compelled to do something, so he started an organisation with a group of friends, called The Holy Land Trust. It wasn't just another political organisation motivated by anger, but something altogether different.

'As an organisation we are not looking for political solutions to the Palestinian–Israeli conflict. We are looking for the human solutions.'

For Sami, that meant engaging with everybody, not across battle lines or in rants over social media, but in communities, talking with, listening to, even serving the other.

'We work with everybody in this land; there is no green line, there are no borders between us . . . We need to truly honour each other in this land.'

He was motivated by one question: 'How can we get the communities to truly recognise and acknowledge the full equal right of the other to be in this land? As Jews, Christians and Muslims who live here, we have a history in this land, we have a desire to be in this land, and we all see a future in this land.'

When they were met with violence or aggression, they responded with creative non-violence. Many of his Palestinian friends lost their homes as illegal Israeli settlements began to spring up in the West Bank. When Palestinian homes were 'in the way', soldiers evicted people at gunpoint and bulldozed the houses, leaving the families homeless. Rather than respond with violence or aggression, Sami and his team simply rolled their sleeves up and quietly rebuilt them.

And then re-rebuilt them.

Some houses have been rebuilt four times.

It wasn't just Palestinians doing the rebuilding. Sami was joined by Israelis and international friends – Jewish, Christian, Muslim and secular – who were inspired by their creative non-violent resistance and wanted to help fight their corner.

It's an image that rarely makes the headlines: Jews and Palestinians kneeling shoulder to shoulder in the dust, driven by the sheer stubborn-hearted desire for harmonious co-existence. For many, it came as a breath of fresh air against the backdrop of political poker games ricocheting around board rooms. In everything they did, Sami called them to stick to their original calling of creative non-violence.

'We fully believe there is a non-violent solution to this conflict. Violence is not the answer,' he told us resolutely. But Sami's early commitment to non-violence was to be severely tested.

MILLENNIAL MAGI

As the new millennium approached, people all over the world started looking to Bethlehem.

'How would Bethlehem celebrate the birth of Christ?' Sami asked us.

We all looked a little blank. Sami longed for the world to see that faith could be a cause for celebration rather than a source of conflict, but to grab the attention of a media obsessed with conflict, he had to do something big. There was no shortage of hair-brained ideas, but one stood out in particular.

'The craziest idea that I loved was when a couple from the US, friends of ours, came and said, "[We want] to enact the journey of the Magi, to walk from Iran to Bethlehem . . . to walk and ride camels exactly how the Magi would have done it."'

They needed people on the ground who could organise this trip, and Sami stepped up.

It seemed to be the final thread that could tie his ambitions for peace and justice together, to show the international community that the Holy Land wasn't just a tinderbox of age-old conflict, but a place where creative minds could come up with peaceful ways of worshipping their God, through ancient journeys of faith . . . even if that meant trekking through the desert.

Turns out my adventure wasn't so original after all.

The journey from Iran's border, through Iraq and Syria, to Bethlehem was far longer and more dangerous than the route I had just walked. I took a slice of humble pie and a puff of shisha and told Sami I'd make the Magis' journey on my next trip. He grinned. I was sort of joking, and he was sort of pretending not to notice. I let out a nervous laugh.

'We had sixteen people walk and ride camels from the Iran–Iraq border all the way to Bethlehem, in ninety-nine days.'

'How many miles is that?' Dan Coe asked.

'I can't remember,' Sami replied, squinting as he tried to do some quick sums in his head. 'About forty miles a day, ninety-nine days . . . ?'

It was in the thousands.

Suddenly my own journey seemed a lot less impressive.

'We had more support than you,' he said generously.

It was a kind reassurance, but if I had the choice of walking a few hundred miles through the Negev or a few thousand miles through Iraq and Syria, I know which one sounded harder.

'It was amazing,' Sami said nostalgically. 'They left in September and arrived on Christmas Day in the year 2000, an amazing, amazing experience. The last leg was ten thousand people walking in a candlelit procession to Bethlehem.'

We had walked their route that very morning. I mentally retraced our footsteps, imagining the endless candles flickering up the hill, a peaceful pilgrimage of thousands of worshippers finishing a journey to honour their king, perhaps the same route a group of Eastern astrologers had taken to worship the same king two thousand years ago.

But their peaceful pilgrimage through the Middle East was dwarfed by a larger crisis.

'In the middle of the Syrian desert, the whole peace process collapsed.'

It had started as a season of great hope, the glimmers of spring after a fifty-year winter, as the Israeli and Palestinian authorities began peace talks in what led to the Oslo Agreement. But despite the agreements being made by politicians in Norway, there was little change on the ground. Israeli forces continued to demolish Palestinian homes, Palestinian governments continued to squander the limited wealth they received to line their own pockets, and leaders on every side began to point fingers at each other. Extremist organisations began to exploit the lack of progress and, as the peace talks collapsed, the land descended into the Second Intifada, the bloodiest battle in decades.

'In October 2000, we went into what is known as the Second Intifada, the second uprising, which created a lot of violence.'

For Sami, the idea that the utter breakdown of law and order could be triggered by a peace process seemed ridiculous.

'It's easy for me as a Palestinian to say, "It's their fault why it failed," but if you meet an Israeli tomorrow they will say, "It is their fault why it failed," and we're both right . . . so for me we had to go much deeper . . . A peace process that is motivated by fear of the other is not really a peace process.'

Sami was compelled to do something, to show there was another way. 'At the end of the day, it's the communities of the land who really determine the peace . . . Politicians can sign any agreement that they want. If the people are ready to invest in that then that peace will be manifested, but if the people don't, then the agreement will just sit on a shelf.'

They decided the solution to hypocrisy at the political level and violence on the ground was to come in the opposite spirit to both.

'For us, the intention wasn't to oppose the peace process; it was to ask, "How can we make it more connected with the peoples of the land?"'

Sami went back to doing what his family had always done.

'After the Magi arrived and we had the celebration, we shifted our focus back to non-violent activism, which is what my uncle was teaching and doing at that time.'

Sami's uncle had taken the baton from his grandparents' generation to fight for peace with creative non-violent resistance. Until one day, out of the blue, he was deported to the US.

Sami was broken. His uncle had taught him more about non-violence than anyone. In a moment, the baton had been passed on once again, but Sami had to decide whether to take it. He was growing tired, disillusioned and angry.

There were several choices.

He could give in to despair, he could leave the land and join his uncle in the US, or he could abandon non-violence altogether and fight fire with fire.

There comes a time.

The words of Marx echo through the ages, 'No great movement has ever been inaugurated without bloodshed.'[4]

TRUE GRIT

The temptation to take up arms must have been huge, but Sami is a Christian, not a communist, and Jesus called the shots in his life, not Marx. The communist revolution collapsed on itself within half a century, whereas Jesus' movement has been quietly growing for two millennia.

You can tell prophets by their fruit.

'Love your enemies and pray for those who persecute you,' Jesus instructed his followers.[5]

It's a tune that has rung through the lives of Jesus' followers throughout the ages, from the early Christians in Roman amphitheatres to the twenty-one martyrs on that Libyan beach.

It's the tune that Sami would continue to march to, however great the temptation for revenge. 'At the end of the day, Jesus was a peacemaker. He came to teach us how to make peace with God and how to make peace with our fellow human beings.'

For some, non-violence is a sign of weakness, of giving up, of failing to fight, but for Sami it's the opposite. The art of creative non-violence requires far greater strength.

One night, as I was struggling to understand all this, one of Sami's friends, the playwright Justin Butcher, pointed me to Walter Wink's masterful commentary on Jesus' teaching about turning the other cheek. The exact line in the Gospel of Matthew is, 'If anyone slaps you on the right cheek, turn to them the other cheek also.'[6]

I'd never noticed the right–left detail before, was I missing something?

In Ancient Near Eastern culture, nobody punched with their left hand. Presumedly, lefties had to be ambidextrous. The implication in the passage, which everyone in Jesus' culture would have understood, is that to strike someone with the right hand on the right cheek would be a backhand, a swing designed not to punish, but to shame.[7]

A backhand demonstrates superiority. When Jesus said, 'Turn to them the other cheek,' the hidden meaning, undetected in western culture is, 'Force them to engage with you as someone of the same status.' Then, when they strike you, they do so as an equal. For an oppressor to slap someone equal to them in public would be to invite shame on the oppressor. Such a move would be highly undignified in Middle Eastern culture.

Jesus' teaching was not so much passive surrender but creative non-violence. To turn the other cheek is to imaginatively outwit your oppressor, to resist the temptation to seek revenge and instead force them to re-evaluate the power balance. It is to show respect and to invite them to do likewise.[8]

Sami would know. 'Getting beaten up, getting arrested, getting detained was a weekly occurrence.'

Despite the aggression he experienced at the hands of some, Sami was strengthened by the fact that there were many others who supported him. He continued to make Jewish friends, both Israelis and internationals, who were inspired by his strength of character and who saw the weakness in the oppressor.

'We had many, many Israelis committed to non-violence and peace work,' he reminded us.

Sami's multi-ethnic team became one of the most powerful peaceful resistance movements in the West Bank. In a world of 'us against them', it became a timeless testament to a different narrative, one of 'peace overcoming hatred'. I might have thought that he would be proud of such a campaign, but he could never be happy when the broader situation hadn't changed. Even if he succeeded in changing some hearts and minds, he hadn't seen the peace he truly sought. Protesting was no longer enough. Rebuilding homes is one thing, but building an entire nation intent on peaceful co-existence is a big step up.

He didn't just want to stand 'against' political oppression; he wanted to stand 'for' something.

'I was really challenged by the calling of Christ to his followers to "love your enemies". For me, I really wanted to understand, what does that mean?'

He started by challenging himself. 'What does it actually mean to love them? Not just make peace with the enemy, not just resolve your conflict, not to sign a peace treaty with your enemy, but to love the enemy?'

One question led to another. 'Who is my enemy? What makes my enemy my enemy? What is the reason this conflict exists? Is it just a political conflict, or is there more to it that created this animosity?'

For Sami, these weren't just philosophical questions; they were personal. And his quest to find answers led him to surprising places.

'The first insight I had, which really opened my eyes, was when I was invited by Jewish friends of mine to go on a retreat, called the Bearing Witness Retreat, which happens in Auschwitz . . . This conflict is very much fuelled by fear and trauma for the Jewish people after what they experienced in Auschwitz and the Holocaust and, of course, the centuries leading up to that . . . They needed someplace to create and protect themselves so that this doesn't happen again.'

He started to understand, at a deeper level, the Jewish desire for peace and security, why they long for a place to call home, to defend and protect, to be safe in. But the creation of a Jewish state was hardly an abstract idea for Sami; the reality was closer to home.

'Thanks to the British, we were chosen,' he said, with a wry smile to the audience in front of him. He wasn't trying to make us feel guilty – he was beyond all that – he was just being honest. That really is what happened. And Sami lost his grandfather in the process.

He understood the Jewish desire to settle in the Holy Land, but he also carried the trauma suffered by his own people, his own family, in the process. Sami realised that if he really hoped to achieve peace on a national scale, he needed to help people find healing and freedom from the trauma that trapped them in a constant fear of the other.

After returning from Auschwitz, he shared his conviction with the team. 'We have to look into the traumas of the communities of this land . . . and how trauma shapes not just behaviour but identity . . . an identity of victimisation, an identity of not trusting, of self-preservation and fighting anybody who we might think could be a threat to this identity.'

Sami realised that if people were controlled by fear, they couldn't even conceive of peace. While young people growing up in Israel would have no living memory of the Holocaust, many are taught to import the collective trauma from the past into their generation.

'The shock in Auschwitz was actually hearing Israeli teachers telling Israeli children, fourteen- and fifteen-year-old children, "If the Arabs, if the Palestinians have an opportunity, they'll do this to you."'

For Sami, who had given everything of himself to respect, to understand, even to love his Jewish neighbours, these words seemed brutally unfair.

My own overwhelmingly positive experiences with both people groups stood in stark contrast to this narrative of fear, reinforced continuously in the media. Stories of Arab aggression are imported into millions of living rooms around Israel, twenty-four hours a day, seven days a week. For some Jews, the only Arabs they see are in the news. No wonder they live in fear.

The tragic irony is that the exact same process is mirrored in Arab homes from the opposite perspective, as Arab news channels pipe stories of Israeli aggression into living rooms across the occupied territories. For some Arabs, the only Israelis they see are soldiers.

The culture of fear is hardly surprising.

It's not even that the stories are made up – most are true. It's just that they are being continuously marketed as the whole picture, quietly leading the viewer into the false pretence that the violent actions of the minority are the stance of the masses. Where are the voices of those calling for peace?

Not in the news.

For me, this seemed ridiculous. On my journey through the Negev and in my encounters in the West Bank, I had personally only seen kindness in every people group. Of course, you could argue that the kindness I received stemmed from the fact that I was a neutral traveller and didn't represent 'the enemy', but that's not necessarily the case.

For a start, as a Brit, I'm hardly neutral. The Israelis I met knew full well that, historically, the British have not always supported the Jewish minority, and in the Arab world I represent the very people who gave their land away in the first place. I spent the centenary of the Balfour declaration in a Palestinian refugee camp, as celebrations were ringing around London for the establishment of Israel. I couldn't have been more vulnerable if I'd tried, yet I was only treated as a friend. In Israel, my host families would often engage me in the tough questions, usually revolving around, 'What do people in your country think about us?'

I would explain that many were supportive of the Jewish nation and happy that a people who'd suffered so much, for so long, finally had a home. But I also shared that, in my experience the Arabs I had met were kind, peace-loving people who wanted to live in their homeland too, and collectively punishing the many for the actions of the few didn't seem fair.

The response I got from most people, was not, 'How dare you crit-icise us?' or 'How naive,' but, 'We agree.' Despite the fears instilled in the population, most Israelis I met had great empathy for the ordinary Palestinians caught in the crossfire, recognising the injustices they faced at the hands of both governments. I remember a lady in Nazareth saying, 'We were refugees once, we know how they feel.'

There is so much potential for peace, yet this groundswell of hope is countered by a barrage of fear dripping from political leaders in the media. It feels like the entire land is caught between the innate desire for peace and the indoctrinating voices of hatred trying to talk them out of it.

How will this battle ever be won?

For Sami, the first step lies in overcoming fear. 'The moment you love somebody, you break fear. There is no fear in love, and so the first act of loving is for me to break my fear of my enemy.'

I couldn't help but draw parallels with the wisdom of Walter Wink in his analysis of Jesus' 'turn the other cheek' teaching. For Sami, loving his enemy isn't a show of inferiority; it is a demonstration of strength and equality.

'To be able to stand in front of my enemy as an equal to them, not to resist them, not to fight them, not to show that I am more powerful than them, but to truly say, "I am equal to you, and I come to you in love."'

Sami draws inspiration from the great peacemakers before him, from Martin Luther King and Mahatma Gandhi to his own grandmother.

But when he wants to help people find healing from the traumas of their past, he learns from the man who inspired many of the great peacemakers.

'In the past, I used to think of Jesus when he was healing like a "superman" figure; you know he has this amazing ability to make miracles and heal people, but then I began to understand . . . when Jesus was healing, he wasn't just trying to show himself off. Jesus was liberating people.'

Sami opened my eyes to something I'd never considered before. What if some people need healing from more than just physical ailments? What if fear can impair us more than injury?

I started looking at the Gospels in a whole new light. Jesus didn't only mend bones; he also changed minds. He didn't only free people from illness; he also freed them from prejudice. He didn't just love his Jewish friends; he also loved their Samaritan enemies. His ministry was more miraculous than I had ever realised.

As Sami explained, 'He never sat in political offices and in fancy hotels doing training and conflict resolution . . . he went out into the communities and met with those who are the enemies, those who were rejected, those who were marginalised, those who were on the edges, those whom people hated . . . How many of us walk into these areas?'

And before I could catch myself thinking this wasn't relevant for me, he added, 'And it's not about you coming to Palestine and doing the walking here; you should really ask in your own neighbourhoods and your own communities . . . how often do you walk to those who are different?'

It's a question Sami asks himself constantly, as he walks out to meet the 'other', freeing people from a lifetime of fear by coming in the opposite spirit.

'The moment you love somebody, you break fear. There is no fear in love.'

18.

RIGHTEOUS AMONG THE NATIONS

ON THE OUTSKIRTS of Tel Aviv stands a brutalist concrete construction called Yad Vashem, the world's Holocaust Remembrance Centre. Inspired by Sami's desire to understand the Jewish story, I entered its dark corridors and immersed myself for hours in the tragedy, soaking in the facts and figures in front of haunting black-and-white pictures. Like many people, I wondered how the rest of the world took so long to come to the aid of an entire people group, and I began to understand the fear imported into the land today.

One encounter stood out in particular.

At the end of the exhibition there is a room dedicated to the 'Righteous Among the Nations', those brave men and women who personally rescued Jews during World War II, at every cost to themselves. Some are famous, like Oskar Schindler, and there are others whose names are less well known but whose sacrifices are equally recognised.

I found myself absorbed by the story of Raoul Wallenberg, the Swedish diplomat who rescued thousands of Jews by smuggling them into Sweden. Witnesses recall him climbing on top of a train to hand Swedish passports through the roof, while soldiers were shooting at him. Gripped by the memorial to his life, with glassy eyes I let out a quiet, 'Wow'.

Without warning, an Australian lady next to me turned and whispered, 'That man saved my mother.'

I let out a second 'Wow'. What else do you say? This lady right next to me wouldn't exist if it hadn't been for the sacrifice of Raoul Wallenberg.

She shared a little of her story in hushed tones, and I thanked her for having the courage to voice it to a stranger. Like countless others, I left Yad Vashem with the conviction that something like this should never happen again.

In the months since that encounter, the inspiration of Raoul Wallenberg has stayed with me, and he isn't the only one. I was struck by the diversity in the 'Righteous Among the Nations'. There were rich and poor, French and German, Muslims and Christians; almost every people group was represented, all risking their lives to save Jews in their darkest hour.

We honour victims by never forgetting them, but should we honour the 'Righteous Among the Nations' by following their lead in our own generation?[1]

Just as there were Muslims like the Veseli family and Christians like the Ten Boom family who rescued Jews in World War II, there are Jews in this generation who risk life and limb for Palestinians.

These countercultural encounters hold the power to rewrite the script of fear and hatred, however deeply it is ingrained in the land. If you've been taught from birth that an entire people group is evil, and then you meet someone from that people group who shows you nothing but kindness, it's impossible not to question your previous prejudice.

From regional conflicts like Israel–Palestine, down to city-level skirmishes between rival gangs, sometimes only *one* positive encounter with a perceived enemy can be a game changer. A 'Good Samaritan' can be the hinge that changes the heart, the force that releases someone from a lifetime of fear. I thought about what Sami had shared about Jesus' approach to his enemies: 'Jesus met with the Samaritans; he went to where they were . . . he didn't go there to judge; he didn't go there to condemn; he understood that people need to be healed.'

For Sami, this healing work leads him on frequent retreats into the wilderness where his team gathers groups of Israelis and Palestinians in reconciliation meetings. They are not negotiations where each side is fighting for its own narrative, but moments of vulnerability where they learn to listen to one another. Both sides get the opportunity to hear the story of the land from a different perspective, to step into the others' shoes and to be part of their healing.

There may never be a way of fully reconciling the opposing narratives, but there are ways of 'bridging the gap', in the words of Salim Munayer and Lisa Loden, authors of *Through My Enemy's Eyes*. Loden is a Messianic Jew and Munayer an Arab Christian, yet despite their ethnic and political differences, for them, the gap is bridged by Jesus' love for both Jews and Samaritans, and in his movement, sacrificial love eclipses political boundaries.[2]

Later in my journey, I met two women with a similar story, one a Messianic Jew and the other a Palestinian Christian. I don't think I've come across a friendship as deep anywhere in the land. They've both known the struggle of following Jesus in cultures that view their faith with suspicion. Yet rather than give in to despair, they've reached out to support each other.

And they're not the only ones.

There are reconciliation ministries all over the land that are bridging the gap through shared experience, such as Combatants for Peace, a joint Israeli–Palestinian movement of former soldiers who have laid down their weapons to love and serve the other. Many of them are good friends of Sami's and have worked closely with his team for years.

For me, one of the most compelling communities is the Parents Circle Families Forum, a network of Jewish and Palestinian parents who have lost children in the conflict and have vowed that they wouldn't wish that on anyone, even someone from the people group who claimed their beloved. It is this utterly rational desire for an end to the suffering that has driven them towards each other, with a solidarity few can understand.

The Palestinian peacemaker Aziz Abu Sarah remembers seeing his older brother taken away by Israeli soldiers when he was just a child. They promised he was just going in for questioning and would be back in a couple of days. Eight months later he returned, beaten and tortured, and later died from his injuries.

For many years, Aziz plotted revenge, but after meeting peaceful and compassionate Jews and Christians on 'the other side', he realised that the actions of those soldiers did not reflect the views of the majority.

While that didn't bring his brother back, it motivated him to choose a higher path.

'I can choose to respond with hatred and violence, or with grace and love . . . First and foremost, I decided to forgive. I forgave, not because the person who killed my brother deserved it (or had asked for it), but because I wanted to be the kind of person who forgives . . . Choosing love crowded out all thoughts of revenge, and I began to act with kindness and mercy.'[3]

Today, he tours high schools with his Jewish friend Nurit, representing the Parents Circle, talking to Palestinians and Jews about the power of peace and forgiveness. They are one of many such friendships I have encountered, rarely in the headlines, in this case an Israeli Jew and a Palestinian Muslim, both bereaved, working together for peace, over and above the bitterness in their personal histories.

'I usually visited high schools with my dear friend Rami, an Israeli graphic designer and fellow member of the Parents Circle. Rami and his wife, Nurit, lost their thirteen-year-old daughter, Smadar, in a suicide bombing when a young Palestinian blew himself up in Jerusalem's Zion Square . . . With Rami and other members of the Parents Circle Families Forum, I have visited dozens of Israeli and Palestinian schools to share our stories of anger and grief and they say that nonviolence is the only way forward.'[4]

A friend of mine in Northern Ireland who was a peacekeeper during The Troubles observed that those who have lost the most are sometimes the ones most motivated to achieve reconciliation. Ironically, it's the 'peripheral supporters' who are more interested in revenge.

There's a lesson in there somewhere.

There are Israeli and Palestinian doctors from both sides who have sacrificed everything to treat the other, against the advice of fearful friends. The Jewish physician Dr Yitz Glick regularly journeys into remote Palestinian villages,[5] despite seeing Jewish friends murdered, for the simple conviction that medical aid should be given regardless of race, creed or national identity.[6] Then there's the magnanimous Gazan doctor, Izzeldin Abuelaish, a world-class fertility expert who continued to serve Israeli parents even after he lost three daughters and a niece when an Israeli tank opened fire on his daughters' bedroom. There is scarcely a dry page in my copy of his landmark book, *I Shall Not Hate*.[7]

The thing that surprised me most about these people fighting for peace is how many there are, from every religion and background. They are not the rare exceptions, the ones or twos. Thousands are rising up with the courage to see the world through the eyes of their enemy and the determination to create a future that is better for the children of both cultures.

It takes great bravery to be a peacemaker but, as Sami reminded us, 'In the Sermon on the Mount, the verse that comes after, "Blessed are the peacemakers" is, "Blessed are those who are persecuted because of righteousness."'[8]

Sami has won hearts and minds on both sides, but he has also faced opposition from Israelis and Palestinians with religious and nationalistic agendas who simply don't want peace.

He sighed faintly, as if recalling some of the struggles he'd endured along the way. 'You should expect persecution, even from your own people, from being in that space of being a peacemaker, where you're standing for truth and justice and healing of the wounds of the communities.'

To be facing opposition from all fronts yet still finding the audacity to love is an extraordinary thing. I wondered how people did it. I decided to seek out the wisdom of another family who have taken on the mantle of peacemakers.

The following day, our intrepid gang of three Dans and a Louise journeyed into the rolling hills on the outskirts of Bethlehem to meet a family who are good friends of Sami.

If anyone knows how to show countercultural love daily, it's the Nassar family.

THE TENT OF NATIONS

We were standing on a kerb under the watchful gaze of a reinforced tower on the separation barrier when an old, beaten-up Mercedes rolled by. We peered in to see a weathered farmer grinning back at us, smile lines framing his grey moustache.

We jumped into the car and were soon weaving around the potholes of Bethlehem's backstreets on the way up to his family farm, the Tent of Nations, nestled on a hilltop on the outskirts of Bethlehem.

It was a long ride, for Palestinians are not allowed to use the main tarmacked road out of town, but it gave us a beautiful panorama of the surrounding hills. Little by little, we climbed into the Judean countryside, once the stomping ground of a certain David, the humble shepherd who took on Goliath.

The farm has been in the Nassar family for more than a hundred years, so when the Israeli government tried to seize it, the Nassars politely refused. They were taken to court and – in a rare victory for Palestinian farmers – they won, thanks to the paper trail that Daher and Daoud Nassar's grandparents had kept from the Ottoman era. Few Palestinians have such paperwork, for they'd rather forget the oppression they faced under the Turkish regime. Unfortunately, that makes it much harder to prove land ownership, even if families have lived in their home for generations. For some reason (Daher doesn't entirely know), their grandfather kept the deeds, and those deeds helped them win the right to stay in their own home.

To say they 'won' is a complicated summary. While they haven't been evicted, they also haven't been fully acquitted. The Israeli authorities bat them between courts at vast expense, hoping that they'll eventually give up, or be unable to afford the court fees. Their cause has attracted worldwide support, and many individuals from Israel, the US, the UK and Sweden have helped pay the fees and fight their corner.

For those who would rather see them kicked out, their continued presence has invited some intense interventions. Their water and electricity supplies have been cut off, and access to the farm is continually blocked, forcing them on ever more elaborate journeys just to visit neighbouring Bethlehem. On two separate occasions, people have broken in and cut down their fruit trees.

In every circumstance, the Nassar family give the standard response. Not revenge or retribution . . .

. . . but love.

'We refuse to be enemies,' is their mantra, and they overcome difficulties with good old-fashioned creativity.

Their innovative resistance reminded me of the words an Iraqi doctor shared with a friend: 'Violence is for those who have lost their imagination.'[9]

Daher showed us around the farm, pointing out the cisterns they had built to harvest rainwater and the solar panels on the roof of the barn. He led us down a set of stone steps, chuckling to himself as he told Swe-Dan, 'Watch your head.'

As our eyes adjusted to the light, we found ourselves in a small cave, beautifully painted by a group of schoolchildren. After the Nassar family were refused building permits on their land owing to 'safety concerns', they came up with an idea.

Move into the caves.

When people visit from Israel, Palestine or further afield, either to support or challenge them, the Nassar family has a common practice: not a sob story or an angry rant, but a hearty meal and the offer of friendship.

Their movement hasn't gone unnoticed. When their trees were chopped down the first time, a Jewish group from the UK came out to help with the replanting. The second time it happened, a different Jewish party from the US joined in. Contrary to the views of the far right, Jewish support for the Tent of Nations is not departing from orthodoxy, but a response to it. Jesus' famous command to 'love your neighbour' wasn't plucked out of the air; he was quoting the Torah.[10] And for Moses, 'your neighbour' meant Jews and non-Jews alike.[11]

The Tent of Nations has become a champion of social justice, a haven for all its neighbours – Jewish, Christian, Muslim and secular. They live to demonstrate to all people that rather than the battle being 'us against them', it can be 'love overcoming hatred', or even 'enemies becoming friends'.

As Daher's brother Daoud explained to us after lunch, there are three standard responses to persecution. In the Middle East, the role of 'oppressor' and 'oppressed' has changed places so many times that almost everyone sees themselves as a righteous victim,[12] and what do righteous victims do? Daoud gave us the options: one – fight back; two – give in; three – run away.

But, as Daoud explained, there's a fourth way, the way of creative non-violent resistance, or, as they call it, the 'Jesus way'. It is the way of Sami's grandmother, who vowed after the murder of her husband that she would never enact revenge, but she would also never stay silent. She showed Sami what it really means to 'turn the other cheek' and, like Sami, the Nassar family has kept this lantern burning.

Like thousands of international friends of the Tent of Nations, we spent the day helping out on the farm. As Lauren Daigle's Spotify play-list serenaded us from my phone, I set to work with Louise and the other Dans weaving cages for new tree saplings, pausing midway for a hearty lunch of olives, flatbread and hummus.

We asked Daoud the question I had been wrestling with since meeting Sami: how do you find the strength to keep up the compassion when the battle feels like it will never end?

His answer was enlightening. 'When we act differently, we force the other to see us also differently, as human.'

What does that mean?

One Sunday, Daoud took his family on the long journey to church in their bright orange VW Campervan. The kids were sleeping in the back as they bumped along endless gravel roads when they were brought to an abrupt halt by a group of Israeli soldiers. Daoud pulled over, and they ordered him to get out.

He obliged.

Nothing to hide.

'Soldiers appeared from nowhere. They had masks, they forced us to stop, pointing guns at us. It was a dangerous situation . . . They forced me to get out of the car; they asked me where I was going, so I told them that we were going to church.'

They demanded that he open the back, but he explained respectfully that his kids were asleep and that being woken up by a group of soldiers, heavily armed and pointing guns at them, would be a little frightening.

'I said, "Let my children sleep; I don't want them to see. It's like a nightmare to see you like that, pointing guns at them."'

The leader of the unit became angry, and as the situation escalated, Daoud agreed to open the van, but asked for a few seconds to wake his children and explain.

They obliged.

He pulled back the van door and gently shook his kids awake.

'I started talking to my children in English. I woke them up and I said, "You will see Israeli soldiers carrying guns, but don't be afraid; they are people."'

Something shifted.

'This sentence changed the whole conversation.'

The soldiers peered into the van and saw some bleary-eyed children smiling back at them, and when the leader of the unit was happy, he told Daoud that he could keep going. But then he paused and offered something extra.

An apology.

Not a short or token apology, but a sincere acknowledgement of respect.

'When the officer called me over to give me my ID card back, he said, "Please apologise to your family; we did something wrong."'

Daoud thanked him and chugged away, but the moment has lingered with his family forever. It would be easy to see the actions of the soldiers as unduly aggressive, but that would miss the point. For a start, Daoud didn't tell us this story to arouse anger – quite the opposite. Behind their masks and guns, the soldiers may have been acting in fear, not fair judgement, and as soon as Daoud hesitated to open his van they assumed the worst. During the Second Intifada, there was a huge increase in the number of suicide bombings from Palestinian terrorist organisations and soldiers ended up suspecting everyone, even a father taking his children to church. But rather than vilifying them, Daoud educated them. He revealed his humanity, and he showed them theirs.

'I always say, this is the powerful message of non-violent resistance, where you are in charge, not the oppressor, and when we act differently, we force the other to see us also differently, as human.'

An encounter that began with armed aggression ended with an assured apology. That's what happens when you remind your enemy that you are human, and that they are too.

Those soldiers were simply carrying out orders, a little fearfully, but when they saw the face of their enemy looking back in love, it changed them.

It reminded me of a bizarre moment in the history of my own people, on the poppy fields of World War I. On Christmas Day 1914, in the heart of a bloody and relentless war, the soldiers heard a sound that nobody could have predicted in months of incessant gunfire.

Singing.

German troops were rattling off a melody of hymns like there was no tomorrow.

As they peered over the trenches, British soldiers were met with German faces, unarmed, standing in the firing line, singing, smoking, laughing, eating chocolate and drinking whisky. They invited the British Tommies into the surreal 'Christmas truce', and before long British and German comrades were exchanging presents, telling jokes and shaking hands with the very men they'd been ordered to gun down the day before.

What must it feel like to look into the whites of your enemy's eyes as he hands you a cigarette and a hip flask?

Memoirs record the intensity of the encounter, broken in a moment as a German soldier in a fake Cockney accent greeted his new British friends with the words, 'Cor blimey, mate,' and watched as the whole gang fell about laughing.[13]

What happened that day?

As the generals watched from a distance, concerned about fraternising with the enemy, gunshots were fired into the air and the troops were called back.

The reaction to being summoned back from the truce was revealing: 'Course that started the war again. Ooh, we were cursing them to hell, cursing the generals and that, you want to get up here in this stuff never mind your giving orders.'[14]

I find it fascinating that it wasn't the 'enemy' they cursed that day, but their own generals. Perhaps the generals were only acting on orders from above themselves – everyone had a job to do, from the greatest to the least – but it must be a little confusing when your job involves turning your rifle on the very man, perhaps a teenager, who has just given you his last piece of chocolate.

Maybe that's the tragedy of every war: young men on both sides, instructed by leaders in their ivory towers to shoot at a mortal enemy, an enemy who, on another day, could be a friend.

I wonder what Jesus felt about his birthday present, a truce between his estranged sons at Christmas?

As I looked for a way to capture everything I had seen and experienced from the peacemakers I have encountered, I was drawn to one of Nelson Mandela's famous mantras:

> No one is born hating another person because of the colour of his skin, or his background, or his religion. People must learn to hate, and if they can learn to hate, they can be taught to love, for love comes more naturally to the human heart than its opposite.[15]

There have always been teachers of prejudice in the world, from the dictators of war to reporters of hate media to leaders who buy influence by instilling fear.

But there are also the educators of love.

At a political level, peace in the Holy Land seems almost inconceivable, but at a grassroots level there are a thousand flickering flames of friendships, families, even whole communities committed to peace, with far more mettle than the perpetrators of violence.

These peaceful revolutionaries, like Sami and the Nassar family, are showing every people group, even former enemies, that in Mandela's words, 'they can be taught to love'.

Part Six
THE DIVINE HUMAN

19.

REFUGEE ROAD

AS THE CITY streets faded behind me and the path wound north and west, descending through ancient terraces and rustling forests, it dawned on me that in the relief of having made it to Jerusalem, I had entirely underestimated the task of walking another two hundred miles to Nazareth.

That's London to Liverpool.

Or New York to Boston.

I had been so overwhelmed by the challenge of crossing the desert, the rest of the journey had seemed like nothing, but on that hot, sticky morning, with my giant rucksack hugging my back, it didn't feel like nothing. I could happily have gone home from Jerusalem, but Nazareth was the final destination, and there would be no tapping out halfway.

I did have one saving grace: Swe-Dan was staying an extra week. In the five-day slog from the rolling hills of Jerusalem to the stuffy plains of the coast, he was the Viking brother I needed.

As we wound our way down through endless miles of crispy woodland, he rumbled around a couple of new tracks, musically processing the emotion of the previous week and strumming his six-stringed guitalele as we walked (it's a tiny guitar; I didn't know, either). My favourite was 'We Refuse to Be Enemies', inspired by our friends at the Tent of Nations.

As the trail trickled on for endless miles, I couldn't help but wonder why Jesus' family had trudged all the way up to Nazareth after their exile in Egypt. They would still have family in Bethlehem, Joseph's original home, and that was only a couple of hours' walk from Jerusalem. Why ditch the ideal location for an insignificant village hidden away up north?

Perhaps there was something I still needed to uncover in Jesus' early life that could reveal something about his vision for peace. It wasn't enough to make a pilgrimage to the land itself; to really get to the truth, as the British scholar Tom Wright likes to argue, you have to make a 'historical pilgrimage to the first century'.[1] And that requires some digging to understand the faith fuelling the peacemakers I had met.

When he entered the world in a feeding trough at the back of a spare room in a borrowed house in Bethlehem, around 6–5 BC, the Roman Empire had ruled the world for sixty years.[2]

Rome couldn't waste its military resources managing Jesus' region when feisty barbarians were waging war in the far reaches of the Empire (c'mon the Scots), so they left Judea in the hands of a local client king. As long as he paid his taxes, the Romans were happy. But finding a 'King of the Jews' who would honour Caesar can't have been easy: Rome was the Jews' greatest enemy. Who would dare?

Fortunately for Caesar, a family of narcissistic traitors stepped up.

The Herods.

The first Herod was 'Herod the Great'. When a leader adds 'the Great' to their name, that should trigger alarm bells. The Russian Tsar Peter 'the Great' took violent control of every facet of society, from the rebuilding of entire cities to the nuances of people's facial hair through the infamous 'beard tax'.[3] That's micromanagement for you.

Jesus lived in the shadow of the notorious Greek king, Alexander 'the Great', who took up mass murder in his teenage years and had conquered the known world by his mid-twenties, leaving a trail of blood all the way to India. Some people have a lot to prove.

To make matters worse, leaders who call themselves 'Thingy the Great' are often paranoid about losing their self-imposed greatness. Those closest to them have a habit of disappearing in the night. Think of an infamous dictator and test them against these characteristics. To be an English peasant under Henry VIII wasn't unlike being a North Korean peasant under Kim Jong Un or a Kurdish Iraqi under Saddam Hussein.

Herod maintained his fragile position by sucking up to Caesar with slimy displays of loyalty, taxing the life out of the Jewish peasantry, building entire cities called 'Caesarea Something' and publicly butchering anyone who refused to flirt with the Romans. He may have produced the biggest temple in Israel's history, but he also dared to erect a golden eagle, the icon of Rome, on top of it. When a public outcry ensued, and a group of zealous young Jewish students took it down, Herod had them burned to death, along with their teachers.[4]

At the risk of stating the obvious, he wasn't exactly the people's king – he was too great for that, apparently.

Imagine turning up for work on Monday morning and seeing an empty chair in the office, or, worse still, coming home to an empty chair around the dinner table.

Jesus would have seen one of those empty chairs after his cousin, John the Baptist, challenged one of the Herods on his family values.[5]

Caesar joked, 'It is better to be Herod's pig than his son,' after Herod had executed multiple family members, including his beloved wife and two sons, just in case they might oppose him.[6] Better to be safe than sorry.

To survive under King Herod (or any evil dictator), you had to work hard, keep your head down, give him everything, criticise nobody and claim no right to anything, especially leadership. Hence Mary and Joseph must have been a little anxious when people started referring to their baby as the next king.

When they carried him into Jerusalem's temple courts on his eighth day, they were greeted by a silver-haired man and woman who'd waited their entire lives to hold Jesus in their arms and say, 'This is the one we've been waiting for.'

There were prophecies about the Messiah in the Jewish Scriptures that seemed to point rather accurately to that young child. Jeremiah predicted that he would be a descendant of David, Micah confirmed that he would come from Bethlehem in the land of Judah, and Isaiah foresaw him being in 'Galilee of the nations'.

Jesus unwittingly fulfilled all of these before he was old enough to read.[7]

I wonder what Jesus' parents thought about all this. Any sane parents would be desperate to keep these prophecies on the down-low when Herod was in earshot. But plans to keep Jesus a secret were well and truly scuppered when a large royal party of Magi rocked up in Jerusalem.[8]

The Magi have always fascinated me. Having just made a desert pilgrimage myself, I have a newfound respect for anyone who would have taken on the shifting sands two thousand years ago, before phone signal or Google Maps. I recalled Sami Awad's expedition on the dawn of the millennium in the footsteps of the Magi through Syria and Iraq. That's a serious journey. You can't keep something like that hush hush.

When the Magi finally descended on Jerusalem with their royal entourage, they asked, 'Where is the *other* king – not Herod, the *real* king?'

That's about as subtle as a slap in the face.

Not good for Mary's nerves.

Herod's response was predictably horrific. He ordered the death of every boy under the age of two in Bethlehem.

No wonder Mary and Joseph fled to Egypt.

As a Roman province with a sizeable Jewish community, Egypt would have been a wise move, notwithstanding the perils of crossing a Middle Eastern desert with a two-year-old. Sometimes, the risk of the road ahead outweighs the danger of the dictator behind.

Perhaps the same is true today.

Not long after Jesus' family fled to Egypt, Joseph learned that Herod the supposedly Great had fallen to the one enemy nobody can outwit: his own death.

The relief must have been overwhelming.

At last, they could return home.

As they started out on that long journey back through the desert, the excitement must have been palpable. They were finally approaching a place where their child could be safe.

Isn't that the hope of every refugee parent?

After weeks on the road, they would have swung east from the coast, probably just north of Gaza, and journeyed up into the hill country of Judea. Jerusalem would have appeared over the horizon as a shimmering city on a hill, the tantalising promise that they were nearly home. If the sight had seemed like heaven for me after three weeks in the wilderness, what must it have looked like to Jesus' young family after years in exile?

Their enemy was gone, their child was safe and their summit was in sight.

Or was it?

Sadly, the sadistic Herod saga didn't end with Herod the Great. When he died, his kingdom was divided between his children, and a large slice of Judea, including Jerusalem and neighbouring Bethlehem, fell to Herod Archelaus, who had the same wilful disregard for humanity as his father.

So close and yet so far.

There would be no returning to Bethlehem with a child who would still be remembered as the next king.

Not yet, anyway.

Joseph made a tactical move for the safety of his family.

Hide.

But where?

The small town of Nazareth, Joseph's adopted home, was the quiet place of obscurity Jesus needed to grow up below the radar. It was up north in the region of Galilee, under the rule of Herod Antipas, who was slightly less psychotic than his southern brother Archelaus. It didn't take much to be the lesser of two evils in the Herod family.

Nazareth would still have its challenges, but it was far safer than Judea.[9]

For me, the extra couple of hundred miles on to Nazareth helped reinforce the reality for millions on the refugee road, both then and now. You can never be quite sure of your final destination. Last-minute changes, unexpected dangers and bloodthirsty political leaders are the inheritance of the refugee life.

As the bright lights of Tel Aviv came into view, I tracked the Yarkon River with Swe-Dan through shady bamboo forests all the way to the

Mediterranean, arriving late in the afternoon to watch the watery horizon wolfing down the sun.

For a few minutes, we sat in silence, lost in the expanse of the water. There is something incomparably majestic about the sea, but it's not always a comforting majesty like the warmth of a summer's day. For some, the rolling expanse is tinged with dread. A stormy sea can turn on you in a moment. A bit like Herod.

In the wake of the Arab Spring, many refugees took their chances with the Mediterranean in perilous boats at the hands of human traffickers, in search of the supposed haven of Europe.

Some, like Zain and Layla, were rescued by EU coastguards.

There were those already in Greece, like Karim, who helped with the rescue.

But there were also people who never made it.

One image brought the world to its knees. The lifeless body of three-year-old Alan Kurdi washed up on the shores of Turkey clung to newspapers across the globe and stopped everyone in their tracks. I remember standing paralysed by the press stand in the supermarket on my way home from work. My nephew was a similar age at the time.

After a few short-lived and ill-conceived conspiracy theories, the international community accepted the image for what it was: a tragedy. And sometimes a tragedy can move the world.

Overnight, the political issue of the refugee crisis became a human issue, a tale of someone's son or daughter lost at sea. In Britain, there was a public outcry and a political U-turn. When people's sense of empathy eclipses their sense of entitlement, the world becomes a kinder place. Streets exploded with signs saying 'Refugees welcome', and the Prime Minister, in response to public pressure, declared that Britain would take 20,000 refugees by 2020.

Sadly, those targets were not met – not even close – but that says more about government bureaucracy than public will. For a moment, people responded with action rather than apathy, and for good reason. That child could have been any of us.

When I was three, the world was no safer. At the climax of the Cold

War, a bizarre coalition of nations were in Afghanistan, fighting the Soviets alongside the Mujahideen, and countless similar proxy battles were mirrored all over the world, from North Africa to Central America to the Middle East, where Saddam Hussein was committing unspeakable atrocities against anyone he didn't like.

How did I, as a defenceless toddler, survive all this carnage?

Certainly not through my own merit. My security came from the fact that, in the great lottery of life, I was born in the obscurity of rural England.

What if I'd entered the world in Afghanistan or Iraq or Libya?

Would I be here now?

Perhaps I'd be standing by a wire fence at a camp in Greece.

Waiting.

Wondering.

What if I'd been born, not in the twenty-first century, but in the first century, in a fishing village on the Egyptian coast? I might have brushed shoulders with another young boy as he set out on a long journey home.

THE COALFACE

For the final leg of the journey from Tel Aviv to Nazareth, I was joined by one last trekking buddy. Family is particularly important in both Jewish and Arab cultures. Kids often stay at home until they get married and then literally build an apartment on top of the family home. Maybe western subcultures that prize individual rights above family values can learn something from the Middle East.

My mum had planned to join me for the final part of the walk to Nazareth, and the trail angels I had stayed with were excited to meet her. I have a small family: my dad died at a young age and my mum took up trail-running in the years after his death. As a veteran of the Camino de Santiago trail, she could easily handle the trek, so she arranged to arrive in Tel Aviv the same weekend that Swe-Dan flew home.

The first night, we stayed with a family who have become close friends of mine. Their grandparents came to Israel from Iraq and Yemen, and their Middle Eastern hospitality was out of this world. They were an intelligent and motivated family: the daughter worked for a law practice in Tel Aviv and her brother was studying biomedical sciences at university. He was fifteen.

They clearly had busy lives, yet it seemed that they were willing to drop everything to make us feel welcome. They ferried Swe-Dan and my mum to and from the airport in the middle of the night and cooked up a feast to prepare us for the journey ahead.

It was a wholly undeserved honour.

I guess that's what real hospitality is.

We shared a traditional Shabbat meal with them on the Friday night, and on the Sunday we took off up the coast, with the Mediterranean on our left, bound for the north.

By this point I had a few hundred miles under my belt and the tender blisters that had plagued my feet for the first week had scarred over like impenetrable leather. Mum wasn't quite so lucky, and her new boots gave her a punishing. I took some weight from her bag to ease the load, in the same way Pete had helped me back in the desert, and cheered her on with the same spaniel-like encouragement that Swe-Dan had shown me the week before. That's the way life is on the road – one day you're the guy in need of help, the next you're the one paying it forward.

I showed Mum the old-school needle-and-iodine approach to blister management, and in five days we made it to Mount Carmel, the site of the prophet Elijah's famous victory over the priests of Baal.

It was a valuable part of the experience for me to walk part of the road to Nazareth with family as well as friends, as it gave me an insight into the life Jesus lived as an adult.

It appears he also lost his dad at a young age. That wasn't unusual in small first-century Middle Eastern towns with no public health service. Joseph would have been older than Mary by quite a margin, and few men lived to what we now consider old age. It can't have been easy for Mary, raising the Messiah as a single parent. I doubt she got any child benefits from Herod.

Although Jesus never married or had children, before he was thirty he would have helped to raise at least six children.[10] Matthew records four brothers and at least two sisters.[11] As the oldest son to a poor widow, Jesus would have had to step up to put bread on the table after Joseph died. While I know what it's like to grow up in a single-parent family, I also live in a country where there's government support for families like ours.

Jesus would have no such luck.

The refugee child became the teenager providing for his family.

He must have grown up fast.

Three times a year, his extended family would have walked the long road to Jerusalem, carrying everything they needed for the annual festivals: food, water, blankets, animals.

As I walked that sandy road myself, with food and water on my back, I tried to capture a snapshot of the journey Jesus took so many times. Admittedly he would have travelled the Jordan Valley route rather than swinging by the shores of the Mediterranean, but I took a detour to drop Swe-Dan and collect mum from the airport. Jesus' journey may have been shorter, but it would undoubtedly have been more dangerous, and I expect he had more to carry.

Did he take the weight of food and water on his back to give his mother Mary a break? Perhaps he had a sibling on his broadening teenage shoulders. There are not many children who will walk a hundred miles or more without growing tired and wanting to be carried, as every parent knows. With six or more younger siblings, Jesus must have had his hands full.

I find this stage of his life so fascinating. How is it that the most famous figure in human history lived completely below the radar for 90 per cent of his life? There is so much mystery. What did he do before his thirties? There are plenty of claims, but little evidence. I've heard the folklores about Jesus travelling through Cornwall, even on to Glastonbury (for the festival, I assume), but in reality, when William Blake's old English anthem, 'Jerusalem', asks concerning Jesus, 'And did those feet in ancient times, walk upon England's mountains green?', the historically accurate answer is, 'Umm . . . nope.'

So where *did* those feet walk in ancient times?

On the final day of my five-hundred-mile journey to Nazareth, I might just have found out.

In ancient times, Jesus walked upon the dusty roads of Galilee as a *tekton*, which in English is translated as a 'carpenter', although the term refers more to a general builder than a master craftsman. There would have been little demand for the Galilean equivalent of IKEA. A *tekton* in those days was the early equivalent of a multi-skilled white-van man (minus the van), with the skills and strength to jump on any job, in timber or stone.[12]

Jesus would have offered blood, toil, tears and sweat to put bread on the table for a growing family, only to see the lion's share of his wages siphoned off to pay three sets of taxes to three sets of corrupt leaders.

It was the humble Jewish peasantry who stumped up the funds to pay for the lifestyles of the rich and the famous, from Herod's lavish building projects to the corrupt temple priests in Jerusalem to the occupying Roman army, whose military might was needed to arm the enforcers of the taxes in the first place.

That's a vicious circle if ever there was one.

Nazareth was a small village, and no doubt Jesus would have had to travel further afield to find work. The main route into the village was up a monstrous hill on the road north, and Jesus must have climbed that hill countless times on his way home from, well, anywhere.

On my last day of this epic journey, I walked that road, and it's still a well-worn commute.

Many pilgrims to the Holy Land testify to a wonderful ethereal experience when they physically walk in the footsteps of Jesus, but I had no such emotion.

I was tired, the road was tough and I had a heavy bag.

I guess that's how Jesus felt.

Every day.

Yet despite the burden of providing for his family and paying his taxes, we never hear that Jesus complained of his hidden years on the coalface. Maybe because it was normal life for a Galilean peasant, nothing to write home about.

But snapshots from Jesus' life show us that providing for his mother and siblings wasn't a chore, but an honour. Before he taught people to love their enemies, he showed people how to care for their families. In his final hour, as he hung bloodied and bruised on a Roman cross, he cried out to his closest friend and made one single request – not for revenge or painkillers (which would have been my last requests), but for John to take care of his mother.

The unselfishness of his final words mirrors his whole working life.

Many people over the years have struggled to understand Jesus' divinity, but, for me, his humanity is equally extraordinary.

If you could choose to live any life on earth, if you could select any time and any place, who would opt for the life Jesus chose?

As I stumbled into a café in Nazareth and sipped a sweet coffee, rich with cardamom, I looked back over the previous five hundred miles. Reflecting on the road I had walked, and the man in whose footsteps I had followed, I was struck by the fact that Jesus modelled the first rule of leadership.

Showing up.

Before he offered any solutions to the conflict and hardship around him, he first embraced it with all its challenges and trials. Modern diplomats often fly into a troubled nation, meet for a few days with the political leaders, offer some wise words, stay in a nice hotel with plenty of security and then fly home.

But that was never Jesus' style. He checked into a dodgy town in a violent neighbourhood, got a job on the coalface and stayed, not for three days, but for thirty years.

When the time came to initiate a new world order, he wasn't bringing a few ideas he'd googled on the way to the meeting; he was bringing the heart of someone who had experienced everything he taught about. Jesus was accused of many things – breaking the rules, mixing with sinners, blasphemy, even terrorism – but nobody accused him of not knowing what life is like in the real world.

Even in the years he spent swinging a hammer, his manual labour was but a side job compared to his real work. The most common title people used for Jesus was not 'carpenter' but 'rabbi', the Jewish word for a teacher.

Every Jewish student knew that God had a habit of calling people from humble backgrounds into positions of leadership. The most famous prophet, Moses, and the most famous king, David, had both been shepherds in the wilderness before they were summoned to rule the nation.

In Jesus' day, a humble student of exceptional intelligence was celebrated in rabbinical circles, and Jesus' intellect was noted at an early age.[13] His brief mention as a carpenter in no way detracts from his repeated status as a teacher, for even the most distinguished rabbis had a trade to which they turned their hand, by way of example if not necessity.[14]

As a young rabbi, Jesus would have spent every waking hour studying the Torah, while grafting to put bread on the table for his family at the same time.

But while his intellect and integrity might hold some inspiration to the modern generation, not all the rumours about him were positive. Born to an impoverished teenage mother in suspicious circumstances, and visited by a bewildered crowd of grubby shepherds, people took some convincing that this fragile baby would grow up to be the long-awaited Messiah.

WAR AND PEACE

After centuries of oppression under six different superpowers, the Jews were looking for a one-in-a-million military leader who could rally the troops and overthrow the beast of Rome. That wasn't the calling of a rabbi or even a carpenter; it was the mantle of a warrior.

The Romans may have given us straight roads, aqueducts and central heating, but they also butchered people from every ethnic group in the known world.

Only the brave dared to fight back.

Few succeeded.

They even had the audacity to call this spread of genocidal mayhem *Pax Romana*, the peace of Rome. If you tried to resist this 'peace', you would be tortured and killed, and if you surrendered, they gave you the honour of working for them, for they had an army to feed. Soldiers get hungry.

For the Jewish people, who believed that God was on their side, this all seemed unbearable.

Where was he?

Why didn't he do something?

Didn't he care?

Unsurprisingly, there were violent resistance movements to Roman rule in every corner of the world, and they've inspired many of Hollywood's sword-and-sandal epics, from the barbarians of Germania in the opening scene of *Gladiator* to the savages of Scotland in *The Eagle*. While Hollywood has taken some poetic licence with history, the real figures behind the resistance were braver than any film can capture. The British heroine Boudica was a force to be reckoned with, as the generals of Rome discovered.[15]

In Judea, the Jewish revolutionaries were so zealous, it was their nickname.

The Zealots carried knives, not olive branches.

The greatest hope of the Jewish people resided in the anointed leader who would finally avenge their enemy and restore Israel to its former glory in the days of David, the shepherd who became a warrior who became a king.

They wanted one of those.

The standard route to 'peace' was to kill all your enemies. Total war. That's how Rome did it, and many in Judea believed it was time they got a taste of their own medicine. Jesus was an ideal candidate; after three decades hauling timber and stone, he would have had the muscle, not to mention the motive of the oppressed masses, and he could quickly build a following among the zealous northern militants of Galilee, a region infamous for its revolutionaries. He fulfilled a ton of Jewish prophecies about the coming Messiah, and some even started calling him 'Son of David', which, technically, he was.

But not everyone was convinced.

Jesus was no soldier, nor was he a politician; he wasn't even a priest. He had no background in national or religious politics or military service. He never held an office or led an army; he hadn't even killed a single Roman soldier, much less a Goliath. He was nothing but a refugee child from Africa who'd spent his life studying the Torah, looking out for his siblings and doing odd manual-labour jobs.

He could have taken up arms and started a guerrilla war against the Romans, like the Maccabees had a century or two earlier against the Greeks, but that was not his way.

He had a different plan.

His reluctance to fight would have lost him the respect of the Zealots, but with a regional accent from the northern hills of Galilee, not to mention a suspicious family history, he had his work cut out to win the respect of the southern Jerusalem elite. Even among his students, his humble beginnings were something of a joke.

'Nazareth! Can anything good come from there?' asked Nathanael.[16]

Nazareth was *that town*.

Contrary to Hollywood's imagination, Jesus didn't even look particularly striking. For westerners, it's difficult not to picture Jesus as tall, slender and distinguished, thanks to hundreds of years of elaborate airbrushing. Da Vinci may have been quite the artist, but he didn't do his history homework.

An anthropologically accurate description would make Jesus short, thick set and coarsely bearded, his olive skin wrinkled and weathered by years under the relentless sun.[17] In his short life of hard graft and constant travel, he would have had neither the time nor the inclination to sculpt his beard or pluck his eyebrows. *Tektons* and teachers were scruffy by necessity. We may have no photographs, but he clearly would have looked similar to the other blue-collar bruisers from Galilee, for when he was later betrayed in the Garden of Gethsemane, the soldiers sent to arrest him needed a signal from Judas to identify him from all the burly fishermen in the gang, so he can't have been head and shoulders above the rest.

When I look at the pensive, wistful depictions of Jesus in stained-glass windows, I can understand the sentiment of their creators. They were master craftsmen trying to portray the beauty of the Gospel stories to thousands of illiterate people. But while I honour the heart of the artists, the historian in me needs to know what his life *really* looked like, not what people want him to look like. The people who have inspired me most on my journey are those who want to become more like Jesus, not those who are trying to make him more like themselves.

That's a world of difference.

Besides, we don't need to 'make' Jesus more impressive by worldly standards, for his power and influence never rested on the delusions of grandeur defined by modern celebritocracies.[18]

Nor was his definition of peace about destroying all the bad guys.

Quite the opposite.

If an unknown, unexpected and unusually compassionate man-of-the-people from an embarrassing town in obscurity can change the world more than anyone else in human history, he clearly had something more than an Instagram filter, the tools of political influence or the ability to kill lots of enemy soldiers.

Something nobody had ever seen before.

20.

SIGNS AND WONDERS

NAZARETH WAS A gift. After the intensity of Jerusalem, the urban sprawl of Tel Aviv and the trials of the desert road, Nazareth was a refreshing antidote to all three. It was therapeutically laid back. There were businesses born out of Jewish–Arab friendships, roof gardens with the sound of laughing families cascading down into the steep cobbled streets, and restaurants spilling out into the town squares with young professionals chatting into the early hours, like a vintage Mediterranean town.

Nowhere is perfect, and no doubt Nazareth has its issues, like any town, but there was a tangible lightness to the place that refreshed my soul.

As fate would have it, a friend from my home town of Taunton was teaching at Nazareth Evangelical College, and we spent hours catching up over lamb kebabs and lemon shisha. He introduced me to his Arab colleagues, and I got lost for a week in a blur of new friendships, fresh hummus and unhurried hospitality.

After writing up the preceding chapters in the quiet courtyards of the enlightened Fauzi Azar Inn, I hiked out to continue my quest by the rolling waters of Kinneret, the Sea of Galilee. It is perhaps the best place of all to take a 'pilgrimage to the first century' for, unlike other ancient landscapes carved up by tourist traps and elaborate shrines, the Sea of Galilee remains largely unchanged. The fields are farmed and the waters are fished, much like they've always been, except with the occasional sound of an outboard motor.

By now, spring was in full bloom and the hills were ablaze with a thousand red poppies peeping through meadows of golden grass. As I emerged over the Western fringe, the entire lake stretched before me, its harp shape unmistakably framed by the hills around it as the sun danced on the rolling waves. As a brisk wind swept down over the cliffs of Arbel, I took refuge in a small cave with a few unsuspecting cows, who seemed far less excited about the view than me. Familiarity breeds contempt, I guess.

This was the sight I had been looking forward to for five hundred miles.

Gazing down at that small glistening corner of the world, nestled in the Jordan Valley, it felt strange to think that this insignificant corner of the planet had hosted a similarly unlikely teacher, who in three short years transformed the world more than anyone else who has ever lived.

How did he do it?

Climbing down to the Sea of Galilee, I passed by the town of Magdala, the home of Mary Magdalene, where Jesus would have preached as he toured the region.[1] Slightly further up the lake is Capernaum, the fishing village where he settled after leaving Nazareth. It was in Capernaum that Jesus built his first team, and there were echoes of the movement I have witnessed all over the world in those early fragile believers.[2]

When Peter first met Jesus, he was doing what he'd always done.

Fishing.

It must have come as a surprise when Jesus called this salt-of-the-earth heavyweight to be the leader of his movement.

The standard practice for respected rabbis was to take the smartest and most prestigious students in the land, usually from the courts of the rich and famous in Jerusalem, the early equivalent of red-brick universities, and say, 'Follow me.'

In Ancient Middle Eastern culture, 'Follow me' meant far more than, 'Come and learn some stuff.' It meant, 'Join me on the road, internalise my teaching and practise my whole way of life.' To be invited to 'follow' a famous teacher was the highest honour; it meant the teacher was putting total faith in you to continue their movement, building on it and applying it to the next generation. It was the same in Greek culture: Aristotle 'followed' Plato, who 'followed' Socrates.

So when Jesus wandered down to the beach and chose Peter, it was a shock. Granted, Peter would have studied the Torah industriously as a child, but to grow up to be a fisherman was an unmistakable sign that he had failed rabbi school. Almost every boy would study the Torah as a child, but only the best would be invited to keep going, and only the best of the best would go on to shadow a prestigious rabbi. Peter didn't make the grade, so he went back to the nets – until a revolutionary rabbi turned up and gave him a second chance.

Succeeding with a dream team is undoubtedly great fun – that's as true for university professors as it is for football managers or film directors – but taking a cast of nobodies and transforming them into something even they didn't expect: that's real leadership.

Jesus had his work cut out. While many looked down on his choice of disciples, the real problem was the way his disciples looked down on *each other*. There was a lot of potential for explosive moments in Jesus' gang. There was Matthew the tax collector, who had worked for the Romans, extracting taxes from hard-working Jews and taking a cheeky cut for himself. Then there were four hard-working fishermen, who would deeply resent paying taxes to . . . Matthew. How did that go down? To really turn up the heat, Jesus recruited Simon the Zealot into his inner circle. A Zealot would think nothing of murdering a traitorous turncoat like Matthew. Now they were on the same side. Supposedly.

What was Jesus thinking?

Unlike the producers of reality TV, Jesus didn't recruit a gang of guaranteed enemies to provide entertainment: he wanted to prove that, if these guys could be taught to love one another, anyone could. It was his training ground for the peace and reconciliation movement he was planning for the whole world.

I wonder if those first students knew what they were getting themselves into when they left their day jobs to follow Jesus.

It was a steep learning curve.

THE DOCTOR OF GALILEE

Before the days of online booking apps, if you needed a place to sleep for the night (not to mention a hearty meal), you could pop into a relative's home unannounced, with all your other friends and family, and stay however long you liked. For free. It worked if you were a friend, or a friend of a friend, or a friend of a friend of a friend, or just a complete stranger.

It sounds cheeky, but Middle Eastern culture is often that hospitable. I've depended on it for months.

When Jesus found Peter's home in Capernaum, he just moved in. Jesus' family may have had their own place in Capernaum, but if Peter was going to lead Jesus' movement, he needed a no-holds-barred education, and for Jesus, that meant living and working from Peter's house (most likely the first-century home discovered by archaeologists in 1968).[3]

It would already have been relatively crowded, for Peter lived with his wife, his mother-in-law and his brother, and those are the only ones mentioned. Doubtless, there would have been other relatives and countless children running around.[4]

Jesus didn't mind. He brought the rest of his students too. Where would they all sleep?

To make matters worse, Peter's mother-in-law was in bed with a fever. So Jesus healed her.

She got up and cooked for them, which was generous but not expected. (While Jesus respected family customs, he loved to challenge societal inequalities, and when he swung by his friends' place in Bethany, he told the women *not* to busy themselves in the kitchen, but to come and join the male disciples instead.[5] He was far more of a feminist than most people realise.)

Word travels fast in a small town. You don't need social media when there are dozens of children running around spreading the word. That night, the whole town showed up at the door, bringing anyone tormented by anything: evil powers, sickness, injuries and 'various diseases', in Mark's words.[6]

Jesus healed them all.

Then he went on to the next town and did the same.

As Jesus travelled around Galilee, he healed hundreds of incurable diseases, cleansed lepers, gave sight to the blind and hearing to the deaf, restored broken limbs and erased debilitating skin conditions. He interrupted a funeral to raise a young man from the dead, performed the same resurrection with a synagogue ruler's daughter and, just to prove the point, he left his mate Lazarus in the tomb for four days until his corpse started to stink, so people would know, when he raised him from the dead, it was the real deal.[7]

No wonder he drew a crowd.

The world of the first-century peasant was one of constant sickness and suffering. You were lucky if you lived beyond your forties, for if the Romans didn't slit your throat, a common cold could finish you off overnight. There was no public health service and no modern medicine; just a meagre, grain-based diet, a lot of germs and the occasional pandemic, to really add insult to injury.[8]

Men died on the coalface, women died in childbirth and children died all the time.

If that was your lot, imagine how you would react if you discovered that a mighty prophet was travelling around the region, healing *everybody* he met of *every* infirmity?

When I first read the Gospels as a teenager, the prevailing view about Jesus' miracles was that they were *metaphorical* miracles. I remember being taught in RE lessons that perhaps the real miracle in the feeding of the five thousand was that people *shared* their lunches. How nice. Let's not spoil that lovely story with the notion of actual miracles.

Most people believed that the 'signs and wonders' reported in the Gospels were either the naive superstition of religious people or they were added in later as an extra veneer of fake news in the Jesus marketing strategy. As time goes on, I was taught, we'll see just how ridiculous all these signs and wonders are.

But in the last few years, the opposite has happened.

The latest historical and archaeological discoveries have strengthened rather than challenged the Gospel accounts. We have a clearer insight into the world of first-century Judea than ever before, and the accuracy of names, dates, places, events, journeys, geographical features, even unique plant species in the Gospels, point to them being simple, honest, reliable, unaltered accounts from the first generation, based on eyewitness testimonies. The suggestion that they were penned in another time and place no longer reflects the evidence.[9]

But what are we to make of the supposed miracles?

I remember at school, my best friend challenged me to read some books about Jesus by atheists to get a balanced view. It was a fair shout. I picked up *Jesus: The Evidence*, by historian Ian Wilson, and made a surprising discovery. While Wilson was not convinced by Jesus' claim to divinity, even as an unbeliever he couldn't refute the evidence for his miracles. Instead, he put them down to a smorgasbord of coincidence, placebo and hypnosis.

Interesting.

If Jesus' critics weren't denying his miracles, the idea that they were entirely fictitious seemed unlikely. It was the same with his original audience: not everyone was superstitious in the Greco-Roman world and many philosophers went out of their way to discredit the supernatural. But with Jesus, the evidence was too abundant to dismiss, so critics opted for alternative arguments. Suetonius called Christianity a new kind of 'magic',[10] Josephus referred to Jesus as 'a doer of startling deeds',[11] Celsus described his miracles as 'sorcery',[12] and the religious leaders claimed his signs were from the devil,[13] which is a little odd. The devil is hardly famous for random acts of kindness.

The late Cambridge professor Graham Stanton pointed out:

In Jesus' own lifetime follower and foe alike accepted that Jesus had unusual healing powers. The question was not, 'Did Jesus perform miracles?' for that was taken for granted. What was in dispute was on whose authority and with whose power Jesus performed unusual deeds.[14]

For me, the alternative theories, from ancient to present, prove that *something* was happening. But if it wasn't a touch of the Divine, what was it?

The 'dark magic' advocates seem to have missed the fact that Jesus was only ever motivated by compassion, and as for the purveyors of solely naturalistic views, it's difficult to explain away the evidence, as Ian Wilson found out.

Was the leper with irreversibly scarred skin healed by hypnosis?

Were blind eyes opened by positive thinking?

What about the people Jesus raised from the dead? Do placebos work when you're dead?[15]

Perhaps the most substantial evidence for Jesus' miracles is not speculation about the past, but the witness of the present. My recent interviews have unveiled the surprising truth that, when people pray to Jesus, the same signs and wonders that line the pages of the Gospels are unfolding today, all over the world, from the bottom of a Chilean mine to military detention centres in the Middle East.

One of the turning points for me was the healing of Steph Lam's left eye. Doctors in Auckland told her she'd never see again, owing to the irreparable scarring of her cornea from the acid burn, and after three days of medical procedures from the best hospital in the country, there was zero improvement. But when her friends and family at church gathered around and prayed for a miracle, her eyesight was completely restored with zero scars.

When Jesus healed the blind man at the Pool of Siloam in Jerusalem,[16] the get-out-of-miracle-free card in a cynical culture is that it was a *metaphorical* healing, that his eyes were opened to a new understanding of who Jesus really was. But if someone's eye can be physically healed in the current generation when people *pray* to Jesus, it doesn't seem unreasonable to expect someone's eyes to have been healed when he was there in the flesh.

Could it be an actual miracle *and* a new understanding?

It was classic rabbinical technique to combine teaching with practical demonstrations. Jesus always practised what he preached.[17]

Of course, this raises countless other questions, not least of which is what about those who don't get their miracle? For many, including me, that's not just a theological question; it's a personal one. But while I cannot explain the miracles I haven't seen, I also cannot explain away the ones I have.

I'm a witness now.

The thing that interests me most about these signs and wonders is not *what* Jesus did, but *why*. When he performed the most extraordinary miracles, when thousands of people were ready to hail him as King . . . he slipped away.

Why did he do that?

Was he embarrassed about his ability?

Did he just want some alone time?

I can't blame him.

I thought back to what Sami had shared with us in Bethlehem: 'In the past, I used to think of Jesus when he was healing like a "superman" figure; you know he has this amazing ability to make miracles and heal people, but then I began to understand . . . when Jesus was healing, he wasn't just trying to show himself off. Jesus was liberating people.'

Sami's insight was the key that unlocked Jesus' miracles for me. He wasn't an ancient illusionist trying to entertain people, nor was he a wannabe military leader, using the supernatural to secure office. He didn't use the miraculous to his own personal advantage; to the contrary, he often asked people to keep quiet about it.

The simplest explanation for Jesus' unusually modest miraculous ministry was that he was healing people because he cared.

He wanted to set people free.

Wouldn't you if you could?

JESUS' DAUGHTER

Standing on the shores of Lake Galilee, with the fresh breeze offering a welcome respite from the intense heat, I tried to imagine what life was like in this exact spot two millennia ago, for Galilee's most vulnerable. Two encounters offer a revealing insight. As Jesus toured the villages around this very coastline, a man with leprosy came and fell at his feet.

Leprosy in the ancient world was an agonising skin disorder that separated people from the community indefinitely. It was infectious, and there was no known cure, so to save your own skin you had to keep a wide berth.

Lepers were quarantined.

Indefinitely.

It was like a first-century version of the coronavirus, except that nobody recovered.

It was a slow and painful death.

Lepers were required to shout, 'Unclean!' at the top of their voices and ring a bell to help people avoid them. After my three weeks of loneliness in the Negev, I can't imagine anything worse – a lifetime of enforced isolation.

Perhaps the most biting edge of this inescapable prison was the tactile separation. Lepers would never feel the comforting touch of a loved one, a pat on the back, a kiss on the cheek, the reassuring hug of a friend.

Until Jesus turned up, that is.

The leprous man implored Jesus with the words, 'If you are willing, you can make me clean.'[18]

Fair point.

'I am willing,' Jesus replied, reaching out and touching the man. 'Be clean!'

No Jewish person had ever been cured of leprosy; it was a miracle that was expected from the Messiah (along with opening blind eyes). Jesus wasn't merely *claiming* to be the Messiah – in fact, he rarely made that claim – he was showing people the evidence. Actions speak louder.[19]

It must have been a remarkable day for the former leper. There were even laws in the Torah about how to give thanks when someone was cured of leprosy, but they had never been applied.

Until now.

The Greek word used to describe Jesus' reaction to lepers is *splanchnizomai*.[20] It literally means 'from the gut' (I've never worked out how to pronounce it). In some translations we read it as 'moved with pity', and in others it is 'moved with compassion', but neither really captures the gut reaction. It means to be so wrought with love, so deeply connected to the suffering of another, that you feel their pain in your own stomach. It's to love someone so much, it makes you sick.

Plenty of people felt sick when they saw a person with leprosy, but not out of compassion. A common belief in the Ancient Middle East was that sickness was a punishment from God, a sort of intensified karma, the rough justice for their own sin or the sin of their parents.

Jesus disagreed.

It's not the fact that Jesus healed the man with leprosy that I find interesting, it's *how* he did it. Jesus had already demonstrated his ability to heal people without making physical contact, yet when he encountered the leper, moved with compassion, 'He reached out his hand and *touched* the man.'

Jesus loved to pick out the most marginalised of people and free them, not just from their disease, but also from the burden of shame that society had placed on them. By touching the leper, people expected the ritual and physical uncleanliness to infect Jesus.

He was happy to take that risk.

When the man was healed, Jesus sent him to the priests to make the thank offerings commanded by Moses, for he respected Jewish law to the letter. Of course, the no-longer-leprous man paid no attention to ceremony; he was busy running around telling everyone what had happened and probably enjoying a few hugs. At least, that's what I would have done.

On another occasion, Jesus was intercepted by an older woman, whom Mark politely describes as having been 'subject to bleeding for twelve years'.[21] She squeezed through the crowd just to touch the edge of Jesus' cloak. Perhaps she knew the prophecy.[22]

She made it. She touched his cloak. She was healed.

End of story.

But Jesus wasn't content with a physical healing. Mosaic law would have declared this woman 'unclean', just like the leper.[23] In fact, her act of squeezing through the crowd to touch Jesus would have made a lot of other people unclean too, so she wouldn't have been popular. She would have carried the same stigma of shame that was attached to many sick people – that her condition was a punishment from God.

Jesus reversed all that judgement.

This woman would have known plenty of labels, but Jesus only saw one.

'Daughter.'

It's an unusual title, especially for a woman who may have been older than him, but he wanted her to know that however sick or desperate she might have been, however great the cloud of shame she laboured under, however 'unclean' she might consider herself, her primary identity in God's eyes was that of a daughter. And he wanted every judgemental bystander to know this.

Sonship and daughterhood triumphs over every other identity, for whatever you become, you never cease to be someone's child. A good parent never ceases to love their son or daughter, whatever labels people attach to them.

Of course, not every parent shows such unconditional love, but Jesus is not every parent. There are no orphans in his eyes, not even old ones. Jesus was demonstrating the heart of a true peacemaker. He recognised that this woman was more than a physical body; she was a human being robbed of dignity.

Peace isn't just an absence of pain or suffering; it's a place of complete wholeness, physically, spiritually and socially. Healing her condition was only the start; what he really wanted to do was restore her honour within the community.

As a final commendation and a lesson to the crowd, he offered some parting words: not, 'Hey everyone, look what I just did,' but, turning the spotlight away from himself, he said, 'Your faith has healed you. Go in peace and be freed from your suffering.'

Jesus replaced the 'unclean' label with something better.

Role model.

21.

CONSUMED WITH ZEAL

BEFORE I FLEW home after weeks on the road, I took one last trip to Jerusalem to stand on the Mount of Olives and watch the sun set over the Old City. Every day, countless pilgrims enjoy the same moment. The view seems to capture the soul of the world, as the towering walls of the Temple Mount rise defiantly from the Kidron Valley, and the gold roof of the Dome of the Rock shimmers in the last rays of sunlight. On the far side, at the Western Wall, Jewish people from every corner of the planet gather to pray, swaying gently like flickering candles, burning with devotion.

For many, Jerusalem is the centre of the world, and at the centre of the centre of the world is the Temple, the apex of three world religions and, for the Jewish people, the very dwelling place of God. It was in this place, for many the most precious on earth, that Jesus did something a little unexpected. He smashed it up.

Few pilgrims come to Jerusalem today to re-enact *that* scene, and they wouldn't last long if they tried. It seems rather out of character for the 'Prince of Peace'.[1]

Standing on the Mount of Olives at dusk as the city lights below started to flicker into life, I continued my 'pilgrimage to the first century' and imagined the moment Jesus rode a humble donkey into Jerusalem from this very spot. Trotting down the Mount of Olives from the east, he entered Jerusalem in triumphant procession, as crowds laid down palm branches and sang Messianic victory songs. As a thousand 'Hosannas' rose into the spring air, Jesus wept over Jerusalem, likening his leadership to the tenderness of a mother hen longing to protect her chicks.[2]

You couldn't create a more peaceful inauguration if you tried, yet moments later he was striding into the temple and throwing furniture.

Why the sudden change of tune?

In ancient times, thousands of people would flock to Jerusalem to celebrate the three annual festivals, and the temple leaders had the honour of shepherding these loyal pilgrims, who had risked everything on perilous journeys to worship God.

That was the theory, anyway.

What the leaders actually did was prey on the humble worshippers and steal their cash.

To say they abused their position is an understatement.

Only perfect, spotless sacrifices could be offered in the temple, and there was a suspicious monopoly on the animals, which were sold at vastly inflated prices. To add insult to injury, only temple currency could be used to buy them and, like the currency exchange desks in the airport, the moneychangers in Jerusalem weren't exactly providing a favourable rate. Having squeezed every penny out of every pilgrim, they even had the audacity to throw in an extra 'temple tax'.

The whole system was set up to make the rich richer and the poor poorer.[3]

For Jesus, this was unacceptable. While the religious leaders had *hundreds* of laws to live by, Jesus had two: love God and love your neighbour. Simple as that. The daylight robbery in the temple courts made a mockery of both.

It was more like, 'Ignore God and rob your neighbour.'

Jesus was rattled.

Given his years of relentless compassion, it would be easy to think of him as meek and mild, sweet and soft, a beta-male who wouldn't say 'boo' to a goose. But his unquenchable kindness is not an indication of weakness, for when Jesus encouraged his disciples to be 'meek', he wasn't using the word in the way we understand the English translation. The Greek word is *praus*, which means 'controlled strength'. We sometimes translate it as 'gentle', but a better translation would be 'composed' or 'disciplined'. The ancient Greeks used the image of a wild horse that had been tamed – one whose strength had been harnessed for battle.[4]

For Jesus, true meekness was about trust.

Like a war horse that chooses to obey its rider rather than running wild, the ancient understanding of meekness was about possessing immeasurable strength but having the wisdom to know how and when to exercise it. For Jesus, it meant to follow divine leading rather than human emotions. It wasn't that Jesus didn't get angry, for he had his moments. The real question when he did clench his fists . . . why?

When Jesus was *personally* attacked, he never lifted a finger. He forgave his oppressors when they handed him over to be executed, and when soldiers spat in his eyes and punched him in the face, he held his nerve and took it on the chin. He could have fought back or rallied an army, but he didn't; he was 'meek', withholding his strength.

Yet when he saw others being wronged, then he flexed some muscle. His selflessness shone through, even when he was angry. And I do mean angry.

In a moment of calculated rage, Jesus stormed into the heart of the temple courts and flipped the tables upside down. As dirty money rolled in every direction, he drove out the animals and booted the money-changers from the temple.

In the words of the psalmist and of one of his disciples, 'Zeal for [God's] house' consumed him.[5]

For a westerner who has been subtly influenced by feeble stained-glass depictions of Jesus, it's a shock to discover that the historical Jesus was, at times, highly intimidating. Of course, those who knew him didn't find him intimidating, for they had witnessed his tender acts of mercy a thousand times. But in his final week, when he trashed the temple courts, nobody dared stop him.

Was this a military action?

So much for being a peacemaker.

Jesus was undoubtedly making a statement, but he wasn't inviting the sort of war that people expected. If the Romans had thought that he was a political threat, they would have intervened in an instant, but they held off – for a few days, at least. His antics didn't go entirely unnoticed.

His volcanic fury in the temple courts wasn't a political act as much as a prophetic act, a sign of what was to come, and a creative protest against the powers that be – like those occupying Wall Street, or the collapse of the Berlin wall or the Arab Spring protests.

There are some demonstrations from which you can't turn back.

'It is written . . . "My house will be called a house of prayer," but you are making it "a den of robbers."'

That statement is worth a thousand speeches.

The 'den of robbers' line was a window into the true desires of the religious elite, the Sanhedrin. They were the ancient equivalent of our government, an eclectic mix of religious leaders from different factions who ran the temple and held the power.

Roman history records the temple being 'covered all over with plates of gold, of great weight', funded by 'all the Jews throughout the habitable earth'.[6]

No wonder Jesus called them a den of robbers.

But he didn't just call them out on where they had gone astray; he also pointed them back in the right direction, to lead 'a house of prayer for all nations'.[7]

The original Jewish mandate was to lead all people groups into an encounter with God – that was the temple's ultimate purpose. In fact, it was God's plan from the very beginning. Abraham was not called 'the King of Israel' but 'the father of many nations'.[8]

That's a big difference.

Jesus' vision of real leadership wasn't about being the guy in charge; it was about serving the Jewish people, and ultimately every people group on earth. For the Sanhedrin to be stealing from the poor to feed the rich wasn't just an injustice; it was an abdication of their true calling.

Jesus took action.

He didn't come to repair the temple; he came to replace it.

'Destroy this temple, and I will raise it again in three days,' he declared.[9]

That meant far more than bricks and mortar.

RAW LEADERSHIP

For many people, Jesus' riot in the temple raises significant questions.

Why did he need to be so violent?

How does this fit with his life of peacemaking?

Perhaps his compassion and his zeal were two sides of the same face.

When you love someone, how do you feel when someone tries to hurt them? I recalled the wolves I had seen in the Negev and thought about the rise in attacks on children. If a parent were to look up and see a wolf leaping out of the undergrowth to attack their child, how would they respond? A rational loving parent would drop everything and charge at the wolf, yet nobody would be daft enough to say, 'Why would such a loving parent be so violent?' It is precisely because of their love for their child that they would vehemently fend off the wolf.

So it was with Jesus in the temple. People who manipulate Jesus' story to disrespect the Jewish people miss the point entirely. It was his love for the Jewish people and his compassion for the poor that drove him to confront their predatory rulers.[10]

It wasn't even the Jewish leadership en masse that Jesus was challenging, for there were good leaders among the ranks and Jesus was quick to befriend them. But at the rotten core of the Sanhedrin were a few corrupt families who ran the whole system like a religious mafia, paying off, killing and colluding with the Romans to get their way.

The archaeological evidence is difficult to avoid.

While the majority of Jewish peasantry scraped by in poverty, the High Priest relaxed in a 13,000 square foot, two-storey mansion with marble floors, elaborate mosaics and multiple bathrooms.[11] Roman historians described him as 'a great hoarder of money' who bribed Roman officials to keep his position.[12]

When soldiers came to collect food tithes from elderly priests, the High Priest instructed them to beat anyone who didn't cooperate. Some died from the beatings; others starved to death, having no food left to feed themselves.[13]

To kill off the elderly so you could enjoy second helpings in your marble-floored mansion was too much for Jesus. The people they were treading on were his people, his friends, his family. And if that wasn't bad enough, some in the Sanhedrin continued to pass judgement on the very people they were violating. Oh, the irony.

Jesus loved authenticity. Most of his teaching can be boiled down to the call to be authentic before God and man – no acting. When he saw the Sanhedrin exploiting the poor while pretending to teach them, he called them 'hypocrites', the Greek word for 'actors'.

For Jesus, there were two types of leader: true leaders and fake leaders. Some served their people, others wanted their people to serve them; some would lay down their life for their flock, others would sacrifice the flock to line their mansion with sheepskin rugs.

Yet while Jesus unleashed his fury on the temple leadership, the door was still open for them to change. He was ready to make peace as soon as they were. If the rich and powerful had repented of their exploitative antics and used their position to serve God and love the people, Jesus would have forgiven their past and welcomed them with open arms. In fact, many in the early Jesus movement did exactly that. Joseph of Arimathea, Nicodemus and Paul of Tarsus were all part of the leadership who joined Jesus' compassionate revolution.

Sadly, not everyone followed. Some rather liked being part of a corrupt leadership; it made for a comfortable life.

Not much has changed.

Corrupt leadership was one of the triggers of the Arab Spring; no people group will put up with being exploited forever. We crave real role models, and people can smell inauthenticity a mile off, even within the most sophisticated propaganda machines. Real leadership is about service, not style. Jesus knew this more than anyone.

'I am the good shepherd,' he told them. 'The good shepherd lays down his life for the sheep.'[14]

This might sound like a cute, fluffy metaphor to a western reader, but to the original audience it was a loaded statement. The 'good shepherd' was always a divine title.

'The LORD is my Shepherd,' sang King David in Psalm 23, and this divine shepherd theme echoed through the Jewish prophets all the way to Jesus.[15]

The prophet Ezekiel learned the 'shepherd speech' from the prophet Jeremiah, and when he saw Israel's leaders exploiting the poor, he pulled it out and gave them a roasting:

> Woe to you shepherds of Israel who only take care of yourselves! Should not shepherds take care of the flock? You eat the curds, clothe yourselves with the wool and slaughter the choice animals . . . You have not strengthened the weak or healed those who are ill or bound up the injured. You have not brought back the strays or searched for the lost. You have ruled them harshly and brutally.[16]

It was a fair assessment; he wasn't pulling any punches. Classic Ezekiel.

But the real surprise of Ezekiel's speech was the solution he promised: 'This is what the Sovereign LORD says: I myself will search for my sheep and look after them. As a shepherd looks after his scattered flock when he is with them, so will I look after my sheep.'[17]

When Jesus said, 'I am the good shepherd,' he was claiming to be the fulfilment of this ancient promise, that God himself would come and shepherd his flock.

And he proved it. There were many 'lost sheep' that the Sanhedrin looked down on – peasants and prostitutes, beggars and lepers, Samaritans and barbarians. Rather than sit back and judge them, Jesus went looking for them.

While the Sanhedrin were inventing pedantic rules in their ivory towers, Jesus was walking from village to village, healing the sick, teaching people to overcome both pride and prejudice, and building new communities of mercy and forgiveness.

This was Jesus' definition of leadership, his way of shepherding.

The Sanhedrin had abandoned the flock, so Jesus was on a rescue mission to get them back. And just to ram his point home, he trashed the temple.

SON OF MAN

It wasn't just the 'good shepherd' that had a divine echo to it; Jesus' favourite title for himself was 'the Son of Man'.

For a western audience, it seems like the least exciting claim you could possibly make. At least the shepherd has a job; a 'son of man' literally means 'a human'.

Wow! Well done. You're a human. That narrows you down.

But Jesus didn't call himself 'a son of man', he called himself, '*the* Son of Man', and there's a big difference between the two. The prophet Daniel was a distant relative of Jesus, and one of the most distinguished figures in Israel's history. He had a vision about a mysterious figure who he described as 'one like a son of man' who, while being fully human, also occupied a divine throne and ruled over an everlasting kingdom.[18]

The renowned Jewish academic David Flusser argues that this is the most potent of all the prophecies, for it promised that the Messianic figure would be not only an anointed human being, but also the very incarnation of God.[19] And as Jesus neared his final hour, he made it abundantly clear that this mysterious Messianic figure who sits on that heavenly throne was him.

Yet perhaps even that wasn't the greatest shock.

After identifying himself as the long-awaited divine human, he immediately stated that he would exercise his supreme authority by serving. Even dying.

'The Son of Man did not come to be served, but to serve, and to give his life as a ransom for many,' he told his disciples.[20]

Now there's a paradox.

In the Greco-Roman world, possessing power meant stamping on the people below you. To claim that you were the most powerful being in the universe and that you were choosing to exercise your matchless authority by *serving* people – that sort of logic just didn't exist in the first century.

Until Jesus turned up.

The 'good shepherd' and 'the Son of Man' both led down the same narrow path – the path of self-sacrifice. For Jesus, greatness and service were two sides of the same coin.

Some have ignored his call to service; others have missed his claim to divinity. Perhaps when we see both together, Jesus' actions start to make sense.

One of the fashionable ideas about Jesus is that he was a sort of inoffensive hippie who wandered around the ancient world saying beautiful things, being kind to cuddly animals and promoting a life of sublime gentleness. He never claimed to be God.

That view makes for a very palatable and convenient Jesus, but it's not the Jesus of history. To ride into Jerusalem to the worship of the masses was more than a suggestion of Messiahship; it was a demonstration. To openly forgive sins was to exercise divinity. To say things like, 'I and the Father are one,' was to claim equality with God. To replace the temple with himself left nothing to the imagination. To claim the divine titles of the 'good shepherd' and 'the Son of Man' was as blatant as it gets.

Jesus took the offices of Messiah, King and God and rolled them all into one, which is not the sort of thing an inoffensive hippie would do.

How do you respond to such wild statements?

What on earth would the Sanhedrin do?

Jesus had them backed into a corner. If they endorsed his divine status and joined his servant-hearted revolution, they would have a lot to lose.

Like a mansion or two.

If they didn't, they risked losing the thin veneer of authority they had bribed their way into, for the whole of Jerusalem seemed to be hanging on Jesus' every word.

They desperately needed to silence him, but that would be easier said than done. He had performed every Messianic miracle in the book and had won the hearts and minds of people all over the nation, even some from within the Sanhedrin who had defected to the Jesus movement when they saw he was the real deal.

But Jesus wasn't the only one with friends in the enemy camp.

The Sanhedrin were about to get a visit from one of Jesus' so-called friends.

Judas.

BETRAYAL

Every Friday night, Jewish families celebrate a traditional Shabbat meal before resting from work on Saturday and enjoying time with their family. Shabbat is an act of looking back and looking forward at the same time. They remember God saving them from exile in Egypt and look forward to the time of ultimate rest when God reinstalls his kingdom on earth.

I had the honour of celebrating Shabbat with several Jewish families during my time in Israel, and I visited the local synagogue with my host in Meitar. Once a year there was a festival like no other, not just a weekly Shabbat but a unique celebration of the day God rescued his people from Egypt, an event marked by the sacrifice of a lamb.

Passover.

Jesus timed his last week to coincide with the Jewish Passover, and the parallels were not missed by his followers.

'Look, the Lamb of God, who takes away the sin of the world!' cried his cousin, the enigmatic John the Baptist, when he saw Jesus among the crowds by the River Jordan.[21]

Three years later, Jesus was about to relate to the sacrificial lamb more than anyone realised. After a traditional Passover meal in the upper room, Jesus took his disciples out to the Mount of Olives for some peace and quiet.

This was common practice for many pilgrims to Jerusalem. Not everyone could afford to stay in the city; youth hostels hadn't been invented and sleeping under the stars in an olive grove was probably quite lovely.

But Jesus wasn't sleeping that night.

'They went to a place called Gethsemane, and Jesus said to his disciples, "Sit here while I pray."'[22]

The doctor, Luke, records that Jesus' sweat was like blood, which medically speaking may have been more than a metaphor.[23] Jesus wasn't hiding his anguish; he was painfully honest with his closest friends, telling Peter, James and John, 'My soul is overwhelmed with sorrow to the point of death.'[24]

In his final hour, Jesus surrendered to a higher purpose than saving his own skin.

That is what made him so different from everyone else that night.

In the cool of the garden, the disciples would have woken up to the noise of a multitude of soldiers weaving their way through the olive trees, flaming torches lighting their path, the silence of night pierced by the tramping of feet and the chink of metal.

Perhaps the quietest sound echoed the loudest.

A kiss.

Judas embraced Jesus with what sounded like the least threatening line in history, 'Greetings, Rabbi!' and kissed him on the cheek.[25]

The soldiers, waiting for the sign, stepped forward.

Some who are sympathetic to Judas believe that his betrayal was an act of faith, that by forcing Jesus' hand against the Romans he expected Jesus to finally overcome the enemy and be the king they were all waiting for. But Judas never called Jesus a king. In fact, he was the only disciple who deliberately avoided doing so, which is why most take a less sympathetic view.

A traitor is a traitor.

His disciples put up a fight, initially.

Brave.

Peter drew his sword and sliced off a soldier's right ear. Not bad for a fisherman. Unless he was going for the jugular. Jesus stepped in, healed the soldier's ear and asked his disciples to step down: 'All who draw the sword will die by the sword.'[26]

He didn't need them to fight for him; only to die with him, if they were willing.

They weren't.

They fled, leaving everything behind them: their past, their promises, their teacher. One guy, wriggling free from the guards, even abandoned his cloak and vanished into the night, naked. When the dust settled, nobody was left except Jesus and 'a crowd armed with swords and clubs, sent from the chief priests'.[27]

This night was destined to end badly.

I stopped for a while in the Garden of Gethsemane when I first visited Jerusalem and pondered the events that unfolded that night. It's one of the few sites in Jerusalem that has some resemblance to Jesus' time. Olive trees haven't changed much – they live for hundreds of years, sometimes thousands.

Peering through the spiny branches across the Kidron Valley, I was struck by the fact that Jesus would have gazed at the same view, knowing what awaited him. In the dead of night, he was bound, beaten and marched up the winding path to the gates of the city, through the narrow streets of Jerusalem to the home of Caiaphas, the High Priest.

CAIAPHAS

'High Priest' was the most distinguished title in Jewish society, apart from the Messiah, of course. The position was held for decades by one wealthy family, who were part of an old boys' club with all the other slimy elitists in Jerusalem, those who wormed their way into office by courting Caesar.

Officially the High Priest was chosen by God and revealed through the prophets, but this family were selected by the Romans, which is a bit different.

The mansion where they gathered was likely that of Caiaphas' family. John mentions his father-in-law, Annas, who continued to throw his weight around even after Caiaphas had taken office. It was always a family affair.

This would have been a special moment for both of them. For the past few weeks, Jesus had outwitted the corrupt priesthood in every argument, demonstrated his divine right to leadership with signs and wonders and won the affections of the very people they had been treading on. Caiaphas was facing the increasing threat of being chased out of office, sucked into a riot, losing face with his people or, worse still, losing favour with the Romans.

He must have feared everything that week.

Except for God.

To see Jesus standing before him, broken, beaten and utterly defence-less, in the marble courts of his mansion must have been a sweet sight to his jealous eyes. He called in a host of witnesses to nail him down and prepared for the planned verdict.[28]

But he missed the obvious flaw in his plan: Jesus was innocent. The witnesses couldn't agree, and there was little evidence that he had ever broken a command in the Torah. Jesus kept all the sacrificial laws, all the Kosher details, even the Sabbath; he just viewed the Sabbath as a day for 'doing good' rather than making up extra rules that only the rich could sustain, and it's tricky to get someone executed for the crime of 'doing good'.

But Jesus was never on trial for his good deeds; Caiaphas had a bigger axe to grind.[29]

'Are you the Messiah, the Son of the Blessed One?'

Jesus called his bluff. 'I am.'

You don't get a clearer confession that that, but Jesus was only just getting started. 'I am . . . And you will see the Son of Man sitting at the right hand of the Mighty One and coming on the clouds of heaven.'[30]

He affirmed the 'Son of God' identity, added Daniel's divine 'Son of Man' figure and threw in a hyperlink to the Messianic ruler that David had sung about in the Psalms.[31]

The High Priest tore his robes and screamed, 'Blasphemy!'

From that moment on, it started to get messy. The religious mafia started spitting in Jesus' face, then they wrapped him in a blindfold and lined up to take punches.

In that moment, as always, Jesus practised what he preached.

He turned the other cheek.

He wasn't passive, for he was quick to question their aggression, but he refused to retaliate with violence.

He had already demonstrated in the temple that he could handle himself in a riot, and he had an army of willing volunteers who would have taken up arms in his defence, if he had called on them.[32]

But he didn't. He chose to walk the path alone.

22.

THE VICTORY OF PEACE

THE FACT THAT a cross is celebrated as the emblem of the world's largest religion is, quite frankly, a bit weird. To its creators, it was the ultimate icon of suffering, humiliation and defeat. If you had suggested to the Persians, Greeks or Romans that a crucified carpenter would be viewed by more than two billion people as the King of kings, they would have died laughing.

Even in the modern secular West, the ultimate goal of a comfortable consumer life makes the idea of suffering for a higher purpose seem a little odd.[1] But not everyone sees a comfortable life as the ultimate goal.

My Syrian friends taught me, more than anyone, that there is more to life than a comfortable existence. Three families I interviewed turned down a quiet life to continue working with the poor and vulnerable on the fringes of the Mediterranean. For them, it was the obvious expression of their faith in another Middle Eastern pioneer, one who himself had turned down a quiet life.

Then there were the twenty-one martyrs on that Libyan beach, who paid the ultimate price for their faith. They made the decision to stand their ground rather than deny their faith, believing that the next time they opened their eyes, they would be in the presence of the one whose name they had uttered with their final breath.

It seems Jesus, like the martyrs who followed him, was no victim.

I wonder when he first saw Good Friday on the horizon.

Perhaps he always knew, or maybe, when his mother told him what an old prophet had spoken over him as a baby, the penny dropped.

Was there an echo of Easter in the first Christmas?

When Mary and Joseph first took Jesus to Jerusalem as a baby, only days old, an elderly man called Simeon held him in his arms and said, 'My eyes have seen your salvation, which you have prepared in the sight of all nations.'

Nice. But the second part carried an unusual tone: 'the thoughts of many hearts will be revealed. And a sword will pierce your own soul too.'[2]

Mary must have spent thirty years fretting about that prophecy. What was the sword bit about? Adversity has a habit of exposing the truth, for when disaster strikes, people show their true colours. Friends who over-promise get found out, traitors reveal their hand and those at the top discover a knife in their back.

But real heroes push forward in adversity, refusing to abandon their post.

'The thoughts of many hearts will be revealed.'

PETER

Peter may have fled in the garden, but he didn't entirely disappear into the night. He followed at a distance all the way through the city with his friend John, and together they snuck into the courtyard of the High Priest to see what was happening. Their entire world had just fallen apart. What was Jesus doing? Why didn't he defend himself? Perhaps he was just biding his time, choosing his moment?

Peter laid low in the courtyard, warming himself by a charcoal fire with the servants and soldiers. His face would have been barely recognisable in the dim glow; he would have looked like any other of the humble servants, hanging around, waiting to sweep the floors. Nobody would have noticed unless one of the real servants called him out.[3]

'You aren't one of this man's disciples too, are you?' It was the servant girl on duty.

Peter panicked and went into denial: 'I am not' Not so brave now. Peter knew what awaited him if he were to confess. Galilee had produced some wannabe messiahs before. When Peter was young, he would have seen the countryside around Nazareth 'decorated' with the crucified followers of Judas the Galilean, the revolutionary who dared to challenge Rome. A few years later, his sons, James and Simon, suffered the same fate.[4]

Now another Galilean Messiah was on trial.

Despite his early bravado, Peter backed down, but denying his connection to Jesus wasn't going to be easy, for Galileans had something of a northern accent. In the wealthy upper quarter of Jerusalem, a working-class Galilean would have blended in like a football hooligan at a royal garden party.

'Surely you are one of them; your accent gives you away.'

Peter kept up the story a second time: 'I don't know what you're talking about.'

Others started to join in the interrogation.

'Didn't I see you with him in the garden?' It was a relative of Malchus, the servant whom Peter had sliced up in the garden.

Now he was really in trouble.

Peter began to call down curses on himself as he denied any connection to Jesus, which can't have helped with the blend-in-with-the-posh-people plan.

As the words left his mouth, a sound echoed through the night, as cold as the kiss in the garden.

A rooster.

This was likely the sound of the temple crier, nicknamed the 'rooster' in Hebrew.[5] For Peter, that cry brought him back to the moment he had promised to defend Jesus to the death, hours earlier, during the last supper. Jesus had called him out on it at the time: 'This very night, before the cock crows, you will disown me three times.'

Peter had denied it passionately. 'Even if I have to die with you, I will never disown you.'[6]

As the rooster's cry rang out across the city, Peter was introduced to himself. At that very moment, his eyes met Jesus' eyes, as he looked up, across the courtyard into the central room of the High Priest's mansion.[7]

What must that look have felt like?

Peter ran away and wept.

I'm not surprised.

PILATE

From AD 6, after Herod Archelaus was dismissed for being too blood-thirsty, Caesar opted to rule Jerusalem with a Roman 'prefect'.[8] The job description was simple; keep the peace. As long as everyone worshipped Caesar and paid their taxes, everything was fine.

The Jews were never going to actually hail Caesar as Lord, so the prefect simply took their taxes and let them do their 'Jewish thing' quietly, as long as Roman soldiers could intervene whenever they felt necessary.

Which they did.

The fifth prefect was a man called Pontius Pilate, who is often portrayed in movies as a nice chap with a difficult job who was forced against his will into ordering an execution. History tells a different story. When Pilate raided the temple treasury for some spare cash, a crowd organised a peaceful protest, and, in an act of premeditated cruelty, Pilate had his soldiers secretly conceal daggers under their cloaks and surround them. On his signal, they cut everyone down with reckless abandon.[9]

That was Pilate's definition of 'keeping the peace'.

His antics had the ring of another supposedly 'Great' leader. There was some bloody déjà vu in first-century Judea. But while Pilate had no qualms with mass murder, he was in a tricky position. Oppression is expensive. The Romans didn't want to waste military resources in Jerusalem that were needed in the corners of the Empire, nor did they want to do anything that would inhibit tax collection. Pilate actually got into trouble with Caesar for being too brutal.[10]

His job description was to suppress the people, but not too much.

How does that work?

How do you win the begrudging favour of the very people you're simultaneously terrorising?

Perhaps a scapegoat can help.

When the Sanhedrin dragged Jesus in front of Pilate, he saw a perfect business opportunity. Jesus' actions were undoubtedly provocative, for he had openly accepted the mantle of king, which to the Romans was like a red rag to a bull. While Pilate rolled into Jerusalem from the west on the eve of the Passover, complete with a military entourage, Jesus was making a rival entry from the east with his own band of loyal supporters.

Only Jesus' followers weren't being paid to cheer his name.

Pilate didn't take kindly to anyone who claimed a degree of authority on his patch, but Jesus' kingship was clearly spiritual, not political, and Pilate knew Jesus was innocent. Jesus worked hard, paid his taxes and cared for people that Rome couldn't be bothered with. He even healed people from Roman households, so if anything he was quite useful. To add insult to injury, Pilate's wife told him that she'd had a dream about Jesus, confirming his innocence.[11]

But Pilate was more interested in striking a deal than defending the blameless.

When he saw a riot brewing, he had the savvy to realise if he sacrificed Jesus and gave the crowd what they wanted, they would calm down, get on with earning him his taxes and, if anything, they might think they owed him something.

To really sweeten the deal, he got to befriend the phoney king, Herod Antipas, who got to finish his father's business.

Everyone was a winner.

Except Jesus.

A small sacrifice for Pilate, so he thought.

All this time, Jesus stayed calm. He was not weak, not cowardly and certainly not a victim. He was the original definition of 'meek': he had the strength and the supporters to take on his oppressors, but he exercised the higher power to hold back, for reasons nobody understood.

Before he handed Jesus over to be crucified, Pilate ordered that he first be scourged, which would have really pleased the crowd.

That's leadership for you.

The soldiers stripped Jesus naked, tied him to a post, took a multi-stranded whip laced with metal and bone, and lashed his body until his bowels and bones were visible, front and back.[12] Jewish law limited the number of lashings to thirty-nine, but Roman soldiers hardly abided by Jewish law. By the time they tired of the torture, ribbons of flesh would have been hanging from Jesus' frame, pools of blood flowing down his legs and out across the courtyard.[13]

Sometimes victims of scourging couldn't even be identified afterwards, they were so marred from the lashing. On other occasions, people died from loss of blood. If the victim survived, they would certainly think twice about committing the same crime again, and so would anyone else who dared to watch. It was as much a deterrent as a punishment.

Before Jesus was scourged, he'd already been beaten up several times by various groups of soldiers, and after the flogging the *entire company* gathered inside for a proper laugh, weaving together a crown of thorns and pretending to worship him. Roman banter was a bit sick.[14]

The irony is, Jesus really did view his final hour as an inauguration of kingship, for he was about to win a victory that nobody expected.

Given their desire to give Jesus a royal mocking, it's clear the soldiers wanted to make an example of him, for Messianic insurrectionists they needed to provide a more significant deterrent than common thieves.

There is no way Jesus would have escaped with the bare minimum in his scourging.

Quite the opposite.

Perhaps the greatest surprise of his crucifixion is that he even made it to the cross.[15]

LAST WORDS

Eyewitnesses recall that when the crossbeam was strapped to Jesus' shoulders and he was marched out of the city, he collapsed on the road. Usually, soldiers would beat the soon-to-be-crucified subject to keep them going, but if Jesus were nearly dead, he would need some help.

The soldiers didn't want to soil their red robes with dirty blood, so on the spur of the moment they recruited a passer-by called Simon who was visiting Jerusalem from modern-day Libya.[16] With Simon's help, Jesus was dragged out of the city and nailed to a post by the side of a road.

Whole books have been written on the physical agony of the cruci-fixion, films have been made to correctly capture the true horror of it, and new language has been invented to convey the pain: the word 'excruciating' means 'from the cross'. But the real question in any murder is not *how* they died, but *why*?

I was taught that Jesus died to 'forgive my sins', which is very generous of him, but in all honesty, did he really need to? Couldn't I just say sorry? Couldn't he just say, 'It's okay, you're forgiven'? Up until this point, Jesus had forgiven people all over the place, he forgave the crim-inal who died next to him, and his mercy even extended to the soldiers who carried out his execution.

As they skewered his wrists to the wooden beam, he whispered through gritted teeth, 'Father, forgive them, for they do not know what they are doing.'[17]

The forgiveness alone was radical enough, but what did he mean by, 'they do not know what they are doing'? Perhaps those soldiers were part of something bigger than they realised.

What if Jesus' peacemaking mission was more than simply reconciling fractured communities? What if he came to make peace between humanity and the Divine?

I thought back to the very beginning of my journey.

In the bottom of a Chilean mine, thirty-three men pioneered the way of forgiveness better than anyone I've ever met. They knelt in the dust and prayed for mercy, they forgave one another for taking too much food or picking a fight, some even forgave the mining company who had got them into that mess. But for all that forgiveness, there was still the unresolved reality that they were buried alive under a lump of rock twice the weight of the Empire State building.

There was no way they were getting out of there by their own efforts, however hard they might try. And they really had tried. They'd entered that underground world, knowing the risk, and they all faced the consequences; that is why they cried out to the God who knew what it was to suffer the effects of a few bad decisions.

Perhaps, more than anything, the cross was about consequences.

If the consequences of every poor decision in human history were pooled into one moment, that would be a monumental burden for one man to carry. It's not that we're all terrible. I have done some good things in life, but I've also done things I'm rather ashamed of. I'm a mixed bag. Who isn't?

But a world of 'mixed bags' is hardly heaven on earth. Every decision has consequences, for better or worse. The world we've built is full of wonder and beauty, I've seen that in a thousand starry skies and in the hearts of kind strangers who've taken me into their homes. But that's not the whole picture, for the world is a long way from what it could be, from what it should be. I've also seen the darker side of human nature on this journey, in other people and in myself. Sometimes it appears in calculated moments, at other times in simple mistakes.

In my first night in the desert, my plan to get water had failed and I hadn't bothered with a backup plan. Pete was quick to forgive me (you find out who your mates are in times like that), but that still didn't change the fact that we were going to get pretty thirsty.

Until a kind stranger came to the rescue.

Isn't that what really happened on the cross?

Jesus didn't just forgive our sins; he suffered the full consequences of them.

The good shepherd became the sacrificial lamb.

By bearing the consequences of human selfishness, Jesus restored the peace with God that humanity had relinquished.

THE END OF SHAME

For followers of Jesus, his victory on the cross is a source of great comfort; it's why the cross is so prolific today, hanging on necklaces, tattooed on biceps and crowning buildings across the world. But have we become so familiar with it that we've forgotten something?

If you type 'Jesus' into Google Images, you'll likely get a few pictures of him on a tall, elegant cross, with a stylish robe to disguise his manhood, as he gazes down at a collection of worshipping figures on a green hill, at sunset. And while that's a very dignified image, it's hardly the truth.

The Romans crucified people naked. The shortage of timber meant that crosses were used repeatedly, so they were scuffed, rugged and soaked in other men's blood. Four-and-a-half-inch nails were driven through his wrists, and his ankles were pinned with another pair of four-and-a-half-inch nails, straddling the upright.[18] Jesus was not executed on the brow of a green hill, but slammed to a beam at eye level by the side of a busy road, where the maximum number of passers-by would see him.[19] His critics lined up to spit in his face, and soldiers sat back and gambled for the shirt off his back.[20]

As fluid slowly would collect around their heart and lungs, those being crucified would drown in their own bodily fluids. To survive longer, crucified criminals would push themselves upwards, gasping for air as their entire weight pivoted on the nails through their ankles.

Sometimes soldiers would slow down a crucifixion to maximise the humiliation by making a seat to support the criminal's torso, nailing their genitals to it so they couldn't move.[21] Other times, when a crucifixion needed to be hurried up, like when a body had to be removed before Passover, soldiers would break the criminal's legs so they'd slump down and suffocate more quickly. This was going to be the case with Jesus, but when they stepped up with the hammer, he was already dead. Some wonder whether this was the mercy of God that he went quickly, but it's more likely that he died faster than expected because the scourging had nearly killed him before he had even got to the cross.

A comparable scene today would see Jesus nailed to a signpost at the side of the main road out of town, so passing cars would see him, pedestrians could throw rocks or take sickening selfies, and stray dogs could lick the blood from his feet.

Why did it all have to be so vulgar?

Partly, that was just the Romans. They might have left us some straight roads, but their sense of justice left a lot to be desired.

But for Jesus, the cross was about another battle.

Every society in the ancient world agreed on one thing: the cross was for the shamed.[22]

That's why revolutionaries were crucified rather than just beheaded, for the axe was too quick. Rome wanted to shame them, for that would provide a greater deterrent. What could be more humiliating than hanging naked in front of your critics as you die slowly?

But Jesus turned that shame back on itself. As one first-century writer put it, 'For the joy that was set before him he endured the cross, scorning its shame, and sat down at the right hand of the throne of God.'[23]

That's the paradox of the cross, it had the power to shame its victims, but Jesus used it to remove the power of shame itself. He can now say to anyone who has been mocked and scorned and humiliated, 'I know how you feel; I've been there.'

But the whole ordeal was more than divine solidarity; it was the promise that there is life after death, there is dignity after shame. Friday may have been worse than anyone imagined, but Sunday was just around the corner. By going through hell and coming out the other side, Jesus demonstrated that shame never has the final word.

When Jesus looks at a football hooligan with a life of violence, on his knees pleading forgiveness, he doesn't just see a sinner; he sees a son, and he runs out to greet him. For anyone who feels ashamed of the hours they've spent indulging the images on their screen, or for anyone who's lied, cheated or stolen and been found out, or found *that* photo of themselves on social media, for those who have been abused, or have been the abuser, the sense of shame is crushing.

But rather than let us pickle in the poison of shame, Jesus drank that bitter cup on our behalf. He didn't go through it lightly; he went through it to win a victory we never could. By seeing beyond the shame of the cross, Jesus saw beyond the shame in all of us, and when shame is forgotten, peace can be fully restored.

Jesus' intention from the very beginning was to save people from their own poor choices. People missed it at the time, for what they thought they needed saving from was the Romans. No oppressed people will want to hear that you've come to save them from themselves.

But while Rome seemed like an insurmountable enemy at the time, it ultimately crumbled under its own weight. Every empire rises and falls, however undefeatable it might look at the height of its power. The British should know.

The full consequence of collective human selfishness is a far greater enemy than any one empire. Jesus wasn't interested in defeating the Romans and installing another government that would eventually become just as corrupt as the one it had overthrown.

His battle was not with the 'evil people'; it was with the evil *in* people – in all people.

Having lived the purest and most selfless life possible, he stepped into the firing line and absorbed the consequences of every sin, except his own.

RESCUE MISSION

In western cultures, our overexposure to the cross has inoculated us to the paradox of it, but in eastern cultures, this isn't always the case. The late teacher and scholar Nabeel Qureshi knew both. He grew up in the US, but within a strict Islamic family from Pakistan. He understood the clash of worldviews better than most, and the message of the cross was understandably ridiculed in his subculture. Why would the holiest power in the universe shame himself in such a way as to embrace the dirt and grime of humanity and suffer such an insidious end?

It's a fair question. I've been asked it myself.

Qureshi answers with another question: 'Let's imagine that you are on your way to an important ceremony and you are dressed in your finest clothes. You are about to arrive, just in time, but then you see your daughter drowning in a pool of mud. What would you do? Let her drown, and arrive looking dignified, or rescue her and arrive at the ceremony covered in mud?'

I have shared this story with people from all sorts of cultures over the years and they always have the same response: 'I would run in and rescue her.'

Qureshi presses the point a little deeper. 'Let's say there were others with you. Would you send someone else to save her, or would you save her yourself?'

The answer is obvious, but therein lies the true meaning of the story. As Qureshi explains, 'If you, being a human, love your daughter so much that you are willing to lay aside your dignity to save her, how much more can we expect God, if he is our perfectly loving Father, to lay aside his majesty to save us?'[24]

Qureshi's story resonated with me, for I drew parallels with the great escape of the Chilean miners. They too were trapped in a muddy pit; they too needed help to get out. The escape route was far from safe, so on the day of their rescue, one brave man went down with the capsule to check the tunnel for potential obstructions and prepare the miners for the ascent.

As Manuel González, the chosen rescue miner, descended into the deep, the mountain rumbled and groaned around him. A multitude of things could have gone wrong at any minute, but for González, it was a risk he was willing to take, for thirty-three men. Thirty-three fellow humans. Over the next twenty-four hours, he got to see every one of them walk free.[25]

For me, González's descent into the belly of the earth echoed that of another great rescue mission, by one who also came from the world above, who knowingly descended into a disaster zone, driven by a courageous love for those who could not rescue themselves.

But Jesus didn't just check in for twenty-four hours; he stayed for thirty-three years. He embraced the darkest corners of the world, with all its injustice and corruption, and suffered the indignity needed to pull us out of the grime we'd got ourselves into. Rather than just saying, 'I forgive you,' which would have been nice but ultimately powerless, he went a step further and absorbed the full consequences of our actions. He could have fought back against the Romans as they hammered him to the cross. He had both the right and the resources to do so. But he didn't.

He was meek. He harnessed his strength.

At three o'clock on a dark Friday afternoon, he made peace between humanity and God, defeating the real enemy with a final cry.

'It is finished.'

23.

LIFE

IN A SECLUDED spot a stone's throw from the Damascus Gate lies one of my favourite places in the world, The Garden Tomb. It's often left out of the tourist trail, and fortunately it hasn't been buried under a mountain of religious relics or caked in gold. It's just a garden. That is why I like it. An oasis of calm hidden from the hustle and bustle of the city streets.

In my pursuit of a 'pilgrimage to the first century', there was something about visiting a garden, free from surging crowds with cameras and flags, that felt more genuine. It may not be the site of the actual tomb – that's probably in the nearby Church of the Holy Sepulchre – although the gardeners didn't seem overly fussed either way. They were happy for people to experience something quietly authentic, as the women would have discovered at the tomb outside Jerusalem on a Sunday morning two millennia ago.

I took Louise, Dan Coe and Swe-Dan to visit early in the morning on their last day. It was before dawn and gloriously peaceful: a sanctuary in which to reflect on the morning when a small band of loyal sisters hurried to a garden tomb, armed with a barrel-load of spices to anoint Jesus' lacerated corpse and pay their last respects.

Of course, what they discovered was an empty tomb.

And the world has never been the same since.

The resurrection is the pivotal event of the Christian faith and, more than anything else, it is the event that has shaped my life too.

I didn't grow up in an especially religious world. I went to a standard comprehensive school, my mates were generally atheists and religion wasn't ever taken that seriously. My mum was convinced that there was 'something out there', and she had been faithfully searching for answers her whole life. The rest of my family didn't share her curiosity, and I doubt my sisters or I would ever have given it a second thought if it hadn't been for an enthusiastic vicar called Peter Hall. He was visiting our school to take an assembly and I remember him being brighter and more fun than my stereotype of boring religious people, so I went along to his youth camp. In between laps of go-karting and games of football, someone explained the thing Christians call 'the gospel', which is basically the story of Jesus. It means 'good news'.

I was always convinced it was exactly that – good news. Jesus was undoubtedly a stellar guy, that much is clear, but the real question for me was not, 'Is it good?' but, 'Is it true?' Britain may have a long supposedly Christian past, but few in the modern generation assume that the Gospel stories are actually true.

I decided to find out.

It was the late 1990s and the Alpha Course was just starting to take off.[1] Millions of people have now done Alpha all over the world, but in the early days it was an experiment of sorts. The idea was that people with no religious background could meet for dinner, hear about the life of Jesus and have a safe space to chat it through with other curious agnostics over coffee. It started at Holy Trinity Brompton in London, but within a few years it had reached the distant lands of my West-Country village, so I went along to my old school hall to hear what all the fuss was about. I even dropped out of rugby training so I could make it every week (I was never that good anyway, as my schoolfriends would happily tell you).

The resurrection came up on the first week, and I was relieved to discover that they didn't waste time discussing it as a nice philosophy or a theological idea. They cut to the chase.

'Did it happen?'

The conversation was only ever about the evidence.

That night started me on a journey to investigate the facts, and I haven't stopped in more than twenty years. It's the foundation I always come back to, the evidence I keep examining. When I sent a draft of this book to my good friend Matt, a fellow geographer and self-confessed atheist, he told me, 'You have to keep this chapter in, otherwise you're skirting the primary issue.'

He was right.

None of the stories in this book mean anything without the resurrection. The Chilean miners didn't pray to a dead God. Steph Lam's eye wasn't healed by positive thinking. The twenty-one martyrs on that Libyan beach held their nerve because they fully expected to meet their Saviour that very day.

Neither the miracles nor the martyrs make any sense if Jesus is in the tomb.

If he's still dead, then he would never have been victorious on the cross. The point is not that he identified with human suffering but that he overcame it. The scandal of Easter isn't just a rugged cross; it's an empty tomb.

Of course, this puts the whole thing in a rather precarious position. If the resurrection is a fairy tale, then my life has been in pursuit of an illusion, this journey has been for nothing, and two billion people worship a myth. Many believe this to be the case.

Including Christians.

It's the one thing ardent sceptics and passionate believers agree on. The resurrection matters. If it's not true, Christians are painfully deluded; if it is true, it changes everything.

I remember being part way through a stag do in London when a couple of lads were giving me a grilling about my faith. They were top lads and it was good chat. We were just a few drinks in, everyone's guard had dropped and there was slight fascination with someone who 'believes this stuff'.

One guy piped up, 'Of course, it doesn't really matter what you believe; the important thing is that your faith has helped you.' He was a kind bloke, and I appreciated the heart behind his reassurance. But if I believe a lie, whether it makes me feel nice or even inspires me to do good things is irrelevant. Granted, many Christians are good people, but so are many atheists. Faith in Jesus is infinitely more than a feel-good motivator to niceness – it's a living faith in a living God.

So if Christians are wrong about the resurrection, then, in the words of Paul of Tarsus, 'we are of all people most to be pitied'.[2]

But surely, in the twenty-first century, we can't believe that someone actually rose from the dead? It sounds so silly, it's easy to dismiss it without a second thought. Many have. But those who make a careful study of the evidence are often surprised to discover just how difficult it is to explain away the events of that Sunday morning.

Libraries of books have been written on this subject, and I can't summarise them all in one chapter, but sitting on a stone bench in a lush garden by an empty tomb on a cool February morning, as Louise hummed a tune next to me, I reflected on the few simple facts that changed my thinking.

THE EMPTY TOMB

Let's imagine that, two thousand years from now, somebody reads the story of the San José mine rescue and believes it to be a work of fiction. They would rightly point out that it's impossible that anyone could have made it out alive from that toxic underground dungeon, let alone thirty-three men. Consequently, they might assume that the 'rescue story' was added in later, as a better ending, perhaps by someone working for the Chilean government.

The first step in their search for truth would be to drill down and see if they could find thirty-three skeletons. Let's suppose that after a painstakingly careful dig, using the shiniest tools available in the year 4020, they make it down to the refuge and find . . . nothing.

No skeletons in the San José closet.

Suddenly the rescue story has a bit of weight to it. Of course, the bodies might have been stolen, but you can no longer dismiss the miracle of San José as complete fiction.

Two millennia ago, the powers-that-be in Jerusalem faced a similar situation. From the Sanhedrin and their spin-offs, to Herod and his cronies, to Pilate and his soldiers, the last thing any of them needed, having finally nailed down this rogue Messiah, was an account of a resurrection to give people hope again. Hope is dangerous. They needed to quickly dismiss any talk of a resurrection, and there was one sure-fire way to do that.

Find a body.

They never succeeded.[3]

Any suggestion that they went to the 'wrong tomb' fails to consider just how determined the authorities were to find the body. They would have left no stone unturned in the search. The 'tomb theft' theory is similarly far-fetched for it's difficult to conceive how any of his disciples could have overpowered the elite group of soldiers who were guarding the tomb and stolen the body without a trace. And this is not to mention the fact that the disciples were in hiding, for fear that they'd meet the same fate.[4]

But still, an empty tomb alone doesn't prove a resurrection. We need some more concrete evidence.

THE SURPRISE OF THE RESURRECTION

Then, as now, one of the key sources of evidence for any detective is the testimony of eyewitnesses, and the interesting thing about the eyewitnesses to the resurrected Jesus is how surprised they all were to see him. There was no danger of confirmation bias in their testimonies. To the contrary, their shock and scepticism is recorded in embarrassing detail.

In fact, one of the key witnesses had doubted Jesus from the beginning.

His little brother.

James lived and worked, laughed and cried, toiled and sweated with Jesus his whole life. I caught a glimpse of that sort of proximity to someone on the first frontier of the desert trail. Pete and I shared every moment. We endured the long, hot days and the ice-cold nights shoulder to shoulder, like brothers.

But that was only a week.

James lived shoulder to shoulder with Jesus for the best part of thirty years, and when Jesus announced his Messianic mandate, James thought he was crazy.[5] He even tried to talk him out of it, and for good reason. They both grew up seeing what happened to so-called Galilean messiahs.

When Jesus was pinned to a rugged cross, James' worse fears were confirmed – that his big brother had become yet another revolutionary, paying the price for delusions of grandeur.

But after meeting the resurrected Jesus in the flesh, James was utterly transformed. He went on to lead the first church in Jerusalem, and he lived and died for his testimony to the resurrection.[6] In fact, he no longer called himself 'James, the little brother of Jesus', but 'James, a servant of God and of the Lord Jesus Christ'.[7]

No brother would make that kind of confession, let alone experience that sort of change of heart, without some concrete evidence. And he wasn't the only one.

When the disciples first heard the report of the empty tomb from Mary and Joanna, they considered it 'nonsense', and Thomas claimed, 'Unless I see the nail marks in his hands and put my finger where the nails were . . . I will not believe.'[8]

Far from rebuking his lack of faith, Jesus was happy to oblige.

In fairness to the disciples, their initial shock is understandable, for nobody was expecting Jesus' resurrection. In first-century Jewish thinking, 'resurrection' meant the full-scale rebirth of all righteous Jewish people to a new age where Israel rules the world. The idea that the Messiah would come back from the grave halfway through history and inaugurate a different version of this brave new world for every people group was unheard of.

Unless, of course, it happened.

The eyewitness accounts of Jesus' resurrection are like nothing the Jews were expecting, nor do they bear any resemblance to Greek or Roman history. The pagan religions believed the gods were capricious brutes with animal instincts who stepped into the mortal world to rape, pillage and destroy.

Jesus lived, died and rose again to serve people.

This was preposterous in Greco-Roman culture.[9]

On Easter Sunday, Jesus didn't ride into Jerusalem on a war horse, shouting, 'I told you so,' nor did he go on a revenge-motivated killing spree through Rome declaring an alternative political state. Jesus simply turned up, unannounced, to a range of ordinary people and demonstrated calmly and physically that he was alive, and that the cross and resurrection had been his plan from the very beginning. The unexpected, apolitical and very human nature of the resurrection accounts makes them far more credible to the modern historian than sensationalised accounts or Roman-style legends.[10]

They were something entirely new.

Specific, detailed, unpolished eyewitness testimonies.

Highly authentic. And painfully honest.

SHEER HONESTY

If you had wanted to make up a story in the Ancient Middle East and expect people to believe you, you wouldn't have written the Gospel accounts. To start with, the testimony of women was largely ignored in a court of law.[11] Jesus may have viewed men and women as co-equal, but few others did, including the disciples. It would have been incredibly tempting for the Gospel writers to gloss over the women and claim that Peter and John were the first eyewitnesses.[12]

They didn't.

The only conceivable reason that they told the story as they did was that, quite simply, it's what happened. To add insult to injury, the Gospel accounts don't portray Peter, James and John, or indeed any of the disciples, in a very favourable light. The women showed courage, faithfulness and loyalty, but the men acted like cowards. Humility may be valued in some modern cultures, but in the ancient world, to be frightened wouldn't be modest; it would be embarrassing. In fact, embarrassing details are one of the tools historians use to assess whether an account is genuine. People don't fabricate embarrassing details; on the contrary, they tend to downplay them or cover them up. If a story is packed with incriminating confessions, it's a clear indication that they're telling the truth.[13]

Another mark of validity lies in the fact that while the four Gospel accounts agree on the key facts, there are minor differences in peripheral details. While some have seen this as a flaw, the reality is that if all four accounts had been utterly identical, the obvious conclusion would be that someone had 'touched them up'. But no such tweaking was tolerated, minor differences were left in, and the accounts were faithfully recorded as the eyewitnesses gave them. The historian Professor Paul Maier explains that 'variations in the resurrection narratives tend to support rather than undermine their authenticity'.[14]

I experienced the same minor variations in the interviews I gave.

When I met José Henríquez in his home town in the Chilean lakes, he told me how they had survived for seventeen days in the depths of the mine because God had miraculously cleaned the dirty water when they had prayed over it. But the following week, when I interviewed his friend Omar Reygadas in the desert streets of Copiapó, he told us that God had 'put something in our bodies' so they could miraculously survive by drinking heavily polluted water.

Who was right?

Perhaps they were just lucky, or they had tough stomachs?

Whatever your opinion, few people would say, 'Well, they must be making it all up, then; the Chilean mine rescue never happened.' Eyewitness accounts to major historic events always contain minor variations.[15] Fictional writers have the luxury of crafting carefully choreographed accounts where all the details line up perfectly, but real eyewitness accounts of real-life events are far more chaotic. The unpolished nature of the resurrection narratives point, not to a slick scandal, but to honest testimonies that 'reek of a humbling authenticity'.[16]

GOING ON RECORD: WHAT'S IN A NAME?

It takes a lot of courage to go on record. There are stories I encountered on this journey that I don't have permission to share. Some people asked to be left out, others had their names changed, but there were also those who wanted to go 'on record', people who were willing to be named and identified.

It was the same in the first century.

Going on record as a witness to the resurrection wasn't an easy decision. There was no witness protection. Some people chose not to testify and others were given protective anonymity, yet there were also the brave souls who gave the sort of details that meant people could track them down and interrogate their witness statements.[17]

The most common names in Jewish Palestine were Simon and Mary, so to make their identities crystal clear, the Gospel writers gave them nicknames and distinguishing details so that people could find them. We do the same today. You might know a Scottish Sarah, a Man Utd Mike or an Aussie Dave. In the Gospels we have Simon of Cyrene, 'the father of Alexander and Rufus', who carried Jesus' cross; 'Mary the wife of Clopas', who witnessed the crucifixion; Joseph, 'a rich man from Arimathea' and 'a member of the Council' who laid Jesus' body in the tomb. There was also 'Mary Magdalene' and 'Joanna, the wife of Chuza, the manager of Herod's household', who were the first witnesses to the resurrection.[18] These are not vague details; they're 'Come and find me' statements.

Many of the names in the Gospels are given these identifying details. There were 'James and John, the sons of Zebedee', whom Jesus nicknamed, 'sons of thunder', 'Thomas the twin', and, of course, Simon whom Jesus nicknamed 'Peter', which means 'Rocky'.[19] It wasn't long before everyone seemed to know Rocky in Jerusalem. The Gospel writers gave these identifying details so that the eyewitnesses could be tracked down and questioned about what they had seen.

In fact, many of them were questioned.

Many of them were tortured for their testimony.

Many of them died.

None of them broke.

If there's one thing we can tell from the resurrection accounts, it's that the eyewitnesses were utterly transformed by what they had seen. Even Peter, whose faith up until that point had always been, well, a little rocky.

TRANSFORMERS

Despite their fear and disbelief when Jesus died, within a few days the eyewitnesses made a shocking announcement: the cross was Jesus' plan to overcome sin and death, and his resurrection proved that it was 'mission accomplished'.

What causes a transformation like that?

The disciples went from petrified mourners, hiding behind locked doors, to fearless witnesses proclaiming a risen Saviour with unbreakable joy.

The writer Philip Yancey reflects:

> That eleven men who had deserted Him at death now went to martyrs' graves avowing their faith in a resurrected Christ . . . this remarkable sequence of transformation offers the most convincing evidence for the Resurrection. What else explains the whiplash change in men known for their cowardice and instability?[20]

Yancey echoes the conclusion that many of the great scientific minds of history have reached. The French mathematician Blaise Pascal argued in his famous, *Pensées*:

> The human heart is singularly susceptible to fickleness, to change, to promises, to bribery. One of them had only to deny his story under these inducements, or still more because of possible imprisonment, tortures and death, and they would all have been lost. Follow that out.[21]

Of course, many people in history have been willing to die for their beliefs. But people don't die for a story *they know they've made up*, holding to their little fib under torture and interrogation. In every comparable example, somebody has caved in, but the witnesses to the resurrection never caved in. They told the truth, the whole truth and nothing but the truth, regardless of the consequences.

The Syrian writer, Nadim Nassar, explains:

None of them possessed the intellectual ability to plot and weave such an incredible story, that, 'Jesus rose from the dead.' And which of them would be ready to die for such a self-created fantasy? We know that most of the disciples died for their faith. During my life in the Middle-East, I met many people who were ready to go to their deaths for their political or ideological beliefs. But none of them would have done that while knowing that their beliefs were false.[22]

Most historians, religious and non-religious, now agree that the disciples must have seen *something*, so those who don't believe in the resurrection resort to 'other' explanations for the disciples' experiences.[23]

Perhaps they were so bewildered by post-traumatic stress that they slipped into a trance and genuinely thought that they had seen Jesus. Of course, spiritual revelations are not uncommon, nor are they disingenuous, for it seems God often speaks to people in dreams and visions – I've seen that at several stages on this journey. [24]

The early disciples were well acquainted with dreams and visions,[25] but what they encountered on Easter Sunday was something altogether different. Jesus didn't appear as a vision, or an angel, or a mysterious figure in a momentary vision; he came back and lived with them for weeks, in full view of hundreds of eyewitnesses, flesh and bone, walking and talking, living and breathing, eating and drinking.[26]

People in hallucinations don't make a fire on the beach and cook breakfast.

The proof of the pudding is in the eating.

AN UNEXPECTED TRUTH

In light of the evidence, some have suggested that maybe Jesus didn't die in the first place, for if he had slipped into unconsciousness on the cross and been taken down early, he might have woken up later in the cool of the tomb.

Perhaps, historically, this is the most questionable theory of all. If there was one thing the Romans were good at, it was killing people. You don't conquer the known world for half a millennium by failing to notice when a dying criminal has simply fallen asleep.

Besides the medical record that Jesus nearly died from loss of blood before he even arrived at the cross, being impaled in four places through several major arteries is not the sort of treatment that allows someone to come back from the brink.

When a victim of crucifixion was dead, the soldiers double-checked the deceased by driving a spear through their lung and into their heart. Besides the lack of response from the body to a giant stabbing, the flow of water and blood demonstrated the accumulation of mixed fluids around the heart and lungs. This pleural effusion caused them to asphyxiate – a common form of death on the cross, if they hadn't already died from loss of blood. Jesus experienced all the above. He was scourged, suffocated and stabbed. Repeatedly.

The Roman centurion whose full-time job was to execute people (and whose life depended on his getting it right) confirmed to Pilate that Jesus was dead, with the full agreement of the other witnessing soldiers.[27]

One of Jesus' secret followers, Joseph of Arimathea, who had defected from the Jerusalem elite, took Jesus' body, with Pilate's permission, wrapped him in linen cloths and buried the corpse in his own tomb, with the help of his friend, Nicodemus.[28]

The idea that an utterly lacerated body, impaled in multiple places, twice confirmed dead, stabbed through the chest with a spear and almost entirely drained of blood, left unhindered in a tomb for three days with no medicine, no food and no water could 'come round' after a little snooze, roll away a tonne of rock and single-handedly overpower all the soldiers, thanks to the unparalleled strength of a good old sleep, is more than a little far-fetched. Even the critics of the Jesus movement have long considered the swoon theory impossible.[29]

Whatever we know about Jesus' body when he went into that tomb, it was that he was dead. And whatever we know about his resurrection appearances, it's that he was in shockingly good health.

All this leads to one rather bizarre conclusion.

It seems that the Jesus whom people met on Easter Sunday was not a corpse or a ghost or an illusion, or even a guy who had woken up from a long sleep looking like it was the morning after the night before.

He was a dead man who was alive again.

He looked a little different from the Jesus they had seen three days earlier, for if he had emerged as a lacerated victim of Roman torture, he would have looked quite petrifying. He had remnants of the old body, but qualities of the new. His scars were miraculously healed, but not entirely hidden, as 'doubting Thomas' discovered.[30]

In the words of C. S. Lewis:

> Christ had defeated death. The door which had always been locked had for the very first time been forced open . . . The Resurrection narratives are not a picture of survival after death; they record how a totally new mode of being has arisen in the Universe: as new as the first coming of organic life.[31]

THE STORY CONTINUES

For me, one of the most convincing indications that something extraordinary happened on Easter morning is that the evidence keeps coming.

In the days that followed, a vast spectrum of eyewitnesses, mostly former sceptics, testified to having met the man himself, restored to perfect health, walking and talking with people in every corner of society. There were Jews and Greeks, men and women, humble fishermen and learned rabbis.

Hundreds of eyewitnesses flooded out across the land, and a movement of transformed souls spread like wildfire through every corner of society.

One guy even met Jesus on his way to kill Christians in Syria.

That was unexpected.

He wouldn't be the last one to share such a testimony.

The military superpower that hammered Jesus to a wooden cross and torched his followers couldn't stop the revolution that began that Sunday morning. In Rome, the Emperor Nero had the Christians rounded up, crucified, torn apart by wild beasts and set on fire on poles to illuminate his garden parties. It was supposed to inject fear and shame into the Christians, but the Roman historian Tacitus reports that the opposite happened. There arose among Nero's guests 'a feeling of great compassion', for everyone knew the Christians were innocent.[32] Within a few years, Nero was chased out of office, while the early Jesus community continued to flourish, until it eventually eclipsed the very empire that had once tried to destroy it.[33]

In fact, every military dictatorship that has tried to destroy it since has ultimately failed. From the amphitheatres of ancient Rome to the beaches of modern Libya, whenever an agent of terror has tried to stamp out the fire, they have only succeeded in spreading the sparks.

The movement is unquenchable.

More than two billion people now worship Jesus in every corner of the world, while Caesar's name is remembered as a chicken salad.

How the tables have turned.

The state's love for relentless power blinded it to a revolution powered by relentless love.

The same is true today.

Some have encountered the iron fist of persecution; others have experienced the velvet glove of compromise. Neither has worked. The movement lives on, the miracles keep coming and the revolution, like its founder, has become rather difficult to keep down.

If Jesus really did rise from the dead on that glorious Easter morning, we really shouldn't be surprised that he's still on the move. Of course, this raises many more questions and I don't have all the answers; if anything, I have more questions now than when I started. But my aim was never to tie up every loose end; it was simply to be a witness, to unearth the evidence in the first century and to interview unsung heroes in the twenty-first century, those who continue to pioneer the movement he inaugurated.

This book is but the tip of the iceberg, the few stories I have obtained consent to share. I have witnessed divine fingerprints in every corner of the globe, and while one story alone could be explained away, as the same patterns have emerged in every culture, for me, the groundswell of evidence has become too big to sweep under the carpet.

Or hide in an empty tomb.

That's why, for me, the resurrection is the ultimate game changer. It's the evidence that points to a higher love, a sign that peace between God and humanity is now possible, and that a brave new world is waiting for anyone willing to embrace it. It's the truth that sits behind all the testimonies on this journey, from the mines of Chile to the deserts of the Middle East.

It's a story that everyone can be part of, anyone willing to lay down their own agenda and follow the way of a carpenter from Nazareth, the refugee who became a rabbi who became a revolutionary, and who sealed the deal with the resurrection.

EPILOGUE

THE BREAKFAST THAT CHANGED THE WORLD

ON THE SANDY beaches of Galilee, after an unsuccessful night of fishing, over a simple breakfast of fresh fish, the resurrected Jesus commissioned the movement that has now spanned the globe.

The disciples had gone back to the thing they used to do, once upon a time, before Jesus turned their world upside down. Fishing.

Why?

For Simon Peter, he must have lived with the genuine fear that he'd blown it. What right did he have to be the leader of Jesus' movement when he had deserted Jesus in his hour of need?

It wasn't just Peter; all the disciples were in the same boat. They'd all failed. And now Jesus was on the beach, calling them in for breakfast.

How awkward must that breakfast have been?

Perhaps Peter's own words were ringing in his ears, 'Lord, I am ready to go with you to prison and to death.'

How long did that last?

What did Peter say as Jesus slapped a fresh fish on the charcoal fire and watched it sizzle? 'Um, by the way, sorry for denying you in your hour of death.'

That would have sounded a bit lame. The silence must have been tangible. It wasn't the first time Peter had met Jesus' eye while standing by a charcoal fire.

Jesus invited Peter for a little walk down the beach. Moment of truth. I bet his heart was beating.[1]

'Simon son of John, do you love me more than these?'

That's got to hurt.

'Yes, Lord,' he said, 'you know that I love you.'

If I had been in Jesus' position, I might have replied, 'THEN WHY DID YOU DENY ME IN MY HOUR OF NEED, YOU COWARD?'

Jesus came up with something altogether different: 'Feed my lambs.'

What?

Nobody saw that coming, least of all Peter.

'Simon son of John, do you love me?'

There it is again.

'Yes, Lord, you know that I love you.'

Jesus replied, 'Take care of my sheep.'

Where was he going with this? A third time he asked him, 'Simon son of John, do you love me?'

Peter couldn't take it any more. 'Lord, you know all things; you know that I love you.'

It's a reasonable defence. If Jesus knew all things, he would know that Peter loved him.

And he did.

'Feed my sheep.'

Jesus was doing what he had done from the very beginning.

Shepherding.

Any shepherd knows that sheep are foolhardy, easily led, liable to get lost and prone to making mistakes. A bit like people. The word 'pastor' comes from the Latin word for 'shepherd'.

Three times Peter denied Jesus and three times Jesus asked him, 'Do you love me?'

But rather than dig the knife in, Jesus did the opposite. He forgave Peter.

And forgiven means forgotten.

As far as Jesus was concerned, his crucifixion had paid the price for Peter's moment of failure, just as it had paid the price for every human failure before and since. Peter's guilt and shame were left behind, like the empty tomb.

But what happened on that quiet Galilean beach was more than just forgiveness. It was a recommissioning, a second chance. If Peter was going to be a pastor, he would have to learn how to forgive people, to give them a second chance. What better way to teach Peter this lesson than for him to experience it himself?

Contrary to all expectations, Jesus doesn't give up on people, even failures like Peter. Peter realised that in his own strength he couldn't even lead himself, let alone a movement, but Jesus wasn't leaving him alone – he was going to help. It was Jesus' plan all along, for he had said so before any of this happened.

During the last supper, Jesus had warned Peter that he would be tested, and he rightly predicted that Peter would fail, despite his bold assurances. But he had also said, 'I have prayed for you, Simon, that your faith may not fail. And when you have turned back, strengthen your brothers.'[2]

Jesus had Peter's second chance planned before he even screwed up.

That's a serious friend.

The way Jesus dealt with Peter is the way I've seen him deal with everybody I have met on this journey. Jesus was obsessed with giving people a second chance. It's the thing that drove him his whole life, and even to his death. He loves to take a team of nobodies with a questionable past, dust them off, forgive their faults and make them something greater than they ever believed possible.

Peter could have spent the rest of his days trapped in a prison of guilt and shame, but instead Jesus set him free. Free to flourish. Free to lead a movement. In fact, Peter went on to become a model 'shepherd'.[3]

It's the same today. I've met people all over the world whom Jesus has released from the most impossible situations and empowered to be pioneers in his servant-hearted revolution. The Chilean miners were freed from a physical prison seven hundred metres underground to become role models of unity in a bickering world. The Syrian refugees I met were released from a prison of tribalism and fear to become voices of love and service to other refugees, regardless of their race or religion. There were the heroes of my home town, the football hooligans set free from a life of violence, and the community houses liberating people from a lifetime of loneliness.

There were the peacemakers I met in Bethlehem, setting people free from a conflict that has existed for millennia, giving a new generation the chance to overcome fear with love.

It's not that every story has ended happily ever after. Jesus never promised that it would, but for those whose husbands and brothers and sons were beheaded on a Libyan beach, the surprising fact is that they are not trapped in a lifetime of bitterness and mourning. To the contrary, they have found in Jesus someone who understands their pain, who has walked the same rough road himself and experienced the same loss.

These people have become the keys to other people's healing, voices of solidarity in a world of other widows and martyrs.

In fact, some of the freest people I've met are those who have suffered the most.

The happiest person I met on this entire journey was Karim, the man who was almost burned to death as a boy in Syria. Never have I met someone so free from hatred, so full of love. I still remember his scars; I can still see his beaming face.

When I met him, I felt free, too.

That's the freedom Jesus calls everyone into. Virtually his last words to Peter were the same as his first words to him: 'Follow me.'[4]

It's the same invitation he gives to all of us. Not, 'Obey these rules,' or, 'Say these words,' or, 'Support this political group,' or, 'Oppose these other people,' or even, 'Join this religion.'

Just, 'Follow me.'

Peter left his nets and followed Jesus, and three years later, after all his faults were forgiven and he was offered a second chance, he did the same again.

That's really all Jesus asks of us.

It's a big ask, to surrender everything, but it's only what he's already done for us. As always, he practises what he preaches. At no stage did he hold back for us, in life or death. So, more than anyone else, he can be trusted when he asks us to take the same leap of faith.

For some, following Jesus is about 'getting into heaven', but it seems Jesus was more interested in getting heaven into earth.[5] Everything he modelled in his earthly life – sacrificial love, radical forgiveness, kindness to his enemies, freedom from tribalism, healing from sickness, courageous humility – was an echo of the culture of heaven, a culture he wants us to embody right here, right now. He calls his followers not into a boring life of sitting around, waiting to be taken up into the clouds, but a dangerous life of bringing life and freedom into the darkest of places on earth.

For me, the starting moment in a life of following Jesus was caught in the prayer that has sustained me through this entire journey, the prayer I learned from José Henríquez: 'Lord, I'm not the best of men, but have mercy on me.'

In a moment of humility you can begin a lifetime of adventure. I don't know what your life would look like if you were to choose to follow Jesus. It might be miracles, it might be martyrdom, but I doubt it will be mediocrity.

I don't know what the future holds for me, either. But based on everything I've learned from everyone I've met on this journey; they would all say the same thing.

'It's worth it.'

SPIRIT

How do we access this divine figure, now that he isn't physically walking the dusty streets of Jerusalem? When Jesus left his early team to continue the movement, he gave them the timeless reassurance that he'd be with them in Spirit.

What does that mean?

For me, the phrase, 'I'll be with you in spirit,' is sometimes just a polite cop-out that really means, 'I can't come to your event because I'd rather stay at home and watch the football.'

Is that really what Jesus meant?

His exact words were, 'But you will receive power when the Holy

Spirit comes on you; and you will be my witnesses in Jerusalem, and in all Judea and Samaria, and to the ends of the earth.'[6]

What does that look like?

Fifty days after Jesus had left, it was the Jewish festival of Pentecost, and the disciples were still in Jerusalem. Waiting.

Luke records that 'a sound like the blowing of a violent wind came from heaven and filled the whole house where they were sitting'.[7]

The impact of this on those present was both powerful and comical. Some observers thought that they were drunk, but others noted that the miraculous signs that accompanied them were more than the actions of people who are a bit tipsy. Peter addressed the gathering crowd and informed them in no uncertain terms that what was happening was the fulfilment of an ancient Jewish prophecy that God would finally pour out his Spirit on all people.

That got their attention.

Then he did exactly what Jesus predicted: he became a witness.

'Jesus of Nazareth was a man accredited by God to you by miracles, wonders and signs, which God did among you through him . . . and you, with the help of wicked men, put him to death by nailing him to the cross. But God raised him from the dead.'[8]

It was a bold move.

The same Peter who couldn't bring himself to say to a servant girl on Good Friday that he even knew Jesus was now publicly proclaiming, '*You*, with the help of wicked men, put him to death . . .'

That's not pulling any punches.

Wherever did he get this boldness?

Was it the courage of a man who had physically witnessed the resurrection?

Was he coming good on his second chance?

Or was he simply filled with the Spirit of God, as Jesus said he would be?

Perhaps it was all of the above.

One thing is for sure: from that moment on, there was no going back. The movement that began in Jerusalem on that morning has rippled out across the entire world and the same signs and wonders that accompanied Peter when he was filled with the Spirit have followed countless others who have taken on the mantle of a witness.

Even today.

For some, the mysterious 'wind' at Pentecost may seem like something of a metaphor. But for the Chilean miner Omar Reygadas, the wind is more than a casual turn of phrase. When he cried out to God in the depths of the San José mine, a physical wind literally swept up through the dark corridors of his underground world, restored his breathing and sent the miners on a desperate hunt for the origin of this life-giving breeze.

Its source was never found, but its effects were impossible to deny. If an inexplicable wind can show up at the bottom of a Chilean mine, is it really so surprising that the same should have happened in Jerusalem when people cried out to God, just as Omar did?

Of course, not everybody who chooses to follow Jesus gets caught up in a divine whirlwind. It's not my experience, but the evidence I have seen certainly suggests that when Jesus said, 'I'll be with you in Spirit,' he really meant it.

Some have experienced life-giving miracles; others have radiated a divine presence even at the point of death.

The Celtic believers, praying on the fringes of Ireland through centuries of British oppression, described the places where people sensed God's presence most powerfully as 'thin places'. Their experience was that in certain areas, especially areas with a long history of prayer, the barrier between heaven and earth became so 'thin' that miracles seemed to flow like a river.

Perhaps I found one of those 'thin places' in the dark valleys of the Negev, when a sudden and gentle conviction led me out of a dead end and on to a hidden path to safety.

For some, it's not so much a sense of God's Spirit that awakens their attention, but a tuning in to his voice. How did a mysterious prophetess from Argentina know that José Henríquez would emerge from his underground prison and then travel the world testifying about Jesus?

That's a bold prophecy for an ageing Chilean miner who doesn't even like flying – especially one whom people had given up for dead. But as he boarded a plane to The White House at the start of a world tour, who could doubt that this prophetess had some uncanny insight?

And she wasn't the only one.

What about the Middle Eastern believers? And what about the dreams of Layla, Zain's wife, or the miraculous healing of their daughter? To this day, I've encountered many extraordinary miracles in the life of the Middle Eastern church; the ones in the book are only the beginning.

Perhaps the most exciting thing about the mysterious presence of God is that we're no longer bound to times and places and religions. If God can turn up by his Spirit at a crowded house at Pentecost, or in the middle of a desert or at the bottom of a Chilean mine, then nobody need travel from far and wide to offer sacrifices, at great expense, to a religious hierarchy in an old temple.

Those days are over. As King David sang, in his shepherding days:

> Even though I walk through the valley of the shadow of death,
> I will fear no evil,
> for you are with me.[9]

Can the 'valley of the shadow of death' really play host to the presence of God? Is anywhere off limits? David clearly didn't think so, for in another of his vintage lyrics he sang:

> Where can I go from your Spirit?
> Where can I flee from your presence?
> If I go up to the heavens, you are there;
> if I make my bed in the depths, you are there.[10]

José shared these exact words with us as he summed up his journey with thirty-three men who '[made their] bed in the depths' and knew God's presence with them.

It was the same divine presence that transformed a bunch of frightened fishermen into a team of fearless revolutionaries two millennia ago.

He seems to have a knack for bringing an unbreakable peace to the most unlikely of people. And by 'peace', I don't mean the mere absence of conflict, but a deep joy, a state of complete wholeness and harmony, even in the midst of hardship. When this peace takes root in people, it starts to show, they become peacemakers themselves and, little by little, they transform the world around them.

They are part of a movement that is still unfolding, right here, right now.

The question is, will you join it?

ACKNOWLEDGEMENTS

This book would never have seen the light of day, if it weren't for several people for whom I am eternally (and daily) grateful for. Special thanks to:

My community in Bristol for journeying with me in the long days of research and writing, and for being there when I phoned from the desert for prayer reinforcement, especially Em and Chris, Anna, Ellie, Kirstin and Alison.

Dieks Anthony and Pete Torrance whose wisdom, prayers and brotherhood kept me strong, and to the rest of the Torrance family, especially Margaret, for championing this from the beginning.

Martin Ouvry for your astute and formative feedback on the earliest draft, Julie Sheldon for your soul-strengthening support and advice, and Matt Jones, for poring through the script and asking me the questions that others were probably thinking, but you were kind enough to voice.

Elisa Cunningham, my illustrator, for your creative genius, and Julie Timlin for your literary skill, especially in sifting out the many rogue hyphens I added for reasons I cannot-explain.

The illustrious team of editors at Hodder, especially Jessica Lacey whose hard work and talent transformed these words from a scattered draft into a crafted script.

My family, Mum, Lucy and Emma for believing in me from the early days and my pastors at City Church, especially Ben Welchman for your leadership in the highs and lows of this journey. Thanks also to my friends at Severn Vineyard, for your faith and encouragement, and to the generous staff at Trinity College for giving me the space and grace to pen this script.

Special thanks to the brave souls who travelled with me in the field: Ross Vardy and Louise Glenn in Chile, Dan Green in the Middle East, and Pete Kessell, Dan Coe and Daniel Abrahamsson in Israel–Palestine. Some of you literally saved my life at times. Yes, literally.

And of course, thanks to the heroes whom I had the privilege of interviewing in desert towns and bustling cities all over the world, whose stories line the pages of this book. Your faith, hope and love have captivated me over the last few years and my deepest desire is that your lives will inspire many others through these pages. Thank you for the honour of sharing your stories.

More than anyone, I thank Ye'shua, my Saviour and God; this book is ultimately for you.

ENDNOTES

Chapter 1

1 Jonathan Franklin, *The 33* (Doubleday, 2011), p. 34.
2 Héctor Tobar, *Deep Down Dark* (Sceptre, 2014), p. 104.
3 Mario Sepulveda in a video message to the Thai boys, BBC News, 5 July 2018, https://www.bbc.co.uk/news/av/world-asia-44720617 (accessed 27 August 2020).
4 The courage and sacrifice of Thai diver Saman Gunan enabled the twelve boys and their teacher to walk free.

Chapter 2

1 Héctor Tobar, *Deep Down Dark*, p. 30.
2 *ibid.*, p. 37.
3 *ibid.*, p. 36.
4 Jonathan Franklin, *The 33*, p. 11.
5 James 4:6.

Chapter 3

1 Héctor Tobar, *Deep Down Dark*, p. 133.
2 Robert Ingersoll made this comment about Lincoln in 'The Exchange Table, True Greatness Exemplified in Abraham Lincoln', *Unity: Freedom, Fellowship and Character in Religion*, 11.3, 1 April 1883.
3 To respect the miners' pact, I have only included names and details that have been independently verified by Héctor Tobar in *Deep Down Dark*. The miners I interviewed took no payment for their interviews, nor did Marta Contreras or Alf Cooper. I also have not profited from this book, for my royalties are going to support the work of A21 towards its work in rescuing victims of human trafficking.
4 Psalm 95:4.

Chapter 4

1 Héctor Tobar, *Deep Down Dark*, p. 143.
2 Jonathan Franklin, *The 33*, p. 257.
3 Exodus 33:11.

Chapter 5

1 'The Nobel Peace Prize 2015', The Nobel Prize, https://www.nobelprize.org/prizes/peace/2015/summary/ (accessed 19 August 2020).

2 Lydia Wilson, 'What I Discovered From Interviewing Imprisoned ISIS Fighters', The Nation, 21 October 2015, https://www.thenation.com/article/archive/what-i-discovered-from-interviewing-isis-prisoners/ (accessed 19 August 2020). For an excellent summary of the wider evidence see John L. Esposito, 'The Origins of the ISIS Conflict', Oxford Islamic Studies Centre.

3 Mourad Wahba and Amin Awad, '3RP Regional Refugee & Resilience Plan 2018 – 2019, in Response to the Syria Crisis: Regional Strategic Overview [EN/AR]' OCHA Services Relief Web, https://reliefweb.int/report/lebanon/3rp-regional-refugee-resilience-plan-2018-2019-response-syria-crisis-regional (accessed 19 August 2020).

4 Open Doors UK, World Watch List (2020).

5 UN General Assembly Human Rights Council, written statement submitted by European Centre for Law and Justice, 'Requesting that the UN recognise ISIS atrocities against Christians and other religious and ethnic minorities as genocide and take immediate appropriate action', Thirty-ninth session, Agenda item 3 (September 2018).

6 Rt Rev. Philip Mounstephen, 'Bishop of Truro's Independent Review for the Foreign Secretary of FCO Support for Persecuted Christians', 2019, https://christianpersecutionreview.org.uk/report/ (accessed 19 August 2020).

7 John L. Allen Jr, 'The War on Christians', The Spectator, 5 October 2013.

8 Quoted in Paul Vallely, 'Christians: The world's most persecuted people', Independent, 27 July 2014.

9 For a good introduction to the impact of Jesus' life on western civilisation, I recommend John Ortberg, Who Is This man? The Unpredictable Impact of the Inescapable Jesus (Zondervan, 2014).

10 Luke 2:2.

Chapter 6

1 The Qur'an encourages dialogue with Christians (Qur'an 10:94), and describes itself as 'safeguarding' the earlier books (Qur'an 5:48, 10:37, 35:31), especially the Gospels, referred to as the 'Injeel' (Qur'an 5:46). Some scholars speculate that the Injeel refers to another 'uncorrupted Gospel', but there is no evidence for this and no inference to a 'different' Gospel in the wording of the Qur'an. At the time the Qur'an was written, the 'Gospel' was universally understood as the four-part accounts of Jesus' life according to Matthew, Mark, Luke and John.

2 John 14:6.

3 John Helliwell, Richard Layard and Jeffrey Sachs, 'World Happiness report, Chapter 2, Figure 2, Ranking of World Happiness 2016–2018', United Nations Sustainable Development Solutions, 2019.

Chapter 7

1 John 3:3.

Chapter 8

1   Acts 1:8.

2   The archaeological evidence of human remains preserved in ancient bogs show that human sacrifice was common, people were burned alive in a giant wicker man and cannibalism was standard procedure. See R. C. Turner and R. G. Scaife, *Bog Bodies: New Discoveries and New Perspectives* (British Museum Press, 1995). For a concise summary see *Dr Mike Parker-Pearson, 'The Practice of Human Sacrifice', BBC History, 28 February 2011, http://www.bbc.co.uk/history/ancient/british_prehistory/ human_sacrifice_01.shtml (accessed 27 August 2020).*

3   Herodian, *Roman History*, 3, 14, 6–8.

4   Julius Caesar, *The Gallic Wars*, 5, 14.

5   Tacitus, *The Life of Agricola*, 1, 11.

6   Martin Mosebach, *The 21: A Journey into the Land of Coptic Martyrs* (Plough Publishing House, 2019), p. 83.

7   *ibid.*, pp. 14–15.

8   *ibid.*, p. 36.

9   Jonathan Rashad, '"Christian Martyrs Change the World": We Meet the Families of the Egyptian Christians Beheaded by the Islamic State', VICE News, 26 February 2015, https://www.vice.com/en_us/article/nemaqq/christian-martyrs-change-the-world-we-meet-the-families-of-the-egyptian-christians-beheaded-by-the-islamic-state (accessed 19 August 2020).

10 Martin Mosebach, *The 21*, p. 93.

11 *ibid.*, p. 25.

12 Luke 23:34.

13 Mark 15:39.

14 Acts 6:8.

15 Acts 7:60.

16 Billy Graham, 'A Time for Moral Courage', *Reader's Digest*, July 1964.

17 See, for example, Leviticus 19:18; Mark 12:31; Psalm 82:3; Proverbs 31:9; Isaiah 1:17; Micah 6:8; James 1:27; Romans 13:1–7; Matthew 22:15–22; Luke 6:27–8.

18 Open Doors UK, World Watch List (2020).

19 Thanks to Linda Lowry of Open Doors USA for these insights.

20 'Nigeria: Leah Sharibu Still Captive One Year On', Open Doors, 19 February 2019, https://www.opendoors.org.hk/en/2019/02/26964/ (accessed 19 August 2020).

21 Rodney Stark, 'Constantine's Very Mixed Blessings', in Rodney Stark, *The Triumph of Christianity* (HarperOne, 2011), pp. 169–81.

Chapter 9

1   This is more than a metaphor. In response to the Syrian crisis, the Arsenal foundation launched a series of football workshops for Syrian refugees in a Jordanian refugee camp as part of its 'Coaching for Life' programme. Despite being a supposed enemy of the Gunners, I have to say, I respect that.

Chapter 10

1 Referring to the apostle Paul's conversion experienced in Acts 9.
2 Romans 12:21.
3 Martin Luther King Jr, 'Letter from Birmingham Jail', African Studies Centre, University of Pennsylvania, 16 April 1963, https://www.africa.upenn.edu/Articles_Gen/Letter_Birmingham.html (accessed 20 August 2020).

Chapter 11

1 See www.stopthetraffik.org (accessed 20 August 2020).
2 See www.lovebristol.org (accessed 20 August 2020).
3 Survey conducted between 1 and 3 April 2020 in the UK. The Policy Institute of King's College London in partnership with Ipsos MORI, 'Life under lockdown: coronavirus in the UK', https://www.kcl.ac.uk/policy-institute/assets/coronavirus-in-the-uk.pdf (accessed 20 August 2020), p. 40.
4 John 13:34.

Chapter 12

1 From the obituary of George Muller in the *Daily Telegraph* (1898).
2 Charles Dickens, *Household Words. A Weekly Journal*, Volume 16, No. 398 (Ward, Lock, and Tyler, 7 November 1857) pp. 433–8.
3 Hannah More was a Bristol-born playwright and a close friend of William Wilberforce. She championed female education and fought tirelessly for the abolition of the slave trade.
4 The Seven Saints of St Pauls are a group of pioneers who fought for racial equality and integrated communities. Local artist Michele Curtis created seven giant murals around the St Pauls neighbourhood to recognise their heroism and inspire people to follow their lead. I met Michele by chance when her team from Paintworks were finishing the Delores Campbell piece, and she shared the vision with me. Delores Campbell was the first female member of the Commonwealth Coordinated Committee, and Bristol poet Miles Chambers described her as the 'mother of Black British culture'.
5 The survey was conducted by the charity 52 Lives on behalf of Gala Bingo. See Natasha Hinde', 'Revealed: Bristol Is The Kindest City In The UK', *Huffington Post*, 20 February 2019, https://www.huffingtonpost.co.uk/entry/kindest-city-in-the-uk-revealed-as-bristol_uk (accessed 20 August 2020).

Chapter 13

1 Tom Holland, *Dominion: The Making of the Western Mind* (Little, Brown, 2019).
2 This is a combination of two quotes by Desmond Tutu. The first is, 'Freedom and liberty lose out by default because good people are not vigilant,' which he penned in *Hope and Suffering: Sermons and Speeches* (Fount, 1984). The second is, 'If you are neutral in situations of injustice, you have chosen the side of the oppressor,' attributed to Tutu in Robert McAfee Brown, *Unexpected News: Reading the Bible with Third World Eyes* (Westminster John Knox Press, 1984), p. 19.
3 Christine Caine, *Undaunted* (Zondervan, 2012), p. 161.

4   *ibid.*, p. 163.

5   Luke 10;25–37.

6   The English translate the third book of the Bible as 'Numbers', but 'wilderness' is a better translation from the Hebrew *midbar* found in the first sentence of the book. See Jonathan Sacks, 'Bemidbar (5768) – The Wilderness and the Word', 31 May 2008, http://rabbisacks.org/covenant-conversation-5768-bemidbar-the-wilderness-and-the-word-2/ (accessed 20 August 2020).

Chapter 14

1   Sarah Townsend, Heejung Kim and Batja Mesquita, 'Are You Feeling What I'm Feeling? Emotional Similarity Buffers Stress', *Social Psychological and Personal Science*, Vol 5, Issue 5, 2013.

2   UK Government Press Release, 'PM commits to government-wide drive to tackle loneliness', 17 January 2018, https://www.gov.uk/government/news/pm-commits-to-government-wide-drive-to-tackle-loneliness#:~:text=Today%20(Wednesday%2017%20January)%20the Jo%20Cox%20Commission%20on%20Loneliness (accessed 20 August 2020).

3   Former US Surgeon General Vivek Murphy outlined his findings in an interview with *The Washington Post*: 'Why former U.S. Surgeon General Vivek Murthy believes loneliness is a "profound" public health issue', 15 May 2018, https://www.washingtonpost.com/video/postlive/former-surgeon-general-dr-vivek-murthy-people-who-are-lonely-live-shorter-lives/2018/05/15/4632188e-5853-11e8-9889-07bcc1327f4b_video.html (accessed 20 August 2020).

4   Cited in Malcolm Muggeridge, *Something Beautiful for God* (HarperCollins, 1986).

5   James Lee, 'True Friendship', delivered at City Church, Bristol, UK, 15 July 2018.

6   Will Smith made this comment during a conversation with Stephen Colbert during *The Late Show* in August 2016.

7   Red Cross and Co-op, 'Trapped in a Bubble: An investigation into triggers for loneliness in the UK', December 2016, https://assets.ctfassets.net/5ywmq66472jr/5t-KumBSlO0suKwiWO6KmaM/230366b0171541781a0cd98fa80fdc6e/Coop_Trapped_in_a_bubble_report.pdf (accessed 20 August 2020), p. 42.

8   Mother Teresa, *A Simple Path* (Ballantine Books, 1995). p. 83.

9   The concept of 'love anyway' is championed by writer and speaker Jeremy Courtney, pioneer of the 'Preemptive Love' movement. See preemptivelove.org (accessed 20 August 2020).

10   To read stories, download resources and run a Peace Feast yourself go to www.peacefeast.org (accessed 20 August 2020).

11   'Forced labour, modern slavery and human trafficking', International Labour Organisation, see www.ilo.org/global/topics/forced-labour/ (accessed 20 August 2020).

Chapter 15

1   This isn't poetic licence. I really did mutter the 'wolf from the door' comment to myself a few minutes before it ran past. I even speculated that I had heard it howling

in my sleep, and it was there in my subconscious. I guess I'll never know. Funny though. Sort of. Type II fun.

2   Peter Beaumont, 'Campers in Israel warned after series of wolf attacks', *The Guardian*, 20 September 2017, https://www.theguardian.com/world/2017/sep/20/campers-in-israel-warned-after-series-of-wolf-attacks (accessed 21 August 2020).

3   Mark 1:12–13.

4   Luke 2:8.

5   John 10:7.

6   John 10:11.

7   Roald Dahl in an interview with Brian Sibley, BBC World Service, November 1988.

Chapter 16

1   Bernard Levin, *Life's Great Riddle, and No Time to Find its Meaning*, quoted by Nicky Gumbel, *Questions of Life* (Kingsway, 2001), p. 13.

2   Psalm 23:1–4 (ESV UK).

3   Augustine of Hippo, *Confessions*.

Chapter 17

1   Rabbi Professor Menachem Klein, *Lives in Common: Arabs and Jews in Jerusalem, Jaffa and Hebron* (Oxford University Press, 2001).

2   Peace Congress file, 'Memorandum on British Commitments to King Hussein', The National Archives, London. Ref: FO 608/92, 15 March 1919.

3   *The Balfour Declaration* refers to a public letter, penned by Foreign Secretary Arthur Balfour, on 2 November 1917 to Walter Rothschild, leader of the British Jewish Community.

4   Karl Marx, in an interview with the *Chicago Tribune*, Sunday 5 January 1879.

5   Matthew 5:44.

6   Matthew 5:39.

7   See Bava Kamma Chapter 8, Mishna 6.

8   Walter Wink, 'Jesus' Third Way' in *'The Powers That Be: Theology for a New Millennium* (Penguin Random House Publishing, 1998), pp. 98–111.

Chapter 18

1   See Rabbi Jeffrey Salkin, 'Thou Shalt Not Compare Historical Horrors?', 26 June 2019, https://www.redletterchristians.org/thou-shalt-not-compare-historical-horrors/ (accessed 21 August 2020).

2   Salim Munayer and Lisa Loden, *Through My Enemy's Eyes: Envisioning Reconciliation in Israel–Palestine* (Paternoster, 2014), pp. 33–6.

3   Kelly James Clark, Aziz Abu Sarah and Nancy Fuchs Kreimer, *Strangers, Neighbors, Friends: Muslim–Christian–Jewish Reflections on Compassion and Peace* (Cascade Books, 2018), pp. 9–11.

4   *ibid.*, pp. 27–8.

5   Dr Yitz Glick received the Shimon Peres Presidential Award for Volunteerism in 2009 for his ongoing medical work in Palestinian villages.

6   International Federation of Red Cross and Red Crescent Code of Ethics.

7   Izzeldin Abuelaish, *I Shall Not Hate: A Gaza Doctor's Journey on the Road to Peace and Human Dignity* (Bloomsbury, 2012).

8   Matthew 5:9–10.

9   Shane Claiborne, *The Irresistible Revolution: Living as an Ordinary Radical* (Zondervan, 2006), p. 279.

10 Leviticus 19:18.

11 Leviticus 19:33–4.

12 Benny Morris, *Righteous Victims: A History of the Zionist–Arab Conflict, 1881–1998* (Vintage, 2001), p. 5.

13 British soldier Archibald Stanley, from 'Voices of the First World War: The Christmas Truce, The Imperial War Museum, London.

14 British soldier, George Ashurst, from 'Voices of the First World War'.

15 Nelson Mandela, *The Long Walk to Freedom: The Autobiography of Nelson Mandela* (Abacus, 1995). P. 384.

Chapter 19

1   This is a classic Tom Wright invitation and is infused through much of his work. I heard the specific comment about making a pilgrimage to the first century in a lecture he delivered at Westminster Chapel in March 2020, entitled, 'Jesus, Paul and the Question of God', available on the Unbelievable? podcast. See https://unbelievable.podbean.com/e/an-evening-with-nt-wright-live-in-london/

2   For a historically accurate account of the nativity, see Kenneth E. Bailey, *Jesus Through Middle Eastern Eyes* (SPCK, 2008), pp. 25–37.

3   For an amusing and insightful read on the subject see The Church Mouse and Dave Walker, *Beard Theology: A Holy History of Hairy Faces* (Hodder and Stoughton, 2019).

4   Josephus, *War*, 1, 646–56.

5   John the Baptist was executed by Herod Antipas, the son of Herod the Great. The event is recorded both in the Gospels (see Matthew 14:1–12) and by Josephus (*Antiquities*, 18.5).

6   Macrobius, *Saturnalia*, 2:4:11.

7   Jeremiah 23:1-6; Micah 5:2–4; Isaiah 9:1–2. For a good introduction to Jesus' fulfilment of Jewish Messianic prophecy see, https://jewsforjesus.org/jewish-resources/messianic-prophecy

8   For some, the addition of a star guiding the Magi seems like poetic licence, but with the advent of modern computer science, stellar movements are now accurately calculable. British astrophysicist David Hughes noted a rare event (roughly once every eight hundred years) in 7 BC, with the simultaneous appearance of Jupiter (synonymous in the Ancient Near East with kingship) alongside Saturn (representing change or, to Jewish astronomers, a Messianic figure). As the late Latvian Professor Kārlis Kaufmanis argued, the Magi would have read this as signalling the birth of a new Messianic King in Judea. The event was also recorded by the Babylonians, and a clay tablet with this inscription can be viewed in the

British Museum (BM 35429). See David Hughes, *The Star of Bethlehem Mystery* (Littlehampton Books, 1980).

9   Archelaus' bloody reputation, highlighted in Matthew's Gospel, is mirrored in Josephus' accounts of Archelaus slaughtering three thousand Jews during the Passover (*Antiquities*, 17, 9).

10 While the conspiracies surrounding Mary Magdalene make for some interesting books, there is no credible evidence that Jesus ever had a romantic relationship. As a Jewish rabbi, he could easily have married and provided a positive role model to other husbands, yet the reality is that his short earthly life was one of singleness and celibacy. In refraining from one exclusive relationship, however, he was able to offer unparalleled friendship to people from every corner of society.

11 Matthew 13:54–7.

12 There was a good market for limestone products in conservative Jewish towns like Cana and Nazareth, as limestone was considered purer than other rocks, and John notes huge stone vessels at the wedding in Cana. The excavation of a first-century Jewish home in Nazareth turned up significant limestone vessels (Ken Dark, 'Has Jesus' Nazareth house been found?', *Biblical Archaeology Review*, 2015, 41, 2, pp. 54–63), and in 1991, a first-century stone quarry was excavated a short distance from Nazareth (Zvi Gal, 'A Stone-vessel Manufacturing Site in Lower Galilee', *Atiqot*, 20, 1991, pp. 179–80).

13 Luke 2:41–52.

14 Paul of Tarsus, for example, continued to work as a tentmaker, in the tradition of Jewish rabbis before him and undoubtedly inspired by Jesus, not so much by necessity as by example (Acts 18:3; 20:34; 1 Corinthians 4:12; 1 Thessalonians 2:9; 4:11–12; 2 Thessalonians 3:8).

15 Tacitus, *Annuls*, 14.

16 John 1:46.

17 This description is based on the work of Forensic Anthropologist Richard Neave of Manchester University. In 2001 he reconstructed the head of a first-century Galilean by combining X-rays of three ancient male skulls, with the help of local archaeologists, for the BBC documentary, *Son of God*. Neave never claimed to have found the actual face of Christ; his aim was to challenge the European airbrushing of Jesus in popular art by demonstrating what a historically accurate first-century Galilean would have looked like.

18 The concept of Celebritocracy is unpacked by Cooper Lawrence in, *Celebritocracy: The Misguided Agenda of Celebrity Politics in a Postmodern Democracy*, (Post Hill Press, 2020).

Chapter 20

1   In 2009, the remains of a first-century synagogue were unearthed in Magdala. See 'One of the Oldest Synagogues in the World was Exposed at Migdal (9/13)', Israeli Antiquities Authority, http://www.antiquities.org.il/article_eng.aspx?sec_id=25&subj_id=240&id=1601 (accessed 21 August 2020).

2   Peter's testimony of Jesus' life was carefully recorded by his assistant, Mark (1 Peter

5:13; Eusebius, *Church History*, 3, 39; Irenaeus, *Against Heresies*, 3,1; Tertullian, *Against Marcion*, 4, 5).

3   In 1968, the remains of a house church were discovered in Capernaum, likely inhabited by a large family of fishermen and dated to the first century. The walls were graffitied with phrases like 'Christ have mercy'. See 'Ten Top Discoveries', *Biblical Archaeology Review*, Issue 200 (2009), pp.74–96.

4   Mark 1:29–31; 1 Corinthians 9:5.

5   Luke 10:38–42.

6   Mark 1:34.

7   Luke 7:11–17; 8:49–56; John 11:1–44.

8   See R. J. Littman and M. L. Littman, 'Galen and the Antonine Plague', *The American Journal of Philology*, 94:3, 1973, pp. 243–55. Also, Livy, *The Early History of Rome*, Books 3 and 5.

9   See Peter J. Williams, *Can We Trust the Gospels?* (Crossway, 2018), pp. 51–86.

10 Suetonius described the early Jesus movement as 'a new and mischievous superstition', the word 'mischievous' translating *maleficus*, a form of dark magic. Suetonius, *Nero*, 16, and Robert Louis Wilken, *The Christians as the Romans Saw Them*, second edition (Yale University Press, 2003), p. 98.

11 There is understandable speculation about the authenticity of this reference to Jesus, largely revolving around the unusual addition of the word 'Christ'. His identity as a 'wise man' who performed 'startling deeds', however, is far closer to Josephus' language than any Christian writing, and is therefore likely to be original. See James Dunn, *Jesus Remembered: Christianity in the Making* (Eerdmans, 2003), p. 141.

12 The pagan critic Celsus attributed Jesus' miracles to sorcery (Origen of Alexandria, *Against Celsus*, 2, 49). Many of Jesus' Jewish contemporaries explained the miracles as such, see M. Wilcox, *Jesus in the Light of His Jewish Environment* (Aufstieg und Niedergang der romischen Welt 2, 25, 1, 1982).

13 Matthew 12:24.

14 Graham Stanton, *The Gospels and Jesus*, second edition (Oxford University Press, 2002), p. 235.

15 There are several modern resurrections accounts, not all of them credible, but one I find compelling is that of John Smith, who fell through the ice on a Missouri lake and was fully submerged in sub-zero temperatures for forty-five minutes. When his body was retrieved there was no pulse, no breathing and no brain activity, and an hour of attempted resuscitations produced zero signs of life. When doctors invited his mother to 'say goodbye', she prayed for a miracle, and his heart instantly restarted. Despite warnings from doctors that he would be brain dead, to everyone's surprise he regained consciousness, returned to complete health and continues to live a normal, independent life. See Joyce Smith and Ginger Kolbaba, *Breakthrough: The Miraculous True Story of a Mother's Faith and Her Child's Resurrection* (Hachette, 2017).

16 John 9:1–7.

17 The Pool of Siloam, where this event occurred was only discovered by accident in 2004 when engineers unearthed some ancient stone steps while repairing a pipe. Archaeologists Ronnie Reich and Eli Shukron were called in to investigate and,

after a painstakingly gentle excavation, a 225-foot pool was discovered, matching the exact style and location of the Pool of Siloam in John 9 ('Ten Top Discoveries', *Biblical Archaeology Review*).

18 Mark 1:40–5.

19 The Messianic miracles were based on prophecies in the Jewish Scriptures that linked certain actions to the explicit work of God, such as opening blind eyes in Isaiah 35 and Psalm 146. Jesus alluded to this during his inauguration speech in Nazareth (Luke 4:18). For a full explanation of the Messianic miracles, see Dr Arnold G. Fruchtenbaum, 'The Three Messianic Miracles', in Study 17: Ariel Ministries' Messianic Bible Study, 35.

20 Strong's number 4697, in *Strong's Greek and Hebrew Concordance and Lexicon*. In Mark 1:41, the ESV translates Splagchnizomai as, 'pity' and the NLT translates it as 'compassion'.

21 Mark 5:24–34.

22 Malachi 4:2 says, 'the sun of righteousness will rise with healing in its rays'. The word for 'rays' is *kanaph*, which is usually translated 'wings' or 'corners' and was used to describe the tasselled corners of the Jewish garments (Numbers 15:38). Some Jews believed that just touching the corner of the robe of the Messiah would be enough to receive healing.

23 Leviticus 15:25–7.

Chapter 21

1 The 'Prince of Peace' is a Messianic title from a prophecy in Isaiah 9:6, which the early Christians associated with Jesus.

2 See Luke 19:28–48 and Matthew 23:37–9.

3 Marcus Borg, *Conflict, Holiness, and Politics in the Teachings of Jesus* (Continuum International, 1998), pp. 10–15.

4 Strong's number 4239, in *Strong's Greek and Hebrew Concordance and Lexicon*. Aristotle alludes to the measured strength of the war horse in *Nicomachean Ethics*, 2, 6.

5 Psalm 69:9; John 2:17.

6 Josephus, *War*, 5, 5, 6 and *Antiquities*, 14, 2.

7 Isaiah 56:7.

8 Genesis 17:4–5.

9 John 2:19.

10 To suggest that the corrupt leadership was 'predatory' is not my poetic licence. The prophet Zephaniah referred to Jerusalem's rulers as 'evening wolves, who leave nothing for the morning' (Zephaniah 3:3).

11 See Leen and Kathleen Ritmeyer, *Jerusalem at the Time of Jesus* (Abingdon Press, 2010).

12 Josephus, *Antiquities*, 20, 9, 2–4.

13 Josephus notes the abuse of the elderly priests in *Antiquities*, 20, 207, and the cruelty of the high priesthood was recorded by the Qumran community who described a 'Wicked High Priest' who 'robbed from the poor' (Dead Sea Scrolls, 1QpHab 8:8–12; 9:4–5).

14 John 10:11.

15 Kenneth Bailey, *The Good Shepherd: A Thousand-year Journey from Psalm 23 to the New Testament* (SPCK, 2015).

16 Ezekiel 34:1–4.

17 Ezekiel 34:12.

18 Daniel 7:13–14. Daniel was a member of the royal line of David, who was carried into exile after the Babylonian conquest in 586 bc.

19 David Flusser, *The Sage from Galilee: Rediscovering Jesus' Genius* (Eerdmans, 2007), p. 103.

20 Matthew 20:28.

21 John 1:29.

22 Mark 14:32.

23 Luke 22:44. It is likely that Jesus was experiencing hematidrosis, a condition where the capillaries feeding the sweat glands haemorrhage as a nervous system response to extreme anxiety. There are several examples in antiquity and the present. See J. E. Holoubek and A. B. Holoubek, 'Blood, Sweat and Fear': "A Classification of Hematidrosis"', *Journal of Medicine* 27, 3-4, 1996, pp. 115–33.

24 Matthew 26:38.

25 Matthew 26:49.

26 Matthew 26:52.

27 Mark 14:43.

28 The trial before the Sanhedrin is recorded in Matthew 26:57–67; Mark 14:53–65; Luke 22:54–71 and John 18:13–28.

29 John 10:32–3.

30 Mark 14:62.

31 Daniel 7:13–14; Psalm 110:1.

32 John 6:14–15, Matthew 26:53.

Chapter 22

1 In 1960, the American economist Walt Rostow mapped out a rather simplistic road to Modernisation in *The Stages of Economic Growth: A Non-Communist Manifesto* (Cambridge University Press, 1960), and his model has subtly influenced the global political landscape more than he could have imagined. The ultimate goal was the 'Age of High Mass Consumption'. The idea of a moral or meaningful existence was rather clumsily bolted on later, a little too late, perhaps.

2 Luke 2:25–35.

3 Peter's denial is recorded in all four gospel accounts, see Matthew 26:69-75, Mark 14:66-72, Luke 22: 54-60 and John 18:15-27

4 This incident is recorded by Luke in Acts 5:36–7, and by Josephus in *Antiquities*, 20, 5, 2.

5 The Hebrew word is *gever*. Roosters were banned from the temple area to avoid the danger of a bird wandering into the Holy of Holies by accident, so the *gever* here refers to the temple crier whose three calls to prayer would echo across Jerusalem in the early morning (Mishnah, Tamid 3.8).

6   Matthew 26:34–5.

7   If Peter was standing in the corner of the courtyard, he would have had a direct line of sight through two open doorways to the centre of the interrogation room, where Jesus was standing. See Leen and Kathleen Ritmeyer, *Jerusalem at the Time of Jesus*.

8   'Prefect' was Pilate's title in a limestone inscription unearthed in 1961, whereas 'Procurator' was used by Roman historians such as Tacitus. The difference is negligible, and Josephus used both titles interchangeably, even for the same person. The Gospel accounts refer to Pilate as a 'Governor', which renders both titles perfectly accurately.

9   Josephus, *Antiquities*, 18, 3, 2.

10   Philo, *On the Embassy of Gaius*, 38, 299–305, and Josephus, *War*, 2, 9, 2–4.

11   Matthew 27:19.

12   Josephus describes one scourging, saying that they 'brought him to the Roman procurator; where he was whipped till his bones were laid bare', *War*, 6, 5, 3.

13   William Edwards, Wesley Gabel and Floyd Hosmer, 'On the Physical Death of Jesus Christ', *JAMA*, 255, 11, 1986, pp. 1455–63.

14   Various aspects of Jesus' mockery, from the crown of thorns to the purple robe, the continued beatings and the bitter wine, are mentioned in all the Gospels (Mark 15, Luke 23, Matthew 27 and John 19) and are entirely in keeping with the sort or mockery that was commonplace for political prisoners in the Roman world. See, for example, the torture and mockery of the Jewish teacher Eleazer (4 Maccabees 6); the public humiliating of the madman Carrabus, (Philo, *In Flaccum*, 6, 36–9), or the punishment of former Emperor Vitellius (Dio Cassius, *Roman History*, 64, 20–1).

15   Roman law stated that, in theory, people shouldn't be killed when beaten with rods or tortured, but in the same line it confessed that 'most persons, when they are tortured, lose their lives' (*Digesta*, 48.19.8.3).

16   This minor character, Simon of Cyrene, is mentioned in three Gospels (Matthew 27:32, Mark 15:21 and Luke 23:26), so it's likely that he became well known in the early church along with his sons, Alexander and Rufus (Romans 16:13). This section of the narrative is almost certainly the result of Simon's testimony, for most of the disciples had fled.

17   Luke 23:34.

18   This description is based on the examination of a crucified man from the first century, dated to the time of Pontius Pilate. An ossuary containing several bones was discovered by accident in a burial cave in Giv'at ha-Mivtar, in 1968, which included a heelbone still exhibiting a rusty four-and-a-half-inch nail which fully impaled the bone from right to left. (See Joseph Zias and Eliezer Sekeles' detailed examination in, 'The Crucified Man from Giv'at ha-Mivtar: A Reappraisal', *Israel Exploration Journal*, 35, 1, 1985, pp. 22–7). It is unclear whether his hands were tied or nailed, although Josephus cited nailing as the common method of crucifixion where soldiers wished to punish Jewish rebels (*War*, 5, 11, 1).

19   Mark 15:29 states, 'Those who passed by hurled insults at him,' which is fitting with historical records of crucifixion as criminals were crucified at the roadside to

maximise shame and act as a deterrent. (See Appian of Alexandria, *Civil Wars*, 1, 120.)

20 Matthew 27:35; Mark 15:24; Luke 23:34; John 19:23–4. The fact that the soldiers acquired Jesus' clothes is utterly in keeping with Roman law (*Digesta*, 48, 20).

21 Seneca, *Dialogue: To Marcia on Consolation*, 6, 20, 3.

22 Crucifixion was regarded as the worst of punishments by the Persians, Greeks, Romans and Jews. (See, for example Cicero, *Pro Rabirio Perduellionis Reo*, 19.16.)

23 Hebrews 12:2.

24 Nabeel Qureshi, *No God but One: Allah or Jesus* (Zondervan, 2016) pp. 91–2.

25 Héctor Tobar, *Deep Down Dark*, pp. 260–1.

Chapter 23

1 See alpha.org (accessed 26 August 2020).

2 1 Corinthians 15:19.

3 While the Romans left some bodies on the cross, the burial of Jesus is well supported by evidence, for Jews were exceptionally committed to burying bodies, even of crucified criminals (Josephus, *War*, 4.5.2), to protect the land from being cursed (Deuteronomy 21:22–3). It was the Sanhedrin's responsibility to oversee Jesus' burial, since they had condemned him to death (Mishna Sanhedrin 6:5), so it is entirely unsurprising that Joseph of Arimathea stepped up. In keeping with Jewish law, which forbade criminals from being buried in the family tomb, he used his own. While Pilate had a poor reputation for respecting Jewish customs, in the Passover week he would be far more lenient to avoid the risk of a riot when the temporary population of Jerusalem was at its highest. Granting the burial of an obscure preacher would have been no effort; in fact, burials like this are well supported in Roman literature (Philo, *In Flaccum* 10.83; *Digesta*, 48.24.3)

4 The expected path of the Messiah was to overthrow the Romans, not be crucified by them (*The War of the Messiah*, Dead Sea Scrolls, 4Q285). When a so-called Messiah was killed, their followers either found a different one or gave up and went back to their day jobs. In the Jewish mind, if the Romans were still in power, the Messiah had failed, so faking a resurrection would be as pointless as it would be implausible.

5 John 7:5, Mark 3:21.

6 The high regard people had for James, Jesus' brother, is recorded in Acts 21:17–18 and by Josephus (*Antiquities*, 20, 9, 3). James' eyewitness testimony to the resurrection had a similarly transformative impact on Paul of Tarsus (Galatians 1:18–20; 1 Corinthians 15:3–8).

7 James 1:1.

8 Luke 24:11, John 20:24–9.

9 An interesting insight into way the Jesus movement was viewed in Greco–Roman society is captured in the 'Alexamenos Graffiti', an ancient sketch scratched into the plaster of a house in Rome, mocking a Christian who is worshipping a crucified man with the head of a donkey. The tagline is 'Alexamenos worships God'. The piece is now on display in the Palatine Hill Museum.

10 Pagan religions in the Ancient Middle East believed that certain figures were deities, but to suggest that the Gospels were borrowed from pagan myths is to ignore overwhelming evidence to the contrary. Jesus was undeniably a historical figure, and his life and deeds are well attested in credible secular sources from Josephus, Tacitus and Pliny the Younger. The pagan religions have nothing like the historical evidence that exists about Jesus, and the apparent similarities between Jesus and pagan figures such as Mithras or Horus, which still circulate internet forums, are largely based on material written *after* Jesus, especially from nineteenth-century new age material, not ancient historical sources. The historian, writer and confessing atheist Tim O'Neill addresses the mysticism issue comprehensively in his critically acclaimed project, 'A History for Atheists', see https://historyforatheists.com (accessed 26 August 2020).

11 Josephus, *Antiquities*, 4, 8, 15.

12 The account of the resurrection given by Paul of Tarsus in 1 Corinthians 15 conveniently misses the women out, despite mentioning Peter and James. Most scholars date this letter *before* the Gospels, which makes the inclusion of the women in the Gospel accounts even more surprising. The only conceivable reason for their inclusion was that the Gospel writers were recording the exact truth, as reported by the eyewitnesses, regardless of how incriminating it might be to the male leaders. Luke especially appears to have drawn heavily on eyewitness testimony from women such as Mary Magdalene and Joanna (Luke 8:1–3; 24:1–10).

13 Edward Schillebeeckx, *Jesus: An Experiment in Christology* (Crossroad, 1981), p. 93.

14 Paul Maier, *In the Fullness of Time: A Historian Looks at Christmas, Easter and the Early Church* (Kregel, 1998), p. 180.

15 A classic example is the witness reports to the sinking of the *Titanic*. Some thought it broke in half before sinking; others thought it sank in one piece. Despite these irreconcilable differences, few would doubt that the *Titanic* sank. See Justin Brierley, *Unbelievable* (SPCK, 2017), p. 140.

16 Jon Tyson, 'Easter Sunday – Resurrection of Jesus', Church of the City New York, 1 April 2018.

17 Paul of Tarsus informed the believers in Corinth that, after Jesus' resurrection, 'he appeared to more than five hundred of the brothers and sisters at the same time, most of whom are still living' (1 Corinthians 15:6). His indication that the eyewitnesses were mostly 'still living' was an invitation to go and find out for themselves if they didn't believe him. This strict dedication to eyewitness accounts continued into the following generation as Papias, Bishop of Hierapolis, was keen to stress, see Eusebius, *Church Histories*, 3.39.

18 Mark 15:21; John 19:25; Matthew 27:57; Luke 23:50; 24:10; 8:3.

19 Mark 10:35; Mark 3:17; Matthew 16:18.

20 Philip Yancey, *The Jesus I Never Knew* (Grand Rapids, Michigan, Zondervan, 1995). P. 216.

21 Blaise Pascal, *Pensées*, 310 (originally written in 1670, available in English as a Penguin Classic, 1995).

22 Nadim Nassar, *The Culture of God: The Syrian Jesus – Reading the Divine Mind, Sailing Into the Divine Heart* (Hodder and Stoughton, 2018). P. 162.

23 The German historian Professor Gerd Lüdemann, who famously rejected the resurrection accounts still admits, 'It may be taken as historically certain that Peter and the disciples had experiences after Jesus' death in which Jesus appeared to them as the risen Christ.' Gerd Lüdemann, *What Really Happened to Jesus: A Historical Approach to the Resurrection* (Westminster John Knox Press, 1995), p. 80. His thoughts are shared by British historian Professor James Crossley who, like Lüdemann, is convinced by the resurrection encounters but attributes them to alternative explanations.

24 For a compelling investigation into miraculous dreams and visions in the current generation, see Tom Doyle, *Dreams and Visions: Is Jesus Awakening the Muslim world?* (Thomas Nelson, 2012).

25 The disciples believed in angelic visions and visitations. In Acts 12:15, when Peter returns to the house of Mark's family in Jerusalem, they assume, 'It must be his angel,' for they thought he had been killed by Herod. The common view with afterlife appearances was that they were spiritual visions or angelic messengers, which is why the resurrection accounts of Jesus stand out, for they testify to something altogether different.

26 The hallucination theory has been widely dismissed by historians, as it simply doesn't match what psychologists now know about hallucinations, which are generally private, personal and non-physical occurrences. For a physical, demonstrative, multiply attested set of witness accounts, including those who were initially sceptical, the hallucination argument simply falls apart, see Paul Copan and Ronald Tacelli (eds), *Jesus' Resurrection: Fact or Figment? A Debate Between William Lane Craig and Gerd Lüdemann* (IVP, 2000).

27 Soldiers who failed in their responsibilities were almost always executed. See Acts 12:18-19, and George W. Currie, *The Military Discipline of the Romans from the Founding of the City to the Close of the Republic* (Bloomington, 1928).

28 Joseph of Arimathea and Nicodemus were named and identifiable members of the Jerusalem elite, the apparent 'enemies' of the Jesus movement. The fact that they cared for Jesus' body while his supposed followers fled is another embarrassing detail that wouldn't have been recorded if the Gospel accounts were fictious.

29 The swoon theory was decisively disproved by the leading German historian and sceptic David Strauss in *The Life of Jesus: For the People* (William and Norgate, 1879), p. 412.

30 John 20:27.

31 C. S. Lewis, *God in the Dock* (Fount, 1979), p. 170.

32 Tacitus, *Annuls*, 15, 44.

33 The remarkable growth of the early Jesus movement was noted by Pliny the Younger, who governed in modern-day Turkey around 111 ad. He wrote to Emperor Trajan seeking advice on how to deal with Christians, complaining that pagan temples were emptying as vast numbers of men and women were joining the Jesus movement. Despite a systematic trial of all suspects, he seemed unable to fully stamp it out, as many Christians refused to recant their faith, despite torture and the threat of execution (Pliny the Younger, *Epistles*, 10:96). The growth of the early Jesus movement he observed, with its impact on pagan worship, mirrors an account by Luke regarding the riot in Ephesus (Acts 19).

Epilogue

1 In John 21, it is clear this conversation must have occurred after breakfast, during a stroll along the beach, for we read that they had finished eating and that Peter turned and saw that John was following them.

2 Luke 22:32.

3 1 Peter 5:2–3.

4 Matthew 4:19; John 21:19.

5 The idea of heaven as a fluffy place in the clouds where we will go to chill out and play harps is Platonic philosophy, not Jesus' teaching. Heaven in the Jesus movement is more than a distant hope; it's a present reality, and Jesus' overarching message is about bringing the peace and love of heaven into the here and now, through prayer and action. This is perhaps most clearly seen through the opening line of the Lord's prayer: 'Your kingdom come, your will be done, on earth as it is in heaven' (Matthew 6:10).

6 Acts 1:8.

7 Acts 2:2.

8 Acts 2:22–4.

9 Psalm 23:4 (ESV UK).

10 Psalm 139:7–10.

HODDER & STOUGHTON

Hodder & Stoughton is the UK's
leading Christian publisher,
with a wide range of books from
the bestselling authors in the UK
and around the world ranging from
Christian lifestyle and theology to
apologetics, testimony and fiction.
We also publish the world's
most popular Bible translation
in modern English, the New
International Version, renowned
for its accuracy and readability.

Hodderfaith.com   Hodderbibles.co.uk
 @HodderFaith    /HodderFaith